THE AGE OF CONSENT

The Rise of Relativism
and the Corruption of Popular Culture

ROBERT H. KNIGHT

SPENCE PUBLISHING COMPANY · DALLAS
1998

To my wife, Barbara

Published in the United States by
Spence Publishing Company
111 Cole Street
Dallas, Texas 75207

Library of Congress Cataloging-in-Publication Data for the Hardcover Edition

Knight, Robert H.
    The age of consent : the rise of relativism and the corruption of popular culture / Robert H. Knight
        p. cm.
    Includes bibliographical references and index.
    ISBN 1-890626-05-8 (hardcover)
    1. Christian ethics.   2. United States—Moral conditions.   3. Ethical relativism—Controversial literature.   4. Popular culture—Moral and ethical aspects—United States.   I. Title.
BJ1311.K56   1998
171'.7—dc21   98-16697

ISBN 1-890626-26-0 (pbk.)

Printed in the United States of America

THE AGE OF CONSENT

Contents

Foreword

I N MY TRAVELS, I am sometimes asked why America seems to
have a split personality.

If you contrast poll findings against developments in popular
culture, you might conclude that America is schizophrenic. The
polls indicate that we are a God-fearing people with durable traditions
of faith, family, and freedom. But the products of the pop culture
pump out a steady message of self-indulgence, moral confusion,
and loss of faith.

The divide is quite real. But the people themselves are not
schizophrenic. It is the elites who dictate culture who are seriously
out of step with what some of us call the Real America. Commuting
back and forth between New York and Los Angeles, they think of
the rest of the nation as "flyover country" that craves their brand of
enlightenment.

Most Americans are too busy raising families, working hard,
operating businesses, and going to church, Little League, and soccer
games to present much opposition to the elites' cultural blitzkrieg.
So, for the moment, the culture remains in the hands of those who

are at odds with the basic beliefs of the majority of the American people.

As *The Age of Consent* demonstrates, the capturing of the culture by an alienated elite did not take place overnight but has been in the works for more than a century. The sixties, with its Woodstockian excesses of illicit sex, drugs, and rock 'n' roll, provided a dizzying accelerator effect that is still giving us cultural whiplash. The stage was set, however, via the steady march of relativism through the cultural transmitters—the arts, the media, education, and entertainment.

In *The Age of Consent*, which Robert Knight defines as a time when time-tested standards have succumbed to the whims of one, two, or more consenting adults, we see how the rigors of the written word have given way to the seductive media of the senses, particularly the visual. Civilizations are known by what they treasure, and the evidence indicates that America—at least its cultural elite—has lurched from a Judaic-Christian, family-centered culture to one in which individual gratification is the defining factor.

In the mid-nineteenth century, Hans Christian Andersen observed that man, in the name of freedom, fashions his own fetters: "Since the creation of the world there has been no tyrant like Intemperance, and no slaves so cruelly treated as his."[1]

Of course, man was warned early on about the wages of sin. Proverbs 5:22-23 says: "The evil deeds of a wicked man ensnare him; the cords of his sin hold him fast. He will die for lack of discipline, led astray by his own great folly." Contrast this with New Age theorist Marilyn Ferguson's view: "Human nature is neither good nor bad . . . it has only to discover itself."[2]

The gap is widening between those who, wittingly or not, have adopted the self-centered vision of the New Age and those who hold to the Judaic-Christian tradition. The New Age, while professing neutrality, actually views man as inherently good, since man can self-invent and self-correct. Since the individual solely determines his own behavioral standard, he is the evolving master of all he surveys. Or so he thinks. The biblical view, however, is that man is helpless—and delusional—when he turns to his own devices instead of to God for guidance. Knowledge of one's own need for redemption can happen only when God is recognized as the ultimate authority. Without such an acknowledgment, man becomes slave to his own self-justifying whims.

In the New Age of relativism, even many churches have modified their message to compete in a self-oriented consumer culture. Television ads often portray local churches as centers for personal development rather than the outstretched arms of the Body of Christ. The armed forces long ago ceased appealing to simple duty and patriotism and began selling the military as a one-stop, personal-improvement program. As job opportunity became the defining element, military standards—particularly the virtue of honesty—fell before the legions of social reformers who saw the military life as a hermetically sealed social laboratory. Feminist pressure took the consumer message further and made career advancement for women a more important element than military readiness. The result is a Navy with a flotilla of "love boats" and watered-down training to accommodate different physical standards for women. Awash in adultery, sexual harassment, and sexual tension, the military was specifically targeted in June 1997 by Representative Barney Frank, who proposed doing away with all sexual standards between consenting adults, a New Age "solution" if there ever was one.

The Frank approach typifies the moral relativists' response to slackening observance of traditional standards: just toss them overboard. This formula has played out with tragic results in many areas, from sex education to drug legalization to divorce law to basic standards of decency in the media. Each time the envelope is pushed, creating more social problems, the solution is to stretch it a bit further in the hopes that the problems will all go away. During the Vietnam War, Senator George Aiken of Vermont won plaudits by suggesting that America should just declare victory and then pull out, which is agonizingly close to what eventually occurred. Aiken's idea, delivered somewhat tongue-in-cheek, has become the liberal way of coping. As our standards slip, we are told that we can wish away the damage and not told that we should clean up our act.

As Robert Knight shows, the development of New Age relativism has produced not a neutral common ground but a leveling of the defenses of civilization itself. If we can no longer trust even the idea of truth, opinion is all that matters. We are being tempted to surrender heaven's ideals to a might-makes-right philosophy. This is already playing out on college campuses, where highly respected professors are losing their positions for not toeing the politically correct line of the moment.[3] The double standard is embarrassingly obvious. When a liberal professor takes enormous intellectual liberties by openly promoting an ideological agenda to his students, the cry of academic freedom rings across the quads. But when a conservative professor is punished for publishing an article in a politically incorrect journal, there is no defense of intellectual diversity. What is billed as academic neutrality turns out to be a smoke screen for the relativistic liberal agenda.

Today's relativists could not have gotten away with their double standards in a culture that prized truth. But a gradual, sustained assault on truth has been carried out through the soft underbelly of Western culture: the arts. In film, music, and television, the themes of sensual pleasure and individual choice have drowned out the tried-and-true virtues of faith, family, self-sacrifice, duty, honor, patriotism, and fidelity in marriage. Cultural mechanics have wielded their tools to dull the public's sense of reasonable limits. In an Age of Consent, the silly and the profound are becoming indistinguishable.

Amid all this, there is heartening evidence that we are in for an upturn in spiritual life. Cultural noise can obscure the permanent melody only so long. In fact, technology may have helped create the musical score for a religious revival. As people grow weary of the cacophony, the true notes of faith and reason sound brighter and clearer. Nothing illustrates this better than the meteoric success of faith-based television shows such as "Touched by an Angel," the multimillion-dollar Christian pop music industry, or the return of many baby boomers to the faiths of their childhood.

As the pretenders, deceivers, imitators, and posers deploy their technologically enhanced megaphones, they find to their sorrow and rage that they can never drown out the ages-old symphony. The choices are becoming clearer and clearer, which may be all to the good. As I said, and as this book demonstrates, the fuzzy neutral ground is disappearing.

God willing, the Age of Consent will give way to an Age of Faith and a rebirth of the American spirit so that our children and grandchildren will grow up in a free and prosperous country. The alternative is too terrible to contemplate.

GARY L. BAUER

Author's Note

ONE BEAUTIFUL AUTUMN DAY many years ago, I was reclining on my dorm-room bunk, an eager freshman trying to make sense of a philosophy book.

Eighty pages into Michel Foucault's *The Order of Things*, I was puzzled: Was this guy ever going to get to the point? The philosopher's endless associations of words with ideas with nature's designs with cryptic references to time and space began to resemble a wicked maze from which there was no escape. Little did I know that this was precisely what the author had had in mind.

To Foucault and his fellow deconstructionists, meaning is subjective. What the reader brings to the text is all that matters. And even that does not particularly matter. Reason, logic, truth— it's all relative.

Every reader's interpretation is as valid as the next. The universe pulses with meaning or perhaps meaninglessness, but it all comes from within, not from without. The line between illusion and reality, therefore, is arbitrary. At first, I read with fascination as Foucault, like an intellectual Salome, dazzled by unveiling layer after layer of insights, employing random associations whose meanings were always just out of reach.

As I continued to read, I grew increasingly angry but didn't know why. I started asking myself, Is it me or him? He's crazy, right? But he is supposed to be a great man.

Before long, after I had scratched and clawed my way through most of the book, I came to a juncture: it *was* me or him. Not that I didn't understand the book; I had begun to understand it all too well, recognizing it as intellectual fraud. As a seeker of truth, I felt cheated, my time wasted, and, for some odd reason, my spirit offended.

Suddenly, I hurled the book through the air, thumping it against the painted cinder-block wall of the dorm room. I had freed myself, at least momentarily, from an enormous evil, a palpably diabolical presence.

Eventually I had to finish the book and write a report, but for the moment, I felt as if I had begun a journey out of the oppressive fog of modernist nonsense and was moving toward the light—literally as well as figuratively; I promptly went outside and enjoyed the late afternoon brilliance of an October day, extravagantly provided by the Creator whom Foucault had so pointedly rejected.

Many years later, I learned that Foucault, a committed hedonist, had died of AIDS, still shaking his fist at God. I sincerely hope that somewhere before he crossed the veil into eternity he did a radical reassessment. I know now that it was not Foucault himself who triggered my outrage. None of us has any reason to feel spiritually superior to anyone else. But I sometimes wonder if, wherever he is, he knows how much and in what way I am indebted to him.

Preface

WHAT IS TRUTH? Any thinking person asks the question one time or another.

It is anything you want it to be, answers the cynic, usually with a smirk.

Cynics, who tend to be idealists deeply wounded by unmet expectations, often embrace relativism as a shield against their disappointment. When disagreements arise, they say things like, Oh, it's all relative. Among teenagers and diffident parents, "whatever" is the preferred discussion-ender, often delivered with a shrug. Both expressions convey that there is no point in making an attempt to get to the bottom of things. Indeed, why bother if there is no actual truth to be found? In such a world, opinion is all that matters.

"Whatever" and "it's all relative" are conversation stoppers, the verbal equivalents of calling a truce. Invoked after a healthy exchange of views, they are used as a salve to heal the wounds of disagreement. Increasingly, however, they preempt the exchange. Supposedly proof that we are tolerant of each other's views, the phrases are actually a sign that we are so intolerant we dare not show any disagreement. Or that we do not have any views worth defending.

The abandonment of serious truth seeking is not the result of intellectual torpor. America has been deliberately dumbed down over the past century. This has been done in the name of progress, with the doctrine of relativism clearing the way for a brave new world to replace the old. Who has done all this you might ask? They go by a variety of names: liberals, leftists, left-libertarians, progressives, globalists, Marxists, secular humanists, and even environmentalists. But they all share one characteristic: hostility to the God of the Bible and his ordering of creation.

Rising from the ashes of Christendom is the Age of Consent, a morally obtuse world in which the only factor mitigating human action is mutual consent—as in, "If two or more consenting adults want to (fill in the blank), then it is of no concern to anyone else—period." The code word for the Age of Consent is *tolerance*. Like a magic oath, it is intoned on television, in education, and even in corporate personnel training. Like any other good thing that has been twisted, tolerance was originally a virtue. Now, to an increasing number of Americans, the word has come to symbolize heavy-handed liberalism, officially sanctioned sexual deviancies, group privileges, big government, and hostility toward Judaism and Christianity.

In theory, tolerance of everything is the animating principle of the Age of Consent. In practice, tolerance is selectively applied. Western religion, for example, is openly discouraged, while deviant behavior is celebrated. Anything that challenges traditional morality is not only tolerated but promoted; whatever supports traditional morality is attacked—in the name of tolerance. Ladeling out the elixir of relativism with a spoonful of tolerance, the Age of Consent has been remarkably successful in masking its real agenda.

In virtually every area of life, relativistic reformers have worsened societal problems by weakening morality. The poster children of this effort, by all rights, could be the prostitutes' union COYOTE (Cast Off Your Old Tired Ethics). That prostitutes even have a union is but one indicator of how far the pendulum has swung toward Babylon. Even the strippers in San Francisco have formed a collective bargaining unit, and the sex clubs have reopened in New York, Philadelphia, and Washington, D.C., despite the threat of AIDS. Public health officials actually claim that the clubs, built for group sex, are irreplaceable forums for "safe sex" instruction.

In place of morality, we have been offered the idol of education. The idea is that if we pile up enough information, we can reach to the sun, without all that God stuff, of course.

Age of Consent progressives believe that if people have sufficient knowledge and the rules are relaxed, they will do the right thing, because people are born good and only corrupted by their parents, religion, and other anachronistic influences. Hence, the solution is to liberate people from the suffocating confines of their families, churches, and communities and turn them over to the experts. Tune out mom and dad and say welcome to Dr. Ruth and the World Wide Web.

The progressive solution to most problems consists of attacking tradition in the name of some underprotected right, such as freedom of speech. More education is recommended—at earlier and earlier ages—as if lack of knowledge is the main problem in an information-saturated society. None of this knowledge infusion has worked. Twelve-year-olds are making headlines by committing gang rapes or executing rival drug dealers with Uzis in our crumbling cities. But it's nobody's fault, except those who won't go along with more of the same soul-destroying program. The progressive architects of this utopia, like the thugs they have spawned, refuse to own up to their paternity. They appear remarkably disassociated from their life's work. Guilty deadbeat dads, they blame anybody but themselves for the chaos inflicted by their progeny.

The reason most societal cures do not work is because the Age of Consent policy doctors are incorrectly diagnosing the illness. They cannot possibly prescribe the right medicine because they refuse to concede the truth about human nature. Despite talk about good intentions, it is getting more and more difficult to believe that the destruction of civil society is occurring accidently. There is too much stark evidence to believe that our cultural surgeons haven't noticed the connection between progressive policies and Uzi-toting youngsters. It was once plausible to give liberalism the benefit of the doubt. Good intentions, but bad outcomes, you know. At least they cared enough to try. Could happen to anybody. Okay, fair enough. But now that the evidence is in and the progressive drive to replace religion with centralized government power has not abated, it's time to reassess. Darker motives seem to be at work.

Evil does not just happen. It thrives when men fool themselves into thinking their personal desires are synonymous with the common good. Men of shameful habit find relativism a handy fallback. Without truth, all standards become subjective. Especially the ones that make people feel guilty about what they are doing.

Disdain for truth itself is superficially liberating. When all opinions are given equal weight, we are free from the risk of ever being wrong. We can do whatever we want without need of correction. There is simply no reason to curb one's desires. If your opinion is as good as anyone's—even God's—then the Ten Commandments are reduced to helpful hints, or as commentator Ted Koppel once lamented at a graduation ceremony, the Ten Suggestions.

The progressive impulse to exalt state over religion is really an attempt to create a world in which the progressive's own, personal malfeasance is hidden. The very existence of the church is inconvenient to those who want to indulge in debauchery. The church is a reminder that there may be eternal consequences for rejecting God and embracing sin. The only way to get around this unwelcome nagging is to make the church disappear, make it irrelevant, or capture it for anti-Christian purposes. This can be done three ways: by legislating away freedom of religion; by commandeering the culture and turning it against the church, or by co-opting the church. All have been accomplished to varying degrees. Despite their professed neutrality in religious matters, New Age progressives always side with forces that weaken the church, inside and out. They're for more government if the net effect is to reduce the role of religion in public life. They are for less government if it means opening a hydrant of smut to turn men into moral eunuchs. It is no coincidence that Hollywood, which routinely ridicules or marginalizes Christianity, donates heavily to organizations like the ACLU or People for the American Way. These groups promote sexual libertinism while advocating the expansion of state regulation in virtually every other area of life, from health care to education. As this century has proven, the modern state is the church's—and Judaism's—single greatest enemy. Caesar, after all, is a jealous god.

The only consistency in the Age of Consent is hostility toward Western religion. When it comes to freedom of speech, New Age progressives are very particular. They look the other way when religion is driven from the public square. In fact, they do the heavy pushing. But they cry crocodile tears over the slightest inconvenience to pornographers. As Joseph Sobran has noted, the ACLU is committed to making the practice of religion strictly private and to making pornography public. The reason is simple. Pornography hurts spiritual growth because it produces guilt. Build up enough guilt, and you won't feel worthy to take a moral stance on anything. Never mind the Christian message of forgiveness and grace. Misery loves company. Like the alcoholic who badgers a friend to have just one more scotch, self-styled civil libertarians push porn so that their own vices—adultery, homosexuality, porn addiction, drug and alcohol abuse—will go unnoticed. That is why the homosexual activist movement, the feminists, the abortion industry, the drug legalization network, and the purveyors of pornography work so well together: they all militate in common cause against a God-ordained, marriage-based moral order that encourages deferred gratification. Such an arrangement rebukes their "choices" by its very existence. Every time another man gets hooked on pornography, one more potential moralist who might hinder the state-aided drive toward libertinism is removed. Same for the woman who gets hooked on drugs or booze. In the relentless campaign to promote "tolerance" of vulgarity, dysfunction, and perversity, relativism is used like napalm to carpet-bomb the opposition.

Who is to say what is right or wrong except each individual in the Age of Consent? If there is no eternal template upon which we should conform our souls, then we can make our own standards. It is up to us entirely. In Genesis, the serpent promised his pupils that "ye shall be as gods, knowing good and evil." What the serpent really meant was that men would not merely *know* good and evil but *determine* it. Hence, the only rule in this brave new world of human preeminence is that of mutual acquiescence. Under such liberating auspices, homosexuals—with a straight face—can claim the "right" to marry each other. Pornographers, prostitutes, and drug dealers can stand with open palms, giving the customers what they want. Revenue-hungry state governments can help corrupt their citizens by creating lotteries, donning a blackjack dealer's green eyeshade to rip off the suckers and tax the lucky few winners. Even the libertarians don't seem to understand that this voluntary "revenue source" reduces the incentive to cut government.

In an Age of Consent, everybody's happy, except the countless victims who suffer the collateral or personal damage of marital infidelity, broken families, abortion, venereal diseases, pornography addiction, drug abuse, alcoholism, compulsive gambling, child abuse, crime, confiscatory taxation to pay for the whole mess, and the rest of the litany of social ills. Children are the most vulnerable victims of all. The winners are lawyers (Here's to litigation—a growing industry!) and the vast array of people who administer the therapeutic state.

In the Age of Consent, virtue is found in the pursuit of—not resistance to—vice. We are told that the highest good is to be true to oneself, which is a lofty way to justify self-indulgence. In schools, children are taught to cultivate their own judgment, not submit to the authority of their parents or their faiths. Right or wrong is no longer conveyed, since someone might be offended. So the child is trained to choose the course of action that seems most advantageous at the time. Situational ethics provides an excuse for indulgences, leaving children vulnerable to those who would "liberate" them with sex and drugs. When right and wrong are removed, the most rational course of action might appear to be to take certain risks—some of which have lifelong consequences.

Since the dawn of time, vices have been noisy supplicants tugging at the human heart. The apostle Paul acknowledged that he fought a daily battle with his fleshly desires, as did St. Augustine, whose autobiographical *Confessions* bared the soul of a quite accomplished sinner. Oscar Wilde, on the other hand, had the modern solution: Got a problem with a temptation? Give in to it as soon as possible. Ever since Freud linked mood swings to sexual dysfunction, psychologists have been spoon-feeding us Wilde's advice, wrapping it in the soothing jargon of self-absorption. Resisting impulses may cause conflict and pain. In the absence of eternal implications, the pursuit of pleasure and the avoidance of pain would appear to make the most sense. The latter part of the twentieth century might best be thought of as a massive, brutal hangover from the God-is-dead party.

If the highest good is personal pleasure, one's divine duty is to fixate on personal needs and wants. Pop singer Whitney Houston echoed this theme in "The Greatest Love," which struck a platinum vein in the American sensibility. The greatest love, it turns out, is to be found in the mirror. It seems to matter little that self-centered people tend to be miserable. Once a vice, and even a mortal sin, self-worship is now a cultivated skill.

But this doesn't quite work out for everyone's good. Crime scholars have stumbled onto the fact that criminals, far from lacking in self-esteem, consider themselves a sort of underground elite who break the law because it is for lesser folk. Like the cultural elites who regularly flout sexual morality, the criminal class sees itself as smarter ("ye shall be as gods . . .") than the lumpen proletariat who mindlessly play by the rules. Charles Dickens, whose many colorful criminal characters often lost their heads on the scaffold of human vanity, gave us Ebeneezer Scrooge, who indulged mightily in his greed before getting spiritual shock treatment. But prior to Jacob Marley's ghost lowering the boom, Scrooge didn't need self-esteem lessons. He did what he wanted, which was to enrich himself. Had he inhabited a modern novel, he might well have been contentedly humming "The Greatest Love" while counting his lucre.

The Age of Consent is a time of self-indulgence and moral confusion, fostered by a fundamental misunderstanding of the human heart. If people are born good and merely need to free themselves from oppressive institutions, as Jean-Jacques Rousseau postulated, then the liberationist philosophy of the Age of Consent makes sense. If, on the other hand, people are born criminally self-indulgent and need years of training to live up to a timeless moral standard, then the Age of Consent is a gigantic, cruel hoax. A handy way to check which theory makes more sense is to ask any father or mother if they had to spend more time teaching their children to misbehave or to behave; to concentrate more on themselves or to care about others; to stop taking things from a sibling or to curb those incessant charitable impulses.

Despite the obvious state of the human condition, the Age of Consent's hawkers have persuaded many people to swallow the soul-destroying poison of self-indulgence. Some people opine that it all started in the 1960s, when authority of any kind was challenged, the sexual revolution took off, and hallucinogenic drugs gave millions of people a cracked view of reality. Some trace it to the Supreme Court decision in 1962 removing prayer from government schools or to *Roe v. Wade* in 1973, which unleashed abortion. Others place blame on the Enlightenment or the Reformation. Conspiracy theories have abounded, from the bogus Protocols of the Elders of Zion through the actual Communist Party plot to take over the world. One World theorists see a grand scheme engineered by the world's elites toward the formation of a global government. At the heart of this scheme is the Council on Foreign Relations, the Trilateral Commission, the Rockefellers, and Rothschilds and the bankers and elitists of Europe and America. Apart from the anti-semitic Protocols, there is far more than a grain of truth in some of these theories. For decades, the One World folks have been shilling openly for the United Nations and multilateral treaties limiting national jurisdiction. They have written books and articles that argue for curbing America's independence. All the while, the Rockefeller Foundation and other globalist organizations have helped promote the sexual revolution by bankrolling sex research Kinsey and his colleagues designed to tear apart the moral order. In fact, what disqualifies the drive for global government as a secret conspiracy is that it is no secret. American troops have already been pressed into service wearing blue United Nations helmets, their American flag patches replaced by U. N. insignia. Things have moved so far along that Deputy National Security Advisor Strobe Talbott, a Clinton appointee, once announced in a speech that national borders would soon be a thing of the past.

Although lovers of freedom would do well to scrutinize any policy changes (and oppose them) leading to global governance, the real conspiracy began when man first acquired a conscience. The Fall of Man is not merely an account of a bygone era but a daily battle in every human heart between good and evil. A conspiracy to subvert our better angels unfolds every moment we ponder our options.

Although the battle for the human soul is an eternal struggle, our particular brand of poison was brewed over the past century. It has been doled out through the transmitters of culture—the arts, education, and the media—and even through the churches, in their rush to be "relevant."

Educators Horace Mann and John Dewey combined to concoct what home-schooling defender Michael Farris has called the "Godless monstrosity" of public schools. Mann preached compulsive universality, while Dewey constructed a secular humanist value system. In the hands of progressivistic educationists, most schools have become runaway trains speeding through an endless tunnel of relativism whose light at the end consists of . . . more education.

In the mid-nineteenth century, German Protestant theologian Julius Wellhausen delivered a bomb to the doorstep of the church that is still going off. Wellhausen's systematic critique of the Bible, which was later known as the "higher criticism," consisted of searching for the rational "evolution" of scripture. Instead of divine revelation, Wellhausen inferred, men had constructed the Bible to meet their own needs and prejudices. As Wellhausen's approach seeped into the seminaries and divinity schools, the whole idea of God's authorship became moot: If man alone wrote the Bible, then man needed to reinterpret it according to man's intellectual growth and changing conditions. During the twentieth century, the church, stripped of its claim to absolute authority, has ceded more and more ground to world philosophies based on human whim. Many churches have become driving wheels of all manner of progressive causes, from the sexual revolution to collectivist economics. The more the churches have conformed to modernism, the less vital a role they have played in the cultural debates. By the late 1990s, many mainstream churches had ditched "The Old Rugged Cross" and struck up the siren songs of the Me Generation, in which God, it is said, dwells in all of us. Since we have godlike perception, we need self-made rules that fit each of us best. Like infected tonsils, New Age priests and priestesses set out with enthusiasm to taint the rest of the Body of Christ and the larger culture with the disease of relativism. Lenin would have been delighted with all the "useful idiots" in clerical collars.

The demise of the church as a bulwark against man's conceit is a long and sometimes absurd story that has been told elsewhere. Likewise, many books have been written on the transformation of education into an instrument of social manipulation by the enemies of Judaic-Christian culture. Many others have been written about the inherent bias of the news media.

This book will concentrate on the rise of relativism within the popular culture. The initial chapters explore the practical implications of relativism on the human soul, leading man into all manner of excess. Chapter Four, which deals with the Sexual Revolution, illustrates how the unraveling of the Western moral code has led to a progressively savage, deviant, and predatory sexuality. Chapters Five through Twelve show how relativism has been conveyed through the popular arts—television, film, and art. Chapter Thirteen examines the destructive effects of relativism on architecture, the most visible outward symbol of culture; Chapter Fourteen discusses music, the most pervasive sign of our culture. Lastly, Chapter Fifteen summarizes the society-wide reaction to the loss of faith and the positive manifestations of what amounts to a countercultural resistance.

Taken as a whole, *The Age of Consent* reveals how, when man becomes the sole judge of his own actions, the intolerable increasingly is tolerated. In *Crime and Punishment*, Fyodor Dostoyevsky observed that if God is dead, all things are permissible. The Bible warns, however, that spiritual neutrality is a fatal conceit: "Woe unto them that are wise in their own eyes and prudent in their own sight." (Isaiah 5:21)

Shorn of a common understanding of what constitutes right and wrong, America is losing the will to seek the truth. We are left with hard-core sloganeers who are not interested in a real exchange of views (that takes listening as well as speaking) but a retreat into glitter and trivia. America is becoming a place in which everything matters—and nothing matters. A remnant is rising to fill the vacuum left by the spiritual void. It is carrying the message that America's only hope lies in seeking forgiveness and guidance from a loving God: "Let us fall now into the hand of God, for his mercies are great: and let me not fall into the hand of man" (II Samuel 24:14).

I WOULD LIKE TO THANK Thomas Henriksen and the Hoover Institution for getting the *Age of Consent* off the ground via a Media Fellowship. Thanks also to Gary Bauer, Chuck Donovan and Family Research Council for encouragement and counsel, and to Tom Spence and Mitchell Muncy for their editing and direction. Special thanks to my father, John H. Knight and late mother, Marilyn Knight, for their unbending faith and support, to my children, Derek and Katie, and to my sister Kathy and brother Tom and their families, and my in-laws, the Salvatores, who have always encouraged me. Thanks also to Tom Landess, Steve Lopez, Gene Beauchamp, Christopher Gacek, Laurence Jarvik, Anthony Falzarano, Kristi Hamrick, Bob Morrison and the Ervin family for their wise counsel over the years, and to Mike Minter for his spiritual leadership.

This book is dedicated to my wife Barbara.

ROBERT H. KNIGHT

THE AGE OF CONSENT

I

The Way We Were

*If any one age really attains, by eugenics and scientific
education, the power to make its descendants what it pleases,
all men who live after it are patients of that power. They
are weaker, not stronger . . . Each new power won by man
is a power over man as well.*

C. S. Lewis

ONCE UPON A TIME not so long ago, American children could
play in their neighborhoods without supervision or wander
down to the corner grocery or a ball field. Parents might
have worried that their eight-year-old would run into trouble from
neighborhood bullies but not into some deeply troubled adult with
a criminal record. This was largely the case for all children, not
just those raised in "Norman Rockwell" homes. Even in large cities,
children were free to roam about under the watchful eye of caring
adults. American culture before the 1960s reflected the values of a
family-friendly society in which children were prized.

In school, children would be taught by teachers who reinforced what the children were learning from their parents and in church. When they went to the movies or tuned into television programs, they saw heroes triumph over evil. They saw human frailty but never hopelessness. Bad guys who didn't turn around got their just deserts, usually in this life but most certainly in the next.

Americans felt secure that America was a good country whose people would be respected anywhere on earth. One of the best and most revealing lines in the eighties film *Raiders of the Lost Ark* occurs when Indiana Jones's girlfriend, Marian, is carried off by thugs as she screams in amazement, "You can't do this to me! I'm an American!" Set in the late 1930s, the movie faithfully captures the average American's faith in America's strength and goodness. Why would anyone pick on an American? We're the *good guys!* Americans understood implicitly that the Statue of Liberty was intended to signify America's role as a beacon to the world but also to serve as a reminder of America's unique promise to its own people.

Throughout the American culture in mid-century, virtues were honored, if sometimes in the breach. Western movies gave us heroes who knew the difference between right and wrong and weren't afraid to protect the weak. John Wayne, John Ford, and a thousand westerns taught us that real men do not start fights, they don't shoot even the baddest guys in the back, and they aren't ever cowards. Real men protect the weak, the innocent, and the wronged. This was the least a cowboy could do—and the least a cowgirl would expect.

Comedian Red Skelton, whose comedy hour on CBS in the 1950s and 1960s never ranked below the top twenty shows, refused to do off-color material. "I'd rather have people say, Boy, he's hokey, isn't he?" he said, "rather than, Who was the guy who told all those dirty jokes?"[1] He also declined to swear, even in his stage appearances: "I don't think anybody should have to pay money at the box office to hear what they can read on restroom walls."[2]

There was less public art in America before public subsidies flooded the market, but it was, for the most part, better to look at or hear than much of what is produced under government grants. "Shock art" was confined to the realm of the unskilled, not the federally endowed. Discordant noise was the sound of musicians tuning up, not giving a performance.

In obstetricians' offices, a diagnosis of pregnancy was most often a cause for celebration, not a chance to dictate life or death for a helpless human being. Unwanted pregnancies were far rarer, and they were normally handled in a manner that did not sacrifice life to convenience. Men who made a living by exploiting young women's predicaments were sent to jail, not given government subsidies.

American families had more money to spend on one paycheck because the government was taking far less. Those who worked hard and saved joined a swelling middle class that believed in achievement and lived it. Some Americans were left behind as the rising tide lifted almost all boats. Black Americans struggled against racism and even laws that officially discriminated against them. Their successful climb to full citizenship is one of America's greatest success stories, despite the uneven record that plagues American cities to this day. Before the Freedom Train got hijacked to Quotaville, black Americans were making steady progress in an increasingly tolerant nation. Americans of Asian and Hispanic extraction also steadily added their numbers to the middle class, creating new industries and reviving areas in Southern California, Florida, and elsewhere.

A Cultural Assault

Not all was perfect in America before the Age of Consent, but something happened to change it for the worse, especially for children. A look at American—indeed, Western—culture at the dawn of the second millennium is, for the most part, not a pretty sight. Leaving behind a common code of shared values, America has been spoon-fed the poison of relativism for the past two generations.

This is obvious to anyone who glances through a daily newspaper, watches television news, or even those who watch situation comedies on television. An endless stream of vulgarity, violence, double entendres, sensationalized sex, and cynical materialism is washing over Americans.

Nobody can truly disconnect from this rapacious, valueless culture. On a trip to Lancaster, the hub of Pennsylvania's Amish country, visitors are impressed by the serenity, spirit, and honesty of the people. The Amish have forsworn all but a few modern conveniences, and they live a devoutly religious life. They believe that the biblical admonition that man's eye is never satisfied is a warning that without conscious resistance, they could become entrapped in a materialistic spiral. They drew a line in the sand, accepting some innovations such as medical science, but rejecting material advances that tend to become ends in themselves, such as automobiles. The Amish reason that succumbing to technological temptation might make them materially richer but at the unacceptable cost of making their spiritual lives poorer.

Yet even in the midst of this timeless Amish culture, I was surprised to see an Amish storekeeper watching a large color television behind the counter in a barn where crafts are sold. It was the middle of the afternoon, and the storekeeper had tuned into talk-show host Phil Donahue, who was parading his usual collection of sexual misfits. The Amish man's eyes were wide, and it seemed as if he were a curious alien, watching images from another world being beamed into the barn. Elsewhere around town, I looked at the Amish children. They seemed remarkably mature for their ages, yet were rarely without an adult nearby. As a parent myself, I understood the protectiveness of the Amish mothers and fathers who stayed even closer to their children when tourists from the outer, material culture were around.

Many Americans, especially parents, are starting to feel more and more like the Amish as they disconnect from a culture that no longer validates their beliefs. In the late 1990s an estimated one-and-a-half million children are being home-schooled. "Alternative" publications outside the mainstream news media are thriving, particularly the overtly Christian books, magazines, and radio stations that have audiences in the millions. Many of these people are finding that the finest line to walk is to screen out the destructive elements of the culture without disengaging to the extent of the Amish. For Christians in particular, who are admonished by Jesus to be "salt and light" in their communities, total disengagement would entail ignoring the Great Commission to spread the gospel.

PARENTS AS RADICALS

As the "mainstream" culture gets coarser and coarser, those who resist the trend are increasingly targeted for abuse. In newspaper articles and broadcasts they are called "the religious right," "right-wing extremists," "fundamentalists," or just "ultra-conservatives." We are talking here about normal folks—mostly Christians and orthodox Jews, plus a growing number of Islamic adherents and concerned agnostics—who want nothing more than to mind their own business but are finding it harder and harder to do so. In the name of religious freedom, relativists have banished religion from the public square. They say they have to destroy public displays of religion in order to protect it. The response has been a culturewide gag order on Christianity in governmental and even commercial circumstances. In a short period, between 1990 and 1996, the word "Christmas" was effectively eliminated from public discourse and advertising, replaced by the word "holidays." To wish people a "Merry Christmas" instead of "happy holidays" is considered rude, as if to actively discriminate against non-Christians. In the name of religious freedom, Christians no longer even can mention the word Christ without it seeming like an imposition on people of other faiths or unbelievers. Likewise, the Easter break has been largely renamed "spring break," with a return of pagan customs such as winding ribbons around the maypole (a phallic symbol of fertility).

In the name of freedom of "choice," relativists have banned

one form of protest so that women seeking abortions would not have to hear pleas from pro-life activists on their way into the clinics. They have opposed protection for any other "businesses," such as corporations being picketed by animal rights advocates or environmentalists.

In the name of freedom of speech, relativists on campus have enacted "speech codes" that prohibit expression of ideas with which the relativists disagree.

In the name of sexual freedom, homosexual activists have managed to ban the words "father," "mother," and "husband" and "wife" from school texts so that no one need feel excluded. The nonjudgmental word "partners" is offered as an acceptable substitute.

In Massachusetts, a Jewish father was alarmed to find sexually explicit material in his elementary schoolchildren's textbooks. He helped organize protests at the local and state levels and began drawing media attention. One reporter asked him why "fundamentalist Christians" like himself were so narrow in their views. He politely informed the reporter that he was a Jew who was just trying to protect his children. The next day, he was identified anyway in the paper as a "Christian fundamentalist." That term, it seems, is so handy a way to stigmatize parents that the reporter wouldn't give it up. It complicates things when stereotyped "extremists" decline to stay in the little boxes that they have been assigned by journalists whose creed is New Age relativism.

The values of that Jewish parent haven't changed, nor have those of countless millions of normal, decent Americans who want to raise their children in a safe place, educate them according to their own faiths, reap the rewards of hard work, worship freely, and contribute to their communities. Most parents are too busy shielding their children from toxic cultural pollution to indulge in mass conspiracies. Yet, time and again, commentators say—with perfectly straight faces—that a mother's attempt to shield her child from some bizarre materials in the public library or in a third-grade classroom is an act of "censorship" or that she was part of a "book-burning" mob trying to "impose their values" on the rest of society. Liberal activists, cheered on by liberal media, demand that such parents be muzzled, by law if necessary, all in the name of tolerance. Curiously, one rarely hears the media warning about the "liberal left," or the "irreligious left" or about "ultra-liberals." In the relativists' seemingly impartial universe, in which all views are supposed to be equally welcome, there are no enemies on the left.

A case in point is the way parents are treated in each yearly edition of the liberal People for the American Way's (PAW) "anti-censorship" report, *Attacks on the Freedom to Learn*. The book, which is selectively distributed to liberal media, gets lots of respectful press. An oversized paperback, it consists of synopses of battles around the country in which texts or programs have been criticized. Whenever parents raise objections about materials, they are listed as "censors," even if they never sought removal of a text but merely thought that a book might be appropriate for a twelve-year-old but not for a nine-year-old. Concerns about age appropriateness are lumped in with attempts to have books removed. PAW notes that parents may "opt out" their children from objectionable programs or books but not ever legitimately challenge the content. Like most seemingly neutral enterprises, PAW has a double standard. The organization lends support to the removal of materials that it does not like. In St. Lucie County, Florida, a parental attempt to introduce—not remove—a textbook critical of the theory of evolution was labeled in PAW's report as "censorship." Likewise, PAW called the introduction of the Parental Rights Amendment in South Carolina an act of "censorship" because it might have empowered parents and thereby hindered school officials. The amendment merely states that, "The right of parents to direct the upbringing and education of their children shall not be infringed."

As the cultural envelope keeps getting pushed directly into the face of the average American, we keep hearing that the real problem is . . . the average American. By trying to protect our children, we are told that we are getting in the way of experts who know better than we what is good for our children. By wanting to keep more of our own earnings, we are told that we are acting selfishly. By going to church, we are told that we are perpetuating a narrow-minded doctrine of right and wrong from a God who has been declared dead by the more enlightened elites.

But no culture has survived without guidelines for behavior. No community has thrived without values that govern how people treat each other. No nation has prospered by punishing productive people. As exceptional as America is, it is not exempt from the rules that sustain civilization. America's moral meltdown, courtesy of cultural elites, is directly responsible for an out-of-control welfare state and a national debt that totals in the trillions of dollars.

America's uniqueness stems from its emphasis on freedom and limited government. But as Benjamin Franklin said, the Constitution is designed for a republic with a highly principled population, specifically, "a religious people." A constitutional republic simply will not work when people do not have enough moral clarity to recognize truth and justice, fend for themselves, and look out for others who can't.

Most Americans recognize that government cannot solve all problems. And that things would be even worse if it ever tried. Joseph Sobran once remarked that when the government starts worrying about your health, it's time to start worrying about your liberty.

Take the problem of rudeness. There are times when we've been tempted to think, wouldn't it be great to have a law forbidding some boor from butting into line in front of us at the supermarket? Or talking loudly in a movie theater? But there are some things that the law does not address, nor should it. Often, the law is secondary to the sense of rightness conveyed by the people themselves and by the shame we feel when we violate the rules of civility.

There is no more proof needed of our culture's moral decline into relativism than the crabgrass-like growth in laws and bureaucracy. Government promises to save us from ourselves so we can be free to pursue all manner of pleasure in the Age of Consent. Accordingly, the government is appealing to our worst instincts—with or without the consent of the governed.

2

Relativism:
The Siren Song of Decadence

*There is one thing a professor can be absolutely certain of:
almost every student entering the university believes, or
says he believes, that truth is relative . . . They are unified
only in their relativism and in their allegiance to equality . . .
[I]t is the modern replacement for the inalienable rights
that used to be the traditional American grounds for a free
society.*[1]

Allan Bloom

NEW AGE RELATIVISM is best defined by citing several sources:

- Computer junkies from 1995 film *Hackers*: "There is no right or wrong, only fun or boring."

- Media mogul Ted Turner: "We don't need the Ten Commandments anymore."

- *Playboy* magazine publisher Hugh Hefner: "Sex is the major civilizing influence in our society, not religion."

- Physicist Stephen M. Hawking: "Questions about reality don't have any meaning."

- Students at Stanford, chanting: "Hey ho, hey ho, Western culture's got to go."

- Suspect in a brutal gang rape in Central Park: "It was fun."

- Bob Dylan, from his *Oh Mercy* album: "They're breaking down the distance between right and wrong."

Dylan's lament is what has been ailing America. The spirit of the Age of Consent, "relativism" is the modern philosophy that obscures, rather than clarifies, moral distinctions. Few would describe themselves as "relativists," but many turn to relativism as a shield against "absolutists"—those who take their beliefs seriously. Rather than make important distinctions between competing beliefs, the Age of Consent banishes all to the realm of dangerous myth.

Relativism is the cultivation of ignorance; the gateway to nihilism; a false view of reality constructed by know-nothings for know-nothings; an extremely efficient vehicle for evil, whose existence it denies.

Webster's defines relativism as "the doctrine that knowledge or truth is relative and dependent upon time, place, and individual experience."

Like any effective lie, relativism has a good deal of truth in it. No one who has ever waited in a line with a young child would disagree that a child's grasp of the concept of time is different from that of an adult. But it is something else to define time as each person's perception of it. On earth, two hours is two hours, whether it seems like a blip or an eternity.

Until recently, the search for truth in our age has largely been the effort to eliminate subjective perceptions. The scientific method has become a secular religion—"scientism," which is the application of the scientific method to all aspects of life. Anything not applicable, such as the spiritual, is considered irrelevant.

Now, with the dawning of the Age of Consent, the focus is turned outside in: subjectivity has become synonymous with objectivity. One can count only on one's own perspective, all other standards being arbitrary. According to the logic of relativism, reality and morality are simply creations of the observer, or "myths," as Jungian historian Joseph Campbell has put it.

This vision took off in the 1960s, particularly in California. In 1964, the Esalen Institute was founded by Mike Murphy and Dick Price at a Big Sur resort owned by Murphy's family. Esalen quickly became the center of the "human potential movement." Drawing celebrities such as writer Aldous Huxley and LSD gurus Alan Watts and Timothy Leary, the Esalen invitees ingested psychedelic drugs and conducted mind-control experiments in plush surroundings overlooking the Pacific Ocean. Attempting to blend watered-down Hinduism with concepts of physical science, the group pushed the boundaries of human relationships, becoming advocates for group sex and self-absorption, among other pastimes. One devotee, Werner Erhard, a former Scientologist, went on to found the Erhard Seminar Training course, better known as "EST." In EST sessions, trainers subject pilgrims to abusive comments designed to break down their value systems. The idea is to free people from all moral and psychological limitations. The method, which included forbidding attendees from leaving to go to the bathroom, was spoofed in the 1977 Burt Reynolds comedy film *Semi-Tough*. The upshot of Esalen, EST, and other outgrowths of the "human potential movement" is a turning inward for answers rather than a turning toward God. This means abandoning traditional concepts of right and wrong and making up rules to suit each individual. Advocates of this approach were sobered somewhat in 1969 when, three days before committing the Sharon Tate murders, Charles Manson's group was welcomed as honored guests at Esalen, where they performed music composed by Manson.

At Esalen, which still operates as a center for unconventional psychological techniques, even love was redefined in the 1960s and 1970s as nothing more than an advanced form of self-interest. "When we say that we are in love with someone, what is happening is that around that person we have an experience of our own essence," counsels former EST instructor Stewart Emery in his book *Actualizations*. "When we say we are in love with someone, what is happening is that around that person we have an experience of our own essence . . . We really fall in love with our ultimate self . . . [W]hat you love is your experience of yourself."[2]

In the Age of Consent, all is good except any restraints on the desires of the self. As Emery notes, there is no evil, just ignorance: "There are some people whom you ought to protect yourself from. It is not that they are bad people. Rattlesnakes may not know that they love all living creatures, so if you walk through a field of rattlesnakes who don't know how beautiful they are, you are likely to have an out-of-the-body experience."[3]

The propensity of rattlesnakes to bite is not part of their nature but merely a lower level of consciousness. In the same way, human nature is seen as good, and sin does not exist except in the mind of the sinner, who is prisoner to outmoded ways of thinking. Traditional beliefs about right and wrong are part of a consciousness that should be shucked off in the manner of a crab molting its shell.

Since people appear to have so many different views on morality—all individually perceived—a natural, universal code of human morality is deemed inconceivable.

Relativistic thinking has penetrated many Western institutions and shattered norms, nowhere more than in popular culture. Sex, violence, and the pursuit of material success have become dominant elements in films and television shows.

In today's more "realistic" culture, success for success's sake is the underlying theme. Character development is done cartoonishly, if at all, because the writers are less concerned with the machinations of the human soul than with achieving sensational effects.

As the culture coarsens into a preoccupation with materialism, the moral underpinnings have become increasingly arbitrary. By undermining traditional values—our sense of right and wrong—relativism has damaged our ability to make crucial choices.

The soul of civilization—any civilization—is culture. Culture is where sense is made of life, where values are preserved and presented. It is the soil in which all human institutions grow. Relativism attacks culture the way the AIDS virus attacks the body. When AIDS cells invade the body, they do not kill by themselves; they make it possible for other diseases, such as cancer, to do the job. AIDS cells destroy T cells, the body's early warning system. Unalerted because the T cell sentries have been neutralized, the body's white blood cells remain passive while disease consumes healthy cells. Eventually, there are not enough white cells to fight off even a minor infection.

Relativism destroys culture by neutralizing the cultural T cells—family and religion. The institutions follow, as the arts, media, education, and the legal system are harnessed not to time-honored principles but to prevailing social winds. In legal terms, this means the replacement of Natural Law—timeless, universal, God-ordained—with the Positive Law, which man makes up as he goes along.

As property rights and contracts are redefined to meet group demands, they lose their power of principle. A legalized anarchy reigns in which might makes right. An explosion in frivolous lawsuits has led to a "lottery" mentality with a get-rich-quick ticket. We watch as a woman wrings millions of dollars out of McDonald's for spilling her own hot coffee on herself. Burglars sue their victims—and win. The legal system is increasingly being viewed as a grab bag in which anyone's grievance or even inconvenience is redressed.

I realized one day how far this had gone when I was driving home with my daughter from church. Noticing that a fruit juice machine was missing from its spot at a local gas station, I said that it was too bad they had removed it. My nine-year-old daughter immediately had a solution: "Daddy," she said, "why don't you get a lawyer and sue them to get the juice back?" She was serious. This would be funny had it not reflected a more troubling reality. Respect for the legal system declines when it is seen not as a dispenser of justice but as a vehicle for personal gain. It is no accident that lawyer jokes are fast becoming the most appreciated jests at parties. And judges may well suffer the same fate in the near future, as mountebanks, moral idiots, and would-be Caesars keep popping up in lifetime appointments, issuing rulings that defy logic, law, and custom.

Judges, who are supposed to be the guardians of the law, routinely toss out majority elections if the result is not politically correct or does not suit the prejudices of the judge. (In California in particular, this has become an art form.) Thus entire communities have lost the right to maintain even a minimal moral climate. When a court declares that all forms of expression are constitutionally protected— even hard-core pornography—then the concept of common decency is destroyed, and pornographers become by default the arbiters of public standards. Thus a seemingly "neutral," relativistic position in the culture war is really not a neutral stance but enlistment on the side of infinitely eroding standards. In this way, agents of the Left, such as the American Civil Liberties Union, People for the American Way, and the many captured "mainstream" groups such as the American Library Association, all work to destroy standards while professing to be upholding everybody's freedom. But parents whose children are made to walk a gauntlet of pornography, homosexuality, and violence at the local library or the corner drugstore do not see their freedoms enhanced. And scholars who look to local libraries to carry the classics of Western civilization are finding many of them missing, replaced by pop music compact disks, videos, and self-help books. They are told that they no longer have the freedom to assume that the culture or the government they support with their tax dollars will defend their values as it once did. Thus they are told to be ever vigilant, as if they could spend every waking hour monitoring what their children consume from television, radio, magazines, and an increasingly coarse peer group weaned on "Beavis and Butthead," Howard Stern, and Marilyn Manson.

In such an environment, virtue is seen as a hindrance to the satisfaction of appetite, whether it be for money, sex, or power. The cultural elite, like those of decadent Rome, is losing its patience with those who will not succumb to its carnal attractions. The mainstream press routinely deprecates "religion" by misstating beliefs and reporting on church services and events in a faux neutral tone reminiscent of *National Geographic* examining the exotic carryings-on in an aboriginal village. The reader would have to be mighty dim to miss the point, which is that These People Are Not Like Us.

Before becoming the *de facto* Establishment, the Left used to call such tactics "marginalization." For years, university professors have made fat salaries by accusing the average American of "marginalizing" homosexuals for not celebrating "gay culture" or "marginalizing" women by not buying into the feminists' denigration of marriage and motherhood.

The solution became quota systems against caucasian Americans and straight males in general, despite assurances that each government power-grab in the name of "civil rights" could not possibly detract from anyone else's rights. As merit gives way to counting heads by race, sex, and sexual preference, cynicism eats away at the old moral restraints. People who "play by the rules" find themselves punished for it. So they become embittered. Ask any hardworking parent in an inner city area who watches as his neighbors "play" the system to fund illegitimacy, indolence, and graft. As justice recedes, people see less and less sense in playing by any rules, including personal morality. And as cynicism disarms the moral sentries, decadence steps into the parlor unchallenged because it is unnoticed for what it is—evil.

In the 1987 film *Broadcast News*, Albert Brooks plays a dedicated reporter who is continually passed over for promotion in favor of an empty-headed anchorman (William Hurt) who gets ahead by mastering style, not substance. As the female producer (Holly Hunter) prepares to throw herself at the handsome, amoral anchorman, the reporter tries one last attempt to dissuade her, telling her in desperation: "Tom, while being a very nice guy . . . is the devil."

When the anchorwoman protests, the reporter persists: "What do you think the devil is going to look like if he's around? No one is going to be taken in by a guy with a long red pointy tail . . . He will be attractive; he'll be nice and helpful. He'll get a job where he influences a great God-fearing nation. He'll never do an evil thing, he'll never deliberately hurt a living thing. He'll just, bit by bit, lower our standards where they're important."

Later, the anchorman acknowledges his own moral ambivalence but complains that he cannot observe any moral line because "It's hard not to cross it—they keep moving the little sucker, don't they?"

Evil is the conquering of the good, which happens effortlessly when there is no resistance—when nobody is watching. Social critic Hannah Arendt coined the term the "banality of evil" to describe the soul's defeat by evil because of its cultivated ability to ignore it.

Relativism is the most banal of evils, masquerading as a disinterested party. Relativism destroys the soul of culture by whispering in a thousand ways that justice is a fantasy, that morality is entirely subjective and therefore situational. But morality is not artificial. It is as natural as air and as necessary for survival as the human institutions it sustains.

The higher morality—concern for others, deferred gratification, a principled code of personal conduct, support for marriage and family—is enshrined in most religions and produces maximum human freedom in its Western incarnation, Christendom.

Without the higher morality, might makes right, and morality is the conduct prescribed to the ruled by their rulers. The liberal democratic system, which holds some truths to be sacred, cannot survive in a strictly relativistic culture. For all the brave talk of infinite "pluralism," freedom withers without a God-given common code of conduct.

In recent years, relativism has accelerated a secular trend toward ultra-tolerance, creating a "value-free" environment, a collective insanity in which there is no moral center. Standards of any kind are attacked as a threat to the false freedom of relativism. If beauty is entirely in the eye of the beholder, then art can be anything at all, as Andy Warhol proved with his pop reproductions of soup-can labels. Once aimed at universal appeal, art is now to be enjoyed only by those who swallow the self-serving, jargon-filled explications of the priesthood of art critics. Just as lawyers developed an arcane language partly to ensure a perpetual need to employ them as interpreters, the avant-garde have made "art" sadly remote and irrelevant to most Americans.

As in art, the legal system has lost respect because it is no longer understandable except to those who indulge in its purposeful obfuscation. And it is perceived (correctly) to be oftentimes serving the guilty at the expense of their victims.

A soulless architecture has produced buildings that satisfy neither form nor function. Although the profession appears to be awakening from its long service to ugliness and conformity, many buildings still seem intended as attacks on the past, jarring contradictions in traditional surroundings.

Movies are being made that tell us nothing about the struggle of the human soul. Sex, violence, bright colors, and lush sound take center stage, subordinating plot, character, and allegory to secondary roles. Moral ambiguity turns bad guys into good guys and vice versa. Traditional values are portrayed as stumbling blocks on the way to human freedom. The good guys still usually win, but their standards have slipped considerably. Batman, pillar of propriety, has became a neurotic recluse who falls into bed Hollywood-style after a date with a reporter. In the comic books, the heroes (even Superman and Batman!) have ugly, distorted features—just like the bad guys.

In the schools, educators are grappling with dictates to teach "multiculturalism," which is really multiethics. In order to avoid offending anyone's subculture, Western civilization is presented as one offering—and a particularly evil one at that—in a kaleidoscope of cultural norms. In the relativistic view, presenting Western culture as anything special is tantamount to bigotry or "establishment of religion." In the name of church-state separation, religion's profound role in the formation of the American character has been excised from many textbooks. Pupils find the Pilgrims inaccurately giving thanks to the Indians, not God. And the Rev. Martin Luther King Jr., becomes just another secular progressive, not a cleric motivated by the Christian vision of men's essential equality and dignity before God.

Environmentalists are expanding the notion of prudent stewardship of the earth into the headier realm of "pantheism" (the unification of God with the created universe) and "animism" (the belief that inanimate objects have spirits). Nature films are less about monkeys and trees than about radical ecologists' worship of nature and its flip side—an undisguised contempt for humanity. One *Time* magazine cover illustrates the New Thinking by showing a closeup of a penguin on an ice floe and a ship and two men in the background. The headline reads: "Is Any Place Safe From Man?"

Churches are trading in their mission of eternal salvation for more stylish pursuits, spending their inherited legitimacy on dubious causes such as passing out condoms to save the sexual revolution. The religious trappings remain, but the soul has taken flight from many trendy congregations.

Without beliefs of its own, relativism has fostered faith in the only philosophy left when the others have been vanquished: materialism, the cold servant of instinct.

3

Materialism: The Religion That Fails

The turn introduced by the Renaissance was probably inevitable historically: the Middle Ages had come to a natural end by exhaustion, having become an intolerable despotic repression of man's physical nature in favor of the spiritual one. But then we recoiled from the spirit and embraced all that is material, excessively and incommensurately.[1]

Aleksandr Solzhenitsyn

IN THE EARLY TWENTIETH CENTURY, communism began its drive to dominate the world with its unconditional belief in dialectical materialism. The idea is that history is moving progressively toward new paradigms, each of which supplants most of the old through synthesis. Eventually, the world reaches the blissful state of communism: everyone is equal, there is no property, all is shared, and the state withers away. In actuality, Marxism has proved to be a false prophecy. Far from withering away, communist governments imposed enormous cruelties on their hapless subjects. As we approach the second millennium, the communist world, after more than seventy-five years of misery, has broken apart from within, brought down by the poverty of its centrally planned economies, its own spiritual vacuum, and firm resistance from an American-led Free World.

Watching from afar, Americans are taking satisfaction that the Western ethos has been vindicated; freedom works, coercive socialism (there is actually no other kind) does not.

Outperforming the East in all areas except perhaps the Olympics (where former East Bloc professionals are still whipping Western amateurs), Western nations are basking in their ideological triumph. As the Berlin Wall crumbled and dictators like Romania's Ceausescu fell, the press exulted over the West's superiority. After a costly, painful struggle for seven decades, the West seemed entitled to a little gloating. But pride goeth before the fall, the proverb says.

The West is holding all the cards—economic, technological, philosophical. It is holding so many cards that some Westerners think it safe to throw some of them away, beginning with the military and proceeding to the spiritual and rational. Having wounded religion by falsely pitting it against reason, the Age of Consent is now attacking reason as a purely cultural construct. When faith and reason are removed, Western culture becomes a parody of itself, surviving on a diet of camp humor and cynicism because the real has been made unreal. What is permanent in life is now "corny." David Letterman's raised eyebrow at any and all claims to fame symbolizes the sly skepticism that is the style of the age.

For the truly hip—those who see through the culture at all times—there are publications devoted to irony, a thin veil for cynicism. The now-defunct humor magazine *Spy* could be wickedly funny. Its mission was to be "silly about serious subjects and serious about silly subjects," publisher Tom Phillips once told a college audience.[2] But what made *Spy's* humor different from that of its elder publication, London-based *Punch*, was a carefully conveyed attitude of disdain. *Punch*, while poking fun at Great Britain's stuffiness, does so from within the culture, not from outside it. It is the difference between laughing with someone or laughing at someone. Humor can be found in both, but the latter relies mostly on cruelty.

Cynicism is not confined to magazines like *Spy*, which, to its credit in an earlier incarnation, recognized its own disease by once including a serious article exposing the camp culture and its obsession with irony. Genuine sentiment, the magazine noted, is invoked in many films and television shows, but is often accompanied by apology. Post-modernism, like adolescence, is embarrassed by sentiment, and must jump through hoops to make the old virtues acceptable: "Gosh, I know this is something out of Dickens, but, like, I love you." Figure skater Nancy Kerrigan consented to ride in Disney World's parade after earning her silver medal in the 1994 Olympics but couldn't resist distancing herself from the event by remarking how "corny" it all was.

It is not only adolescents who must mine sentiment from increasingly shallow veins. The success of television shows such as the seventies series "The Golden Girls" shows that audiences of all ages are conditioned to focus on baser impulses. "The Golden Girls" (now in syndication) includes subplots that transcend the sensual, but the tidal wave of double entendres drowns them out.

An undeniably important and exciting part of life, sex has been elevated into a national religion. Magazines at supermarket checkout counters scream the actual word "Sex!" from their covers—even the venerable *Reader's Digest*, which knows a thing or two about marketing. Old people are supposed to be obsessed with sex as much as young people. In a culture in which lust and life are synonymous, it is proof that they are still alive. As Chesterton observed, sex is the materialist's religion. Anyone not obsessed with sex is a loser at best and narrow-minded at worst. Parents venturing with their children into supermarkets find kiosks stacked with *Sports Illustrated*'s annual "Swimsuit" issue, featuring seminaked women on the cover and plenty of flesh inside. Women's magazines such as *Cosmopolitan* show deeper and deeper cleavage on the cover and feature models with sensuous leers, the kind that courts have found to constitute part of the legal definition for pornography. Combined with headlines that incessantly promise to help the reader have a hotter sex life, the overall effect is to create personal doubts about sexual adequacy and to foster complacency toward an essentially pornographic culture designed specifically to create and service dissatisfaction.

When Roger Staubach was the star quarterback for the Dallas Cowboys, he was frequently asked about his "goody-goody" lifestyle. Having achieved stardom, Staubach was still married to the same woman, eschewing the playboy lifestyles of some of his peers. That Staubach and not his sybaritic compatriots was on the defensive shows how far traditional values had been devalued by the 1970s.

It is not that sex is unimportant, Staubach explained in an interview. Sex is great, but it should not be the paramount consideration in life. To Staubach's detractors, this was heresy, right up there with Pat Boone preferring milk over scotch. What a couple of losers. (Pat came back, it must be noted, in leather regalia in 1997 to do a heavy metal album, *No More Mr. Nice Guy*, convincing more than a few skeptics that we are smack dab into the End Times.)

Seers such as Dear Abby, Ann Landers, and Dr. Joyce Brothers have become celebrities by giving advice on social relations, with sex topping the list of subjects. Taken as a whole, the columns appear to support traditional values but actually work to undermine them in the name of "tolerance." Woven into the largely common-sense denunciations of rascally boyfriends and predatory "other" women are the messages that aberrance is only in the minds of the readers and that the pansexual lobby is better equipped to preach sexual ethics to teens than are parents. In one column, Ann Landers proclaims that anyone who does not buy the myth that homosexuals are "born that way" are "haters." She urges the "haters" to change their bigoted ways and get aboard the gay rights bandwagon. One memorable Dear Abby column in 1997 consists of a letter supposedly from an eleven-year-old boy who is happy that he is being raised by his dad and the dad's homosexual lover. The letter deftly hits every talking point made by homosexual activists. Abby closes by telling the boy that he is very "blessed by God" for this arrangement, as if God, who declared in Genesis (later restated by both Jesus and the apostle Paul) that his plan for sexuality is for a man and a woman to marry and become "one flesh," does not have a problem with any of this.

Dr. Ruth Westheimer has gone one up on the "personals" columnists, concentrating solely on sex, or, in her vernacular "good sex." Dr. Laura Schlesinger has built a radio empire by delivering in-your-face common sense to callers on her talk show who confess their stupidities. A practicing Jew, Dr. Laura reserves special derision for whiners and special pleaders, and the audience loves it. It is a refreshing display of common sense, with a major exception being Dr. Laura's one-time unfortunate compliance with the homosexual activist movement's propaganda. Like most public figures, she declined to challenge the moral equivalence of homosexuality with heterosexuality or to acknowledge the burgeoning ex-gay movement. But this changed in 1997 after homosexual activists attacked her for raising questions about pro-homosexual curricula in public schools. She noted in a September 5, 1997, program that her history of support for gay activism was ignored and that she had been cast as a hateful bigot. Having experienced the harsh side of homosexual activism, Dr. Schlesinger now takes a more critical view and has referred callers struggling with homosexuality to Exodus International, an ex-gay ministry which operates eighty-five chapters in the United States and 125 worldwide. For some people, at least, she contends, there is good news: you don't have to be gay.

The popularity of these upside-the-head commentators is testament to the hunger for wisdom that mom, pop, grandma, and religion used to dispense. When the traditional conduits of values are no longer effective, people seek direction elsewhere. The columns and talk shows also serve as proof of man's wicked tendency to delight in the words of a gossip, which, as the Proverbist states, "are like choice morsels; they go down to a man's inmost parts."[3] Hearing how messed up other people are makes our vain human hearts feel more virtuous by comparison. That is one major reason why America has grown so complacent over the vulgarization of the culture.

The sexual revolution, like any false doctrine, is threatened by the very existence of traditional values. Promising freedom, sexual promiscuity has brought misery to many in the form of unwanted pregnancies, abortion, sexually-transmitted diseases, and widespread social pathologies spawned by family break-up.

Sexual freedom is a dangerous myth that is part of a relativism that has fostered an obsession with materialism—the realm of the senses. The only sin is not satisfying The Drive, whatever form it takes, be it sex, intoxication, power, or acquisitiveness. "When the going gets tough, the tough go shopping," a bumper sticker cheerily reminds us. Thousands of years of Western civilization, which had produced a child-centered, family-based culture, has been supplanted by self-seeking adults who follow the 1960s dictum: "If it feels good, do it."

People are subject to many instinctual, sensual impulses. As psychiatrist Jeffrey Satinover observes, these drives are morally neutral unless cultivated toward ends for which they were not designed. For example, if someone indulges in illicit sex to compensate for loneliness or anxiety, the relief is temporary but the effects may become permanent. Instead of addressing a genuine need, such as estrangement from God, the indulgent person (just for old times' sake, let's call him a "sinner") not only does nothing to alleviate the cause but winds up exacerbating the situation. Satinover illustrates this: "When I place my hand in a fire, it burns and hurts badly. The safe and effective response to this pain, obviously, is to remove my hand. But an equally effective—in fact more effective—method of relieving pain would be to kill it entirely, say by taking high doses of pain-killing drugs or severing the responsible nerves. But such an action is hardly safe. It is, rather, very risky. For from that point on I could 'safely' place my hand in the fire without any pain at all."[4]

Rather than denying the strength of material temptations, traditional morality orders them in a socially cohesive hierarchy that answers human needs and protects the interests of children. When someone controls the sexual drive in order to maintain a monogamous relationship, he or she is demonstrating fidelity to something other than immediate gratification. When a lasting relationship is held to be less important than one of its components— sex, for instance—the relationship will fall apart, despite the promises of "open" arrangements. One of the more predictable events of the 1970s was the marital breakup of George and Nena O'Neill, authors of the 1972 best-selling "new lifestyle for couples," *Open Marriage,* which counseled couples to abandon fidelity as part of an old view of marriage that was "antiquated," "obsolete," "unrealistic," "archaic," and "unreasonable."[5]

The ancient Greek philosophers recognized the danger of giving free rein to the senses. Greek tragedies are replete with the wages of excess. Aristotle's Golden Mean was a prescription for a balanced life, in which people do not ignore the senses but do not elevate them to a position they do not deserve. The balance is achieved by internalizing moral values imparted by family, religion, and culture.

Mature sexuality depends on the cultivation of self-control, in which sexuality is placed within a larger context. In Western nations before the Age of Consent, promiscuity had been discouraged by law but mostly through cultural pressure. Polls show that Americans generally feel that people should be able to live any way they want. But they are reluctant to confer more status on non-traditional relationships such as homosexual partners or heterosexual live-ins.

They fear, rightly, that such oxymorons as gay "marriage" would undercut the traditional family's moral, religious, and legal protections. Aggressive gambits in the late 1990s to secure "gay marriage," "domestic partner" benefits, and the adoption of children by homosexual couples appear to have justified long-standing fears that the ascendance of homosexuality occurs at the cost of society's most fundamental moral norms. In December 1997, the state of New Jersey entered into a consent decree fashioned by the ACLU that gave single people, unmarried couples, and homosexual couples the same status as married couples in adoption cases. This meant that marriage could no longer be considered a primary beneficial factor when placing children in adoptive homes, proving that the ascendancy of the homosexual agenda is the downfall of marriage as a legally protected social necessity.

Homosexual rights advocates, who have likened their struggle to that of the black civil rights movement, contend that they are fighting bigotry. They ignore the fact that a homosexual orientation can be controlled, resisted, or even changed. Thousands of former homosexuals give the lie to the idea that anyone is "born gay."

To bolster their cause, homosexual activists have persuaded a willing mass media to uncritically trumpet various "scientific" studies by homosexual researchers that purport to show that homosexuality is both normal and innate. Such studies have fallen apart upon closer examination, but the public has been treated only to headlines proclaiming progress toward the discovery of a "gay gene," or inflated "gay teen suicide" or "hate crime" statistics. A fair airing of facts about homosexuality—its causes, its behavioral manifestations, and its effects on individuals, families, and societies—would settle the debate, but that is unlikely in the current climate. Whichever way Americans finally decide the homosexual issue, its very existence has ignited a reexamination of norms, beliefs, and the moral tightrope between tolerance and acceptance. It is a debate that could happen only in a free society in which tolerance is a primary value.

While America may not be as accepting of open homosexuality

as the activists would like, it is light years from the repressive atmosphere of authoritarian nations. In some Islamic countries, homosexuality is a crime punishable by death. In China, the government has used electric shock on homosexuals to try to force them to change their behavior.

Overly powerful states take it upon themselves to dictate morality—whatever they choose it to be—beyond what is sanctioned by cultural norms. As the federal government in America grows to the point to which it is intruding into every aspect of living, official policies toward such private matters as sexuality are increasingly unavoidable. While this is now helping to advance the homosexual agenda, it carries the risk of backfiring on its adherents. A government that dwarfs all other institutions can easily become a tyrant. As George Washington warned, "Government is not reason; it is not eloquence. It is force. And force, like fire, is a dangerous servant and a fearful master."

THE IMPORTANCE OF THE FATHER-MOTHER FAMILY

A free society, whose strength depends on maintaining moral agents such as the family outside the state, can be liberal and tolerant so long as the center holds. A tree can have its branches bent in different directions without permanent harm if the trunk is solid. Primacy of the family is the trunk upon which the rest of the culture rests, and the success of alternative living arrangements is largely due to how closely they reflect traditional family values. The value of family life is so obvious that homosexual activists, who once scorned marriage as a symbol of conformity, are now fighting for "gay marriage" and adoption of children by homosexual couples. By appropriating the moral capital of the family, they hope to validate their sexual behavior without honoring the core relationship—the joining of the opposite sexes in marriage. By making sexuality seem trivial, as if there were no significant differences between men and women, they ignore what makes marriage essential. An exclusive sexual, legal, economic, and spiritual relationship, marriage provides for continuance of bloodlines and kinship, makes men more productive and women more secure, gives children a family heritage, including grandparents, aunts, uncles, and cousins, and is the basis for lawful property distribution.

The two sexes approach children with different strengths. Rutgers sociologist David Popenoe observes that children have the need for communion—the feeling of being connected, included, and related—and for agency—independence, individuality, and self-fulfillment. Fathers and mothers complement each other in providing for these two sets of needs: "At play and in other realms, fathers tend to stress competition, challenge, initiative, risk taking, and independence. Mothers, as caretakers, stress emotional security and personal safety. On the playground, fathers will try to get the child to swing ever higher, higher than the person on the next swing, while mothers will be cautious, worrying about an accident."[6]

Several decades of social science research reveal that children do best in two-parent, father and mother families, and that any departure from this model diminishes children's chance of success. Without a father in the house, children of both sexes are more prone to peer pressure, early sexual experimentation, use of alcohol and illicit drugs, educational failure, and even criminal behavior.[7]

Analyzing numerous family studies, veteran social analyst Patrick Fagan concludes that

> absence of marriage, not race, is the major factor in explaining crime rates and poverty. The rise in crime is tied to the disintegration of marriage. The impact on the child is significant and can be permanent. Out of wedlock birth and growing up in a single parent family means that the child is more likely to suffer from poorer health as a newborn (if a very young mother), an increased chance of dying, retarded cognitive and verbal development, lower educational achievements, lower job attainment, increased behavior and emotional problems, lower impulse control, retarded social

development, etc. The root cause of these ills lies not in poverty,
but in the lack of married parents.[8]

As relativism reduces "family values" to the status of arbitrary opinions
based on temporary consensus, it eats away at the moral center
that sustains real diversity.

In ancient Greece, Socrates saw that his own extreme relativism
threatened the very social order of Athens and complied with his
own execution by drinking hemlock. His seemingly selfless act
was ultimately narcissistic, however, since he assumed that nothing
in Athens's culture was strong enough to withstand his powerful
questions. For an egomaniac, Socrates was a heck of a citizen.
Though he found Athens's culture ultimately groundless, Socrates
concluded that its civic virtue was so precious that it should be
preserved from the likes of him, the nonconformist.

The late Allan Bloom caused a sensation in the late 1980s with
Closing of the American Mind. Although the book was an engaging
critique of relativism, Bloom ultimately based his idea of the good
society on little more than a shared belief in democracy and free
inquiry. The Bible, he said, is important only because a lot of
people are familiar with it so it can impart shared values—not because
it is true. For Bloom, truth is secondary to cultural consensus.
Hollow at its core, this belief in process is the essence of modern
liberalism, which believes in preserving personal freedom by reducing
all ideas to the same value. The utopian liberal dream, however,
always founders upon the rock of human nature, thus requiring
armed force to achieve the aims of an egalitarianism-spouting elite
against an often unwilling populace. The more the elites work for
an egalitarian world, the more they set themselves apart from the
rest of society.

More on liberal elitism later. For now, let's go back to Socrates.
His self-sacrifice was a noble act. But its morality is suspect for
two reasons: first, it was a denial of the individual's unlimited capacity
to grow and learn; Socrates figured he knew it all and could never

discover a spiritual goodness behind the cultural goodness. Second, he gave the state more authority over the human conscience than it deserves. He was saying, in effect, that the interests of the collective whole gave the city the authority to kill him merely for disagreeing with it. Socrates wittingly or unwittingly gave aid and comfort to totalitarians of all stripes.

Perhaps Socrates should not be blamed. He predated the Judaic-Christian tradition, which proclaims that human life is more important than any political entity and that suicide is an affront to the creator. Socrates humbled himself before the state, which is not the same as humbling oneself before God. The latter is the basis for the American system, whose founding documents tacitly recognize biblically-based, transcendent law, a natural system that is universally applicable.

As American culture descends into relativism, it delegitimates institutions based on natural law. The school of pragmatic philosophy epitomized by John Dewey and William James argues that free institutions can be sustained merely by the fact that they seem to produce beneficial results. We try them, and they work. But that is like saying a successful marriage works only because of its benefits, not because it is founded on love and commitment.

Material pragmatism cuts the heart out of American institutions and then declares that the benefits derived from those institutions are self-sustaining. "Market conservatives" who disdain cultural issues are little different from liberals in their belief that the marketplace (or in the liberals' case, the marketplace of ideas) will somehow produce virtuous, self-governing citizens. Let's call these folks "liberaltarians."

What the liberaltarians, who clamor for drug legalization, free sex, abortion, legalized prostitution, and limitless pornography above all else do not understand is that the sexual revolution that they mistake for freedom is the most serious threat posed to liberty in America.

4

The Sexual Revolution: Relativizing Eros

During the last two centuries, and particularly the last few decades, every phase of our culture has been invaded by sex. Our civilization has become so pre-occupied with sex that it now oozes from all pores of American life.[1]

Pitirim Sorokin

IN THE LATE 1930s, Russian émigré Pitirim Sorokin saw a sea change occurring in Western democracies, most notably the United States. With a rise in sensual music, lurid advertising, and a movie-driven commercialized culture fixated on satisfying the senses, America, he said, was passing from an "ideational" to a "sensate" society. Sorokin, founder of Harvard's sociology department, explained that "ideational" was not idealism, but the priority of spiritual and intellectual goals over those that appealed to the senses.

Sorokin saw the "basic substitution of the dominant Medieval (Religious) values by the Sensate (Secular) values during the past five centuries."[2] Ideational community values help restrain the libido, channeling sex into marriage. Sensate values downgrade marriage and lead to the pursuit of sexual satisfaction as the primary goal.

Many factors were at work in this transformation, not least of which was the rise of a materialistic outlook in the natural sciences, which led to a materialistic view of psychology and sociology. As Francis Shaeffer observed: "Scientists in the seventeenth and eighteenth centuries continued to use the word God, but pushed God more and more to the edges of their systems. Finally, scientists in this stream of thought moved to the idea of a completely closed system. This left no room for God. But equally it left no room for man. Man disappears, to be viewed as some form of determined or behavioristic machine."

Thinkers such as Jean-Jacques Rousseau (1712–1778) and Ludwig Feuerbach (1804–1872) converted this mechanistic view of man into a philosophy of life. Finding no way to link the purely personal whims of the individual to any overarching system such as the God-centered Judeo-Christian order of creation, Feuerbach turned man into a dualistic creature who believed in fables (religion) but was subject to reality (materialism). Rousseau, believing that the Enlightenment's emphasis on reason and logic was largely an illusion, retreated to a view of man as an autonomous machine who prospered when acting wholly on instinct. Recognizing that this could lead to social chaos, he prescribed a totalitarian solution: the community would "force" each man to be free. The glaring contradiction of this idea did little to dissuade subsequent materialistic thinkers, who began to gravitate toward man-made solutions to social problems. No mere individual could be trusted, only the collective wisdom residing in the community (or "village," to update things). Rousseau, who abandoned his own children by his live-in lover, dismissed families as overly restrictive of the individual and prescribed communal child-rearing. This paved the way for the collectivist political movement launched by Karl Marx and Frederich Engels against church and family. The process was accelerated with the arrival of Charles Darwin's *Origin of the Species by Means of Natural Selection* in 1859. If man were merely a collection of molecules assembled by evolution through natural selection, then sexual mores, indeed, all morality, was entirely a cultural construct. Science, the ultimate material arbiter, now said so. If man made the rules, then man could rewrite them à la Rousseau, or dispense with them altogether. It is in this spirit that feminists are now trying to expand the sexes into five "genders" based on psychology instead of biology. By ridding humanity of the male-female order, rooted in generative function, the feminists are creating their own world in which aberrant sexual behavior is regarded as "normal."

Sigmund Freud (1856–1939), whose worldview and vernacular permeate modern life, took a subtheme in the sensate life—sex—and made it the entire plot, with unmet sexual yearnings at the heart of all human action. The materialistic philosophy that accompanied the rise of evolutionary theory eventually became harnessed to Freud's pseudo-scientific psychology in which sex became shorthand to explain everything. It was only a matter of a few years (in the scheme of human history) before Dr. Freud gave way to Dr. Kinsey and then to Dr. Ruth, who has given way to "gangsta" rapper Dr. Dre. Once human beings were freed from responsibility through the magic of psychoanalytic transfer (blame mom and dad and society for what you have become) and subconscious sexuality (it's not my fault that I can't seem to keep my pants on!), the moral anarchy burning through Western civilization was nearly complete.

Many people believe that the sexual revolution began in the 1960s, but Sorokin looked around in the 1940s and 1950s and found a commercial culture awash in pornography, rising rates of divorce, teen pregnancies, and sexually transmitted diseases. The family, he said, was on the ropes, facing extinction in the face of a relativized definition of sexual propriety.

No longer was the highest good in America said to be self-sacrifice, but rather self-fulfillment. No longer were people viewing this world as a way station but as a final destination—a view that would have profound effects on behavior. No longer was sex viewed as part of the procreative imperative but chiefly as a means to romance and pleasure. Sorokin concluded that America was on the precipice over which all major cultures had plunged throughout history—the unraveling of the social order due to sexual excess:

> Among the many changes of the last few decades, a peculiar revolution has been taking place in the lives of millions of American men and women. Quite different from the better-known political and economic revolutions, it goes almost unnoticed. Devoid of noisy public explosions, its stormy scenes are confined to the privacy of the bedroom and involve only individuals . . . It has no great leader; no hero plans it, and no politburo directs it. Without plan or organization, it is carried on by millions of individuals, each acting on his own . . . In spite of its odd characteristics, this sex revolution is as important as the most dramatic political or economic upheaval. It is changing the lives of men and women more radically than any other revolution of our time.[3]

For all his insight, Sorokin was wrong about two things: America was far from hitting bottom, and the sexual revolution was far from being a spontaneous, organic movement of individuals without collective efforts. From Margaret Sanger's Planned Parenthood to Alfred Kinsey's sex studies to the successful efforts by the *Playboy* magazine-funded American Civil Liberties Union and its allies to gut laws against pornography and indecency, to the feminist and homosexual rights movements, to an educational structure designed to wean children from parental values, there was and is a conspiracy against sexual mores, the family, and religion—the final target.

Presidential speechwriter Peggy Noonan concluded after looking at public policy crusades during the twentieth century, that the real goal of every liberal movement is to "make the world safe for fornication." Get enough fornication going and you get a lot of people too frightened to approach God because of their guilt. Hence, you create pressure to loosen the mores still further to make everyone feel better about his own misconduct.

A typical expression of the "free love" that began to flood the culture through psychology, media, and cinema is this piece of advice from Peter Kostenbaum from his 1974 book *Existential Sexuality: Choosing to Love.* Kostenbaum counsels people to experiment sexually before they make a commitment and actually proposes serial polygamy as a serious norm: "[A] society that expects and encourages two marriages of its people is likely to be a healthier one than the one we have at present. The first marriage is experimental; it is a learning experience and a matter of convenience . . . With the advent of easily available contraceptives and legal abortion, the separation between love and sex is now, perhaps for the first time in the history of mankind, final. A new age of freedom for self-definition is upon us."[4]

The most effective propaganda for the sexual revolution exists today in the pages of the popular press and many women's magazines, where the reader is pounded continually with articles about having more sex, better sex, kinky sex, sex outside marriage, multiple sex partners, and lesbian sex. *Glamour* magazine once asked on the cover, "Can Lovers Cheat and Still Be Faithful?"[5] And *Lear's* did a nude photo layout calculated to tease with its article "Bisexuality: Having It All." *Cosmopolitan* customarily has at least one article on the cover each month that promotes acceptance of sex outside marriage.

As with the drug revolution of the sixties and seventies, the key to persuading people to experiment is to give the impression that everyone is already doing it and that some people are doing such bizarre things that what *you* do by comparison is okay. That is why the homosexual rights movement has been promoted and funded by *Playboy* magazine and other purveyors of heterosexual pornography. And why homosexual activists promote pornography of all types. Any breaking down of the barriers in one sector helps all the other forces of decadence make their case.

The high rate of divorce also explains America's supine acceptance of the floodtide of pornography and homosexuality. It's too glib to say that people want as many options as possible, but it is not far from the truth. Well-publicized divorces and live-in situations by celebrities have helped break down resistance as well. One psychologist who studies sexual behavior believes strongly that the sexual liberation practiced by the elites has had an impact: "I think what people are saying is, If it's good enough for the stars, it's good enough for me. They think that if those people can have an affair and still manage their lives, then they can, too."[6]

Over the years, the public has been treated to gossip in the supermarket tabloids, the women's magazines, and in major Sunday supplements such as *Parade* and *USA Weekend* (both claim over thirty million circulation weekly), which matter-of-factly report the births to unwed stars of an astonishing number of bastard children. When the relationships break up, as they inevitably do, the concept of adultery is underplayed. From a position of tolerant neutrality in the early 1990s, *USA Weekend* in particular moved in the mid-nineties toward frequent promotion of homosexuality, recommending pro-gay books, homosexual films such as *The Incredibly True Adventures of Two Girls in Love*, pushing the careers of openly homosexual recording artists such as Melissa Etheridge and dispensing dubious advice to impressionable teens. A February 1996 cover teaser: "Accept your inner misfit, k.d. lang says."

Inside, the lesbian activist singer offers seductively subversive advice under the headline, "Different is O K": "I do what my instincts tell me, but I don't really have a choice . . . Spirituality comes from questioning everything but at the same time accepting everything . . ." For "parents of gays," she advises, "let the kids live their lives. You lived yours. Don't make your kids live your lives again."[7] In other words, mom and dad, leave your children to the tender mercies of homosexuals. Even though you spent years in service to them, raising them, drying their tears, staying up at night with them, and generally sacrificing an enormous amount of personal freedom and capital out of your love for them, stay out of the way. Oh, and your lives are over, by the way, you dinosaurs.

In a genuinely poignant paragraph, the reporter notes that, "When she was twelve, her dad walked out on her family, and the whole town knew it. 'I will forever be learning what the effect on me was,' lang says."[8]

It is not too hard to surmise what effect the sexual revolution has had on families; it has been devastating, particularly to women and children, but also to the drifting boy-men who are not anchored by genuine commitment. In their quest for a false freedom, men have been offered numerous substitutes for family life, most insidiously the vast array of pornography that is everywhere, from the corner store, to the home video channels, to the Internet, and to hotel rooms on lonely business trips. Misery loves company, even if it is only a fantasy. Pornography has freed many men from the exclusive dependence on their wives for sex, without the risks of prostitution. Few who are caught up in porn addiction (for it is as overpowering as nicotine or cocaine) understand that they have traded a benign, self-imposed yoking of the sex drive in exchange for a sensate slavery so powerful that many men have wrecked their families, risked enormous embarrassment, and messed up their lives in an unending quest for satisfaction.

In all the milestones on the road to decadence, each is marked with a sign farther ahead implying that the sexual pilgrim still has a ways to go before applying the brakes. Fueling the notion that sexual license is good is the modern notion of "progress" itself, the faith that we are constantly evolving toward a more satisfying state of living. This "fatal serialism of the modern imagination—the image of infinite unilinear progression,"[9] as C. S. Lewis put it, allows us to mouth such easy lies as "you can't turn back the clock," or "we've progressed beyond that," or "my generation has a new way of looking at things."

Even the 1990s Girl Scout handbook, in a passage promoting feminist careerism, notes with amusement that "some people are so old-fashioned!"

For those who feel that things by nature are always improving, it might be pointed out that the Roman emperor Caligula (A D 12–41) considered himself a progressive, taking Rome from its stuffy preoccupations with marriage, family, and a Republican form of government into an orgiastic frenzy of adultery, homosexuality, violence, and tyranny. And if human progress is inevitable and continual, how do we explain the hundreds of millions of deaths in the twentieth century at the hands of totalitarian socialist governments, or even the evolution of music from Mozart to Marilyn Manson?

The sexual revolution depends on the liberal view that man is good by nature and that the fulfillment of each person's desires outweighs any other claims on his time or loyalties. Ethics, therefore, becomes the relativistic game of rationalizing human action, which is only a more complicated way of saying, "If it feels good, do it." As Planned Parenthood founder Margaret Sanger wrote in 1922, "Instead of laying down hard and fast rules of sexual conduct, sex can be rendered effective and valuable only as it meets and satisfies the interests and demands of the pupil himself."[10]

To facilitate this type of liberation, a number of groups sprang up to fight for changes in the moral, economic, and legal codes during the twentieth century.

Planned Parenthood, the largest and most powerful lobbying force and the largest operator of abortion clinics in America, was founded by Sanger in 1921 as the American Birth Control League. Sanger, who began a career as a radical activist in 1911, was a member of several communist groups. She helped finance the trip of John Reed to the fledging Soviet Union, where he gathered material for his revolutionary tract *Ten Days That Shook the World*, which was later glorified in the movie *Reds* starring Warren Beatty. As a sexual revolutionary, Sanger had a succession of lovers, including sexologist Havelock Ellis and novelist H. G. Wells, and an "open marriage" to Three-in-One Oil magnate J. Noah Slee.[11]

Sanger founded a feminist magazine called *Woman Rebel* and placed below the masthead this statement: "No Gods, No Masters." Described by a contemporary as "an ardent propagandist for the joys of the flesh,"[12] Sanger herself wrote that the mission of *Woman Rebel* was "to look the whole world in the face with a go-to-hell look in the eyes . . . to speak and act in defiance of convention." She claimed that "the marriage bed is the most degenerating influence of the social order . . . a decadent institution, a reactionary development of the sex instinct."[13] As Charles Donovan and Robert Marshall point out in their book *Blessed Are the Barren,* Sanger's solution was "to give women total 'control of their reproductive functions.'"[14]

Sanger had another reason to promote birth control: eugenics, the scientific production of "superior" offspring. This was revealed starkly on the masthead of her *Birth Control Review* in 1921, where she wrote: "Birth Control: To Create a Race of Thoroughbreds."[15]

Working with a variety of left-wing organizations, Sanger began to acquire support for ending the legal ban on contraception, first for married couples, then the population at large. In the 1930s, she turned her attention to blacks in the nation's urban areas, where she put into place a team of black "leaders" who would persuade pastors and other influential people that birth control was necessary. Although, as she wrote, "colored negroes" respect white doctors more, a cadre of black doctors and clergy should be recruited so that, "We do not want the word to go out that we want to exterminate the Negro population and the minister is the man who can straighten that idea out if it ever occurs to any of their more rebellious members."[16]

Sanger and her movement were not the only ones interested in creating a purified population during the 1930s. In Sweden, socialized reproduction was becoming part and parcel of the welfare state. And in Germany, Adolf Hitler eagerly absorbed the racialist writings of Richard Wagner's son-in-law, Houston Stewart Chamberlain, author of *Foundations of the 19th Century,* "a panegyric of the Aryan race wherein Europe is saved from the chaos of Roman decadence by the Germanic invasions."[17] Chamberlain was the mentor of Alfred Rosenberg, whose seven-hundred-page book *Myth of the 20th Century* outlined the theory of the purification of the Nordic races that greatly influenced Hitler in his campaign to seek a "final solution" by eliminating the Jews.

Ironically, historian William Shirer writes, Sanger's books were among those ordered burned by the Nazis in their purge of "decadent" works that undermined "the root of German thought, the German home, and the driving forces of our people."[18]

In 1942, the various affiliates of the Birth Control Federation of America, which evolved out of Sanger's American Birth Control League, voted to form the Planned Parenthood Federation of America, Inc. The New York State chapter's old bylaws said their object was to "develop and organize on sound eugenic, social, and medical principles, interest in, and knowledge of birth control." Under the new organization, "birth control" was replaced with "planned parenthood," and the word "eugenics" was dropped "because in 1943 it had unpopular connotations," as Donovan and Marshall relate: "With the United States at war with a German government founded in large part on race-improving eugenic theories that were implemented through forced sterilization and segregation of the 'unfit'—in short, measures Planned Parenthood leaders had advocated for many years—it indeed was prudent for the organization to drop mention of eugenic goals from its bylaws, if not from its policies, at least for the duration of the World War II."[19]

During the early 1940s, the National Research Council began channeling Rockefeller Foundation money into sex studies by Alfred C. Kinsey at Indiana University. The result in 1948 was *Sexual Behavior in the Human Male*, which was treated to an explosion of uncritical media coverage. In 1953, Kinsey added a female volume, *Sexual Behavior in the Human Female*. Serious scientists had examined the data and methodology and had concluded that Kinsey had skewed his samples and worse. But their protestations went unheard, and Kinsey was cited continually over the next few decades as "proof" that Americans were awash in adultery, homosexuality, and other behavior destructive to family life. At the heart of the Kinsey research is a little-mentioned chapter in the male volume called "Early Sexual Growth and Activity," which contains graph tables showing children as young as five months old having "orgasms" that were timed with a "secondhand or stopwatch" by "technically trained" pedophiles.

In 1981, Dr. Judith Reisman delivered a paper on the Kinsey child sexuality data at the International Conference on Sexuality held in Jerusalem. Instead of being hailed as an investigator, she was attacked viciously by her colleagues. In 1990, she co-wrote, with sex therapist Edward W. Eichel and Drs. Gordon Muir and John Court, the book *Kinsey, Sex and Fraud.* The book's findings "demolish" the Kinsey credibility, according to the British medical journal *The Lancet.*[20] Among other things, the book exposes the use of children in experiments, shows that perhaps one-quarter of Kinsey's sample of men consisted of prison inmates, many of them sex offenders, and reveals an overall sloppiness and clear ideological intent on Kinsey's part to dethrone traditional sexual morality.[21]

In his chapter on animal contacts, Kinsey's hostility toward Western religion could not have been any clearer. Concerning people being dissuaded from having sex with animals, Kinsey writes: "These taboos were well established in the Old Testament and in the Talmud . . . [T]he student of human folkways is inclined to see a considerable body of superstition in the origins of all such taboos, even though they may ultimately become religious and moral issues for whole nations and whole races of people."[22]

Adored by the liberal media and liberal academics, Kinsey is quoted in everything from sex manuals to court cases as "scientific" proof of the normalcy of aberrant sexual behavior. Portrayed in the media as a dispassionate scientist and strait-laced husband and family man, Kinsey was in reality a seriously disturbed person whose secret sexual life included homosexuality, voyeurism, exhibitionism, masochistic self-mutilation, and group sex. Despising religion, Kinsey disparaged the value of traditional morality as a cultural construct that served to keep man miserable. There is considerable evidence that Kinsey's homosexuality drove him to formulate a science of sexology that validated his behavior. James H. Jones, a former Kinsey Institute board member, revealed in an exhaustive biography of Kinsey in 1997 that Kinsey even had Mrs. Kinsey filmed while having sex with Kinsey staff and that Kinsey pressured staff members and their wives to be photographed and filmed while having sex.[23] Kinsey's own view of sex was that it had no moral content and was merely a physical urge that needed to be satiated. Jones summarizes: "Privately, Kinsey believed that human beings in a state of nature were basically pansexual. Absent social constraints, he conjectured, 'natural man' would commence sexual activity early in life, enjoy intercourse with both sexes, eschew fidelity, indulge in a variety of behaviors, and be much more sexually active in general for life."[24]

There seemed to be no restraint on sexual behavior that Kinsey would acknowledge: "Kinsey's deep-seated animosity to traditional morality led him to take a benign view of child molestation and incest . . . Whenever possible, Kinsey provided encouragement to advice seekers, stressing that most of their difficulties would vanish if they refused to allow social taboos, prejudices, and meddlesome laws to control them."[25]

It would not be a stretch to compare what Kinsey did for sex to what Hugh Hefner did for pornography, which was to mainstream immorality. As America entered the fifties, Planned Parenthood's agenda received new support from the fast-growing soft porn industry. As the Henry Ford of skin magazine publishers, Hugh Hefner made pornography respectable and easy to obtain. As Judith Reisman reveals in her book *Soft Porn Plays Hardball*, Hefner cited Kinsey as his inspiration in the formulation of his "*Playboy* Philosophy," crediting Kinsey with helping to break down his own Methodist-spawned inhibitions.[26] Working with Planned Parenthood and the ACLU, Hefner's Playboy Foundation helped fund the legal challenges that resulted in the 1973 *Roe vs. Wade* Supreme Court decision that struck down abortion laws in all fifty states.

In 1964, Planned Parenthood Medical Director Mary Calderone founded the Sex Information and Education Council of the United States (SIECUS) in New York City. While Planned Parenthood handled the drive for legalized abortion, *Playboy* hooked its first generation of teen boys and young men into voyeurism and masturbation. SIECUS directed the effort to force Kinsey-style sex education into the public schools. Calderone was joined on the SIECUS board by Alfred Kinsey's co-author, Wardell Pomeroy, as well as William Genne, commissioner on Marriage and Family Life of the National Council of Churches, Wallace Fulton of the Equitable Insurance Company, David Mace, executive director of the American Association of Marriage Counselors, and Lester Kirkendall, an author and lecturer at Oregon State University who wrote approvingly of the advent of "intergenerational" sex—that is, sex between children and adults.

From the criminally obtained child sexuality data, the Kinsey-inspired team at SIECUS formulated a view of child sexual competence that led to an essentially pedophilic philosophy in sex education. Age limits had no meaning, only the child's own sexual competence and ability to make sexual decisions. Beginning in colleges and then high schools, and finally grade schools, sex instructors began to introduce children at younger and younger ages to sex, all in the name of education. With the advent of AIDS, sex educators were able to expose children to more and more graphic materials on the grounds that the children were at risk if they didn't know all the different ways that they could contract HIV—from anal sex to oral sex.

Meanwhile, Planned Parenthood became the beneficiary of hundreds of millions of federal dollars through the Title X program beginning in the early 1970s. Title X became the prime money source for Planned Parenthood and was funded through the Carter, Reagan, Bush, and Clinton Administrations. The money allowed Planned Parenthood to expand its empire of clinics and abortion mills and to concentrate on a worldwide effort through the United Nations and other international organizations while SIECUS promoted "comprehensive sexuality" education at home.

As the pro-abortion movement gained strength and was institutionalized, it became increasingly clear that a major component was homosexual rights activists, particularly lesbians. Feminist organizations such as the National Organization for Women made abortion something of a sacrament, and the acceptance of homosexuality became an animating creed. At the same time, male homosexuals began orchestrating the successful hoodwinking of the population through the manipulation of science and the media

THE HOMOSEXUAL MOVEMENT

Although they had been secretly meeting since the late 1940s, homosexual activists began their push for acceptance during the 1950s. The Mattachine Society, the first gay rights group, recruited

UCLA psychologist Evelyn Hooker to do comparison studies on heterosexual and homosexual men in order to prove that there was no psychological difference. As later interviews and statements in her own studies make clear, Hooker set out to "prove" that homosexuality was normal and was keenly aware of the political implications. Tom Landess, former academic dean at the University of Dallas, who wrote a report for the Family Research Council dissecting the Hooker studies, notes that, "From Hooker's own report—and from a follow-up interview in later years, we see that homosexuals were not only eager to participate, but indeed were the instigators of the study."[27]

Mattachine sent over forty handpicked subjects, and Hooker recruited the "straights" willy-nilly. Because so many of the subjects had mental problems, the sample was cut to thirty homosexuals and thirty heterosexuals. Hooker then administered three common psychological tests—the Make a Picture Story (MAPS), the Thematic Apperception Test (TAT) and the Rorschach. In two of the three studies, MAPS and TAT, the independent judge picked the homosexuals out easily. They were the only subjects who eroticized the inkblots and pictures. In the Rorschach, the judge found a nearly normal correlation—except in regard to one area—sexuality.

Despite the fact that the tests, overall, had convincingly proved the opposite of her hypothesis, Hooker's studies were publicized loudly and uncritically as scientific evidence that homosexuality was as normal as heterosexuality. As Landess notes, "For many commentators and activists, the Hooker study effectively ended the debate over whether or not homosexuals were in any way abnormal in their relationships with each other and with the community at large."[28]

While Hooker's findings were sinking in, homosexuality became a favorite topic in the counterculture, as hippies consumed the writings of French libertine Arthur Rimbaud, American hedonist William Burroughs, and beat poet Allen Ginsburg. These and other homosexual writers found their way onto college reading lists, usually in the English departments, where homosexuals could exert influence by their sheer numbers.

In 1969, the Stonewall rebellion signaled the beginning of the official Gay Liberation Movement. A New York bar catering to drag queens and "chicken hawks" (homosexual men who seek underage male partners), the Stonewall Inn was also a haven for drug-dealing. When the police began to question some of the patrons on June 27, 1969, the bar patrons—many of them drag queens—responded by throwing rocks and rioting. It was the first mass "resistance" against the establishment by homosexuals, and it serves today as their sacred totem, with gay pride parades and numerous rites held annually on the Stonewall anniversary. Few gay activists, most of whom deny that pedophilia plays any part in the homosexual "community," acknowledge that Stonewall was known as a meeting place for pedophiles.

In the early seventies, homosexual activists lobbied hard at the American Psychiatric Association and the American Psychological Association to have homosexuality rediagnosed. Commandeering the nomenclature committee, threatening violence at the national convention, and mounting an extremely aggressive campaign, the activists managed to secure a vote from the psychiatrists to remove homosexuality from the list of diagnostic disorders. As pro-gay writer Ronald Bayer recalls, "[The APA] had fallen victim to the disorder of a tumultuous era, when disruptive conflicts threatened to politicize every aspect of American social life. A furious egalitarianism . . . compelled psychiatric experts to negotiate the pathological status of homosexuality with homosexuals themselves. The result was not a conclusion based on an approximation of the scientific truth as dictated by reason, but was instead an action demanded by the ideological temper of the times."[29]

It didn't matter that most developmental psychologists and psychiatrists continued to regard homosexuality as a treatable emotional disorder resulting from an underdeveloped gender identity. It didn't matter that the change was a triumph of politics over science, with the flawed and misrepresented Hooker studies carrying most of the water. The media picked up the refrain that "gay is normal, gay is good," and continue it to this day, portraying homosexual rights activism as an extension of the black civil rights movement. The distinction between skin color and sexual behavior is an inconvenient fact easily overlooked by journalists in an Age of Consent. More than any other issue, the media collectively have thrown overboard any pretense of objectivity when dealing with homosexuality. At the 1994 and 1995 conventions of the Gay and Lesbian Journalists Association, where more than six hundred homosexual journalists gathered, all major media companies—NBC, CBS, ABC, the *New York Times, Los Angeles Times,* the *Washington Post,* AP, UPI, National Public Radio, etc.—were represented by attendees, speakers, recruiting booths, sponsorship dollars, or all of the above. In 1995, Knight-Ridder, publisher of the *Miami Herald,* the *Philadelphia Inquirer,* and other large papers, led the way with a fifteen thousand dollar donation. Even the Army Times Publishing Company chipped in one thousand dollars.[30] By 1997, the association claimed a membership of 1,200 journalists.

Over the years, beginning with the erroneous, Kinsey-derived 10 percent estimate of homosexuality in the general population, the media began publicizing a steady stream of "gay studies." Conducted almost entirely by homosexual activists, the studies purport to show that homosexuality is genetic; that children in gay households are not affected in any way (as if a boy cannot tell the difference between his own father and a lesbian lover); that a third of all teen suicides consist of "gay youth"; and that the military's ban on homosexuality is wrong because "studies show" that homosexuality has no effect whatever on morale, unit cohesion, strategic concerns, public health, the military blood supply, morality, or the privacy concerns of the rest of armed forces personnel. Dr.

Charles Socarides, a prominent New York psychiatrist, summarizes the absurdity of the gays-in-the-military campaign: "You'd think that homosexual priests could control themselves. But many of them can't. And if they can't control themselves, what makes us think that gay marines can?"[31]

As for the other contentions, they are all flawed, misrepresented, or fraudulent, but one would never know it by paying attention to the daily press. A case in point is the wildly exaggerated claim of "eight to thirteen million children" being raised by gay parents. During a December 28, 1997, edition of CNN's "Crossfire" on the issue of homosexual custody of children, the figure was flashed on the screen, with the ACLU named as the source. There are fifty to sixty million children in the United States. If the ACLU is correct, then one in five children is being reared by homosexuals. Considering that the most reliable surveys indicate that the total homosexual population of the United States is below 2 percent, this would mean that every single homosexual is raising four or more children. Few reliable statistics on "gay parenting" are available, but a reasonable estimate based on census data would put the figure below one hundred thousand. But repeating an inflated figure makes the phenomenon seem so widespread as to be . . . normal.

While heaping uncritical attention on any aspect of the homosexual agenda that the activists deem strategic, the press persistently omit not only the bizarre and unhealthy physical realities of homosexual sex but purposely ignore the burgeoning ex-gay movement, which has helped thousands out of the homosexual lifestyle. When former homosexuals like Anthony Falzarano of Transformation Ex-Gay Ministries in Washington, D.C., do get invited to do interviews, they are pelted with hostile questions. On talk shows, they are often far outnumbered by homosexual activists in front of audiences primed to abuse the ex-gays. Still, despite the unfairness, ex-homosexuals are chalking up impressive victories, one soul at a time. After the *Washington Post* did a catty cover story on Transformation in its "Style" section, treating the ministry with a skeptical tone that would be unthinkable if the subject were, say, the Lesbian Avengers, twelve people came to Anthony Falzarano's ministry for counseling because they had read the article. As allies of the gay rights movement, the press understands implicitly that ex-gays are the activists' worst nightmare, so they generally ignore them. Thus, many people who are struggling with homosexuality are robbed of the chance to learn about genuine alternatives.

Driven by the overall cultural plunge into moral relativism, homosexual activists, pornographers, serial polygamists, and sexual adventurers of all stripes have managed to persuade a majority of the press and academia that any resistance to a radical sex agenda cannot possibly stem from motives higher than hatred and bigotry. Like a drumbeat, the words "hate," "bigot," and "extremist" are used daily to characterize Christian conservatives and others who dare to question the latest sexual onslaught, much less oppose it. On the receiving end of incredible abuse are parents who have the audacity to ask school officials why their seven-year-old sons and daughters are being taught about condoms, anal sex, and the pros and cons of "clean" needle exchange programs in the name of "AIDS education." Or why the local library is celebrating "gay pride" month at a time when more than half the homosexual men in America are carrying the HIV virus.

As the sexual revolution claims more victims, its pedigree and its consequences are slowly being discovered. It is to be hoped that a measure of sanity will prevail before it becomes illegal in the Age of Consent to write a chapter like the one you just read.

5

Television's Relativistic World

Beyond simply reflecting our changing sexual mores, television has endorsed the changes, and may have accelerated their acceptance . . . It has lately played a leading role in questioning traditional moral standards before a vast national audience.[1]

S. Robert Lichter, Linda Lichter,
and Stanley Rothman

IN THE MID-1970S, a television show called "The Waltons" chronicled the lives of a fictional family in the Virginia hills during the Depression. Based on the memories of series creator Earl Hamner, the Walton family tackled everyday problems from first love to financial uncertainty to the realities of old age and prejudice. Underneath it all, the show was buoyed by a rock-hard faith in God and in the healing powers of family love.

For several years, "The Waltons" was among the top shows in the Nielsen ratings. Suburban and rural families tuned in, but so did many urban dwellers. One feminist reporter confided to me that she looked forward to Wednesdays, when "The Waltons" brought her a sense of sanity. In the Age of Consent, it was her guilty pleasure, and she didn't exactly trumpet that fact when surrounded by fellow journalists at parties.

Reaction to "The Waltons" fell along fairly predictable lines. Fans saw the show as a realistic portrayal of a loving rural family whose traditional values enabled it to thrive amid adversity. Cynics saw "The Waltons" as a Pollyanna soap opera populated by impossibly good hicks who satisfied Middle America's craving for nostalgia. ("Little House on the Prairie," another mega-hit family drama, was also relegated to this category.) For those who wouldn't buy the premise that people could sincerely love each other the way the Waltons did, the series was pure Norman Rockwell on video— a sticky-sweet paean to an American way of life that liberals believed never was.

Neutrally bringing up the topic of "The Waltons" at social gatherings in the Age of Consent still reveals volumes about people and their values. The cynics roll their eyes, and some snort audibly. Those who consider themselves "progressives" are contemptuous of anything traditional unless it is blessed by someone verifiably hip, whereupon it becomes avant-garde, or at least campy.

THE TUTOR THAT FAILED

When television was in its infancy, many viewed it as the key to a better-educated populace. In glowing terms that are now being liberally applied to the Internet, television would cure the masses of their ignorance and bring about a new age of information.

NBC founder David Sarnoff predicted that "the ultimate contribution of television will be its service toward unification of the life of the nation, and, at the same time, the greater development of the life of the individual. We who have labored in the creation of this promising new instrumentality are proud to have this opportunity to aid in the progress of mankind. It is our earnest hope that television will help to strengthen the United States as a nation of free people and high ideals."[2]

In 1949, a trade journal writer was even more effusive: "With the combination of motion picture film and the television camera, coupled with the television receiver in the American home, John Q. America is about to receive the greatest treasury of enlightenment and education that has ever before been given to a free man."[3]

NBC executive Pat Weaver saw children as the prime beneficiaries of the new technology, creating "a generation of informed youngsters whose great point of difference from us will be that they accept diversity, individuality, differences in belief, custom, language, et cetera, as wholly natural and desirable."[4]

Almost no one today is as unequivocally happy about the actual effects of television on the nation, except perhaps those who have a vested interest in social chaos (come to think of it, that is a lot of people). But some observers early on saw the threat that television posed.

In 1949, a group called the Southern California Association for Better Radio and Television monitored one week of television in Los Angeles and found ninety-one murders, seven stagecoach holdups, three kidnappings, ten thefts, four burglaries, two arsons, two suicides, one case of blackmail, and assaults and batteries "too numerous to tabulate."[5]

In 1950, the National Council of Catholic Men urged broadcasters to develop a code of standards to prohibit programs "detrimental to the best moral interests of televiewers, especially the family group and the children of the family."[6] The group devised its own ratings system to inform Catholics about television content. Other Catholic spokesmen also saw television as a lethal missile aimed at families. Boston Archbishop Richard J. Cushing observed that "some television programs have sunk to a new low in breaking the laws of morality and decency."[7] Harvard anthropologist Ernest A. Hooten complained in 1951 that television constituted "an easy correspondence course in crime, a visual education in how to do wrong. Such vicious programs result from the ignorance and venality of movie, radio, and TV producers."[8]

Apart from the portrayal of violence, some critics saw more sweeping cultural threats. On an ABC radio "town meeting" discussion in 1951, social critic Charles A. Siepmann blasted television as a "liability." Seeing economic concentration in the network-dominated industry as a threat to the kind of "diversity" that others predicted, Siepmann described television as

> almost exclusively a medium of mass entertainment, with the accent on mass. It will, in other words, compound all of radio's many felonies, eschew the long-term cultural view in the interest of quick returns on sponsors' money, measure quality by the quantity of audience response, sell cultural minorities short, and give art, intelligence, and excellence the silent treatment . . . Left to itself, commercial television is likely to turn us all into a race physically distinguished by a hyperthyroid look about the eyes, and fannies flattened by excessive hours in easy chairs. A nation of passive gawkers, instead of active intelligences, credulous instead of critical, mass-minded instead of individual, more and more dependent upon outside stimulus, and progressively devoid of inward resources. And we shall continue to see our children graduate prematurely to the immaturity of their elders.[9]

Some television performers were keenly aware of their newfound power—and their responsibility to use it wisely. Comedian Red Skelton ended his squeaky-clean family variety radio and television shows with the humble sign-off: "Thank you for letting me into your homes . . . Goodnight and God bless."[10]

In the 1940s, the early television stations broadcast a variety of cultural fare that seemed to meet the promise that television could be uplifting. WRGB in Schenectady featured presentations of Shakespeare's *Taming of the Shrew*, Tschaikovsky's *Pique Dame*, a black gospel revival meeting, light opera, a real circus, and experimental dramas and topical discussions. The station also pioneered two soap operas, a precursor to the networks' successful daytime television dramas.

But for better or worse, television quickly became almost solely an entertainment medium, with advertisers flocking to highly rated programs. During the 1950s, the Golden Age of television, many radio stars made their way to the video screen, including comedians Jack Benny, Lucille Ball, Eve Arden, Bob Hope, Dean Martin, Danny Thomas, and Red Skelton. "Amos 'n' Andy" also made the switch, but with black actors replacing the original white actors, Freeman Gosden and Charles Correll. Detective shows such as "Ellery Queen," "Dragnet," and western stars such as Hopalong Cassidy, Gene Autry, Roy Rogers, and the Lone Ranger also made it big on television. As in radio, variety shows boomed, with Sid Caesar and Imogene Coca's "Your Show of Shows" leading the pack along with Milton Berle, television's "Uncle Miltie," and the king of the variety hour, Ed Sullivan.

The standards were high, and there were no television offerings that the entire family could not watch. The now-defunct DuMont network, which featured live programming only, was especially stringent. Television historian J. Fred MacDonald relates that DuMont "maintained bouquets of flowers for those emergency situations when a female star or guest arrived at the studio with too much cleavage exposed. In such cases the network ordered the woman to use one of the bouquets as a corsage to cover her bosom."[11]

In 1950, DuMont posted placards in its control rooms and studios with this message from network president Mortimer W. Loewi and program director James L. Caddigan: "Attention, producer, directors, and talent: Your audience is the average American family— Mom and Dad—Junior and Sis—Grandma. You are a guest in their living-rooms. Any violation of this privilege through the use of material in bad taste, immoral business, situations, dialogue, lyrics, routines, or costuming will not be tolerated by the DuMont Television Network."[12]

Ten years later in 1960, by the time 87 percent of U.S. households had at least one television set, DuMont was out of business—not because it had high moral standards but because it failed to take advantage of technological advances. The filming of situation comedies allowed for more familiarity with the characters and subtle thematic developments. The filming of dramas allowed for more diversity of locale and higher production quality. Even the popular variety shows were defunct by the late fifties. "Your Show of Shows" was canceled in 1954, and Milton Berle was off by 1956. Red Skelton bucked the trend by keeping his show to a half-hour and by affecting a variety of characters, from Clem Kadiddlehopper to Junior, "the mean widdle kid." But the situation comedies became king, easily out-drawing the variety shows and music shows. "The Adventures of Ozzie and Harriet," which debuted in 1952 on ABC and ran until 1966 (435 episodes) was the longest-running situation comedy. Others included "The Jack Benny Show" (CBS, 1950–65), "Make Room for Daddy" (ABC, 1953–64), "The Donna Reed Show" (1958–66), "The Burns and Allen Show" (CBS, 1955–58), "The Life of Riley" (NBC, 1949–50, 1953–58), "Leave It To Beaver" (CBS, 1957–63), "The Real McCoys" (ABC, 1957–63), "Father Knows Best" (CBS, 1954–62), and "I Love Lucy" (CBS, 1951–57).[13]

As television got off the ground in the late 1940s and early 1950s, it quickly became the defining means of communication. In the affluent 1950s, television was the megaphone for a progressive future of technological advancement that Americans saw as their special contribution to the world. The accent was on youth and shows that appealed to youth. During the early fifties, ABC unveiled "Disneyland," "The Mickey Mouse Club," "American Bandstand," "Maverick," "77 Sunset Strip," the "Rifleman," "Adventures in Paradise," and "The Untouchables."

Television's very popularity triggered societal changes, much as the introduction of the automobile near the turn of the century effected major cultural transitions.

As historian MacDonald relates, "By 1949, government statistics suggested that TV was the cause of major declines in movie attendance, book purchases, admissions to professional sport events, radio listening, and attendance at the theater and the opera. Cab drivers complained that since the arrival of television fewer people were using taxis in the evening hours. Restaurant operators and bar owners blamed the attractiveness of television for business losses. Educators claimed that video was undermining the study habits of students."[14]

It wasn't until the 1970s that the term "cocooning" came into vogue, but the television-induced stay-at-home routine was well underway two decades earlier.

FAMILY TIME

America's families watched television together right up until the late 1960s, when the sea change began to take place. It was in the early seventies that television began to behave more like an intruder than a guest in the nation's living rooms. Somewhere between "Make Room for Daddy" and "All in the Family's" debut on CBS in 1971, the Hollywood creative community began to absorb and transmit the radical notions of the psychedelic sixties. Television became a shill for the Age of Consent: increasingly crude, morally relativistic, violent, sex-laden, and hostile to marriage, families, and children.

It was "All in the Family" that spawned the new emphasis on novelty and breaking barriers. In its first three months, the show examined sexuality, miscarriage, race, feminism, and cohabitation. It did so in an artful and humorous manner, vaulting to No. 1 in the listings by the end of the season. The primary mode of thought on the show was one of an unfolding moral relativism. All ideas, particularly those that fit under the "traditional" rubric, were up for grabs. But "All in the Family" was not, at bottom, relativistic; the tone and topics moved ever leftward, even as Archie Bunker grew in popularity. Portrayed as a narrow-minded bigot by Carroll O'Connor, Archie nonetheless, and however inartfully, defended the values that television liberals were constantly pounding. In television, the ratings rule and the networks took note of the success of this iconoclastic show.

In assessing the new television season in the fall of 1972, *Time* magazine observed:

> TV has embarked on a new era of candor, with all the lines emphatically drawn in. During the season that began last week, programmers will actually be competing with each other to trace the largest number of touchy—and heretofore forbidden—ethnic, sexual, and psychological themes. Religious quirks, wife-swapping, child abuse, lesbianism, venereal disease—all the old taboos will be toppling . . . An upcoming ABC Movie of the Week will feature Hal Holbrook explaining his homosexuality to his son . . . NBC's "The Bold Ones" will be getting bolder, mainly by knifing into such delicate surgical issues as embryo transplants and lobotomy.[15]

Notice that no liberal themes were open to question, and "taboos" are treated as morally neutral, whether it be wife-swapping (adultery) or "ethnic" themes (racism). This grouping ensured the progressive vision of a constantly changing morality, with millennia-old sexual morality being cast as disposable just like the odious sin of racism. Although many Americans were caught flat-footed by "All in the Family's" rapid success, they didn't perceive the show as a threat to their values. Archie, after all, was lovable in his bigoted way. And his liberal son-in-law "The Meathead," played by Rob Reiner, often got his comeuppance. But in 1972, the spin-off series "Maude" presented America with a liberal frontal assault. Played by actress Beatrice Arthur, Maude found herself, at forty-seven, pregnant with an unwanted child. For two weeks she pondered the situation, finally opting for an abortion.

As CBS president Robert Wood boasted, "Maude breaks every

rule of television from the start . . . she's on her fourth husband, and she is living with a divorced daughter who has a son. It's not so long ago that you couldn't show a woman divorced from one husband, let alone three."[16]

What seemed to be mostly an exercise in pushing the envelope had its roots in a more serious effort to change American values. In 1969, the Population Institute, a clone of the Planned Parenthood Federation, was set up to influence public opinion to accept population control. As television historian Kathryn Montgomery explains: "The plan to use entertainment television for such educational purposes was the brainchild of two Methodist ministers, David Poindexter and Rodney Shaw. Prime time programming seemed to be the ideal vehicle for public education. Not only could it reach large numbers of the American public in an instant but it could also package political and social issues in an entertaining context."[17]

In 1971, the Population Institute held a luncheon in New York with television executives. The purpose was to persuade them to include population control themes in their shows. "Maude" creator Norman Lear attended, as did the presidents of all three networks. Also in attendance were John D. Rockefeller III, chairman of the President's Commission on Population Growth and the American Future, Senator Bob Packwood (R-OR), and George Bush, who at the time was chairman of the Republican National Committee.

In the winter of 1971–72, the Population Institute got the cooperation of the National Academy of Television Arts and Sciences to be "a sponsor of TV population education,"[18] and it held conferences in New York and Los Angeles at which "the leading creative people in the TV industry discussed with population experts means whereby population education might be advanced and attitudes changed."[19] Cash awards were offered, with ten thousand dollars going to "the best prime-time entertainment program of sixty minutes or longer," five thousand dollars for "the best half-hour prime-time entertainment program," and five thousand dollars for "the best daytime serial episode or series of episodes during the 1972–1973 season."[20]

As Montgomery concludes, "The Population Institute's efforts to educate Hollywood played an important role in the genesis of the "Maude" abortion episodes. The organization succeeded in stimulating Norman Lear's personal interest in doing a show about the population issue."[21] Perhaps it is no coincidence that years later, Norman Lear's estranged wife founded *Lear's*, a magazine for older women that promoted abortion, lesbianism, and other feminist topics before folding.

When Hollywood's doors opened to the Population Institute, a slew of left-wing groups followed. Feminists, environmentalists, homosexual activists, peaceniks, consumer groups, and even animal rights organizations set up shop. They now lobby producers, vet scripts, advise writers, and keep count of any scores to settle.

The Environmental Media Association (EMA), with such heavy hitters on its board as Disney Chairman Michael Eisner, was set up in the late 1980s to inject environmentalist themes into films and television shows. "On some projects we're out there brainstorming with the producer," boasts EMA President Andy Spahn, who hopes to see projects about "environmental criminals."[22] Other groups that lobby Hollywood include Women in Film, which promotes feminist themes, People for the Ethical Treatment of Animals, the American Indian Registry for the Performing Arts, the NAACP, and even the National Stuttering Project, which took issue with the way a stutterer was portrayed in the film comedy *A Fish Called Wanda*. A fledgling Christian influence is being rebuilt in Hollywood, and the American Cinema Foundation has been trying to bring more balance to political discussions. But most conservative religious influence has been coming from outside Hollywood, via organizations such as Donald Wildmon's American Family Association, CLEaR-TV, the revived Moral Majority, and Terry Rakolta's Americans for Responsible Television. The threat of boycotts has staved off some of Hollywood's more destructive instincts, such as open promotion of abortion, and it has created pressure from sponsors stung by their inclusion on "bad corporate neighbor" lists.

Homosexuality Comes Out of the Closet

In 1972, ABC broke another barrier with its made-for-TV movie *That Certain Summer,* which featured Hal Holbrook as a homosexual father who "comes out" to his son.

Activating a powerful weapon in their campaign to normalize homosexuality in America, several homosexual activist groups began meeting with the networks to ensure a positive spin on their cause. The first target was an upcoming episode of "Marcus Welby, MD," the folksy but serious drama starring the avuncular Robert Young, who played the dad in the earlier hit series, "Father Knows Best." The script called for Dr. Welby to counsel a man whose homosexual tendencies were threatening to destroy his family. Welby assures the man that as long as he suppresses these urges, he can continue to be a good family man. The New York–based Gay Activist Alliance (GAA) went ballistic, planning a counterattack before the show aired. As Kathryn Montgomery relates, "Instead of waiting for an appointment with ABC executives, the activists—with the help of another network insider—'took over' the network executive offices." GAA media director Ron Gold recalls that, "We know somebody who worked there who gave us a kind of plan of the place and we did a little scouting in advance and we managed to sneak into the offices. The confrontation at ABC headquarters was hostile and explosive. This unexpected visit from twenty-five angry activists was hardly the manageable kind of meeting network executives preferred to have with advocacy groups."[23] ABC officials agreed to meet with two of the group, but the activists insisted on keeping everyone in the meeting. The situation ended with a protest and arrests outside the station. Although ABC aired the show, the activists made their point. From then on, ABC invited homosexual activists to comment on any scripts dealing with homosexuality. In another "Welby" episode a few months later dealing with a molestation of a teen by a male teacher, homosexual activists managed to have the script rewritten. References to homosexuality were dropped, and entire scenes were removed. After this capitulation, the networks found themselves under a siege that continues to this day and has had an enormous impact on the product.

Beginning with the comedy "Soap" in 1977, homosexual characters became mainstays of prime-time series, such as Steven Carrington, whose "Dynasty" was the top-rated show in 1984–1985. Other homosexual characters included a neighbor on "Cagney and Lacey," a police officer on "Hooperman," a nurse on "Heartbeat," two homosexual men parenting a teenage daughter on "The Tracey Ullman Show," and a college professor on "Doctor, Doctor." The tide receded a bit in the early nineties, after "thirty-something" lost hundreds of thousands of dollars in sponsorship when it featured a bed scene with two men. In 1990, NBC lost five hundred thousand dollars on an episode of "Lifestories" that was about a homosexual newscaster's battle with AIDS.

Public television picked up the beat, however, broadcasting numerous shows that promoted homosexuality, such as the "Lost Language of Cranes," "Tongues Untied," "Tales of the City," "Portrait of a Family," and "Moll Flanders."

When the sky didn't fall in, the networks opened the floodgates. By 1996, the commercial networks came full circle, promoting homosexuality with a vengeance. Virtually all top-rated situation comedies featured sympathetic, recurring homosexual characters, and "gay marriages" were performed on "Roseanne" and the top-rated "Friends."

The interplay involving most homosexual characters has two themes: either the character's homosexuality is presented as making no difference whatever, or "bigoted" characters come to accept homosexuality as normal or even superior ("Friends") by the end of a show. Religious, medical, and societal objections are swept aside or ignored in a tide of engineered "tolerance."

As one bisexual screenwriter told the *Los Angeles Times*, in dismissing concerns of parents and conservative pressure groups, "These people think that a kid will see two guys kiss and suddenly turn queer."[24] Perhaps not, but a reasonable concern could be that normalizing a behavior on television may tempt impressionable teens into unwise experimentation. And a steady diet of propaganda could radically alter their values. If television has no impact, then why would the bisexual writer care how homosexuals are portrayed?

Despite the homosexual onslaught, much of it engineered by the Gay-Lesbian Alliance Against Defamation (GLAAD), a handful of shows continued to portray homosexuality as either a humorous condition or a liability, most notably Fox's "In Living Color," which had flamboyant homosexuals in its Men on Film segments. But a couple of years later, Fox caved into the gay activists and used "Melrose Place" and "Beverly Hills 90210" to promote homosexuality and even an end to the military ban on homosexuals.

Easily the most effective special interest in Hollywood, the homosexual rights movement ensures uniformly positive portrayals of homosexuality. As Marty Kaplan, a screenwriter and producer for Walt Disney Studios remarked, the case made by homosexuals "falls on receptive ears because it's consistent with the values of this community."[25] In 1997, more than thirty openly homosexual characters inhabited prime time, and Ellen Degeneres became the first lead character of a network show to "come out" as a homosexual.

According to *Los Angeles* magazine writer David Ehrenstein: "There are openly gay writers on almost every major prime-time situation comedy you can think of, including 'Friends,' 'Seinfeld,' 'Murphy Brown,' 'Roseanne,' 'Mad About You,' 'The Nanny,' 'Wings,' 'The Single Guy,' 'Caroline in the City,' 'Coach,' 'Dave's World,' 'Home Court,' 'High Society,' 'The Crew,' and the new 'Boston Common' . . . In short, when it comes to sitcoms, gays rule."[26]

Ehrenstein, a professed homosexual, cheerfully admits that gay writers are attempting to influence viewers with a homosexual agenda: "[T]he gay and lesbian writers of today have been pushing the envelope any chance they get. In fact, they're encouraged to do so. Since current comedies are positively obsessed with the intimate sex lives of straight young singles, who better to write them than members of a minority famed for its sexual candor . . . As a result of the influx of gay writers, even the most heterosexual of sitcoms often possess that most elusive of undertones—the 'gay sensibility'— 'Frasier' being a case in point."[27]

The "gay sensibility" consists, according to two homosexual writers, of "a very urban, very educated, ironic, detached, iconoclastic attitude." Plus, a deliberate overdose of sexuality. This has been going on since the 1970s. According to New World Pictures' openly homosexual casting vice president Joel Thurm, the subtheme of the "Golden Girls" was very gay: "As far as I'm concerned, Blanche [the earthy grandmother] was gay. And I know for a fact I'm not the only gay man who feels this way. Blanche spoke frankly and openly about sex the way many gay men do. In fact, I identify with Blanche, especially now that I'm getting older . . . and hornier."[28]

In contrast to the constant sexual innuendo of virtually all prime-time situation comedies dominated by homosexual writers, the seventies mega-hits "Mary Tyler Moore Show" and "The Bob Newhart Show" depended on clever, family-friendly writing. Thurm says he was the only homosexual writer on the staff of Newhart's show and that he knew of no gay writers on Mary Tyler Moore's program: "None of the writers were gay. It was very much a boys' club. Not homophobic, mind you, but a real football-watching crowd."[29]

Even the top-rated "Seinfeld," which began as a clean clone of Jerry Seinfeld's remarkably tasteful stand-up comedy routines, quickly devolved into risqué material under the guidance of homosexual writers. In one episode, the father of George's bisexual girlfriend reveals that he has love letters written to him by the late novelist

John Cheever, whose homosexual affairs were revealed posthumously. Veteran comedy producer Mel Brooks marvels at the ease in which such esoteric knowledge is sold to bread-basket America: "Could anything be more arcane? Imagine—referring to John Cheever's bisexuality on a mass-market TV show. Amazing!"[30]

Meanwhile, public broadcasting is offering up a steady diet of gay-flavored commentary and shows devoted to homosexual themes. "In the Life," which is carried by most PBS stations, is a newsmagazine devoted entirely to the promotion of homosexuality. The show, like any gay-oriented program, assiduously avoids covering the ex-gay movement. Only topics that fit the homosexual activist agenda are featured, such as the latest news about AIDS.

During the 1990s, the red AIDS ribbon has been displayed prominently on the lapels of most stars taking part in Emmy and Oscar award ceremonies. Given the enormous influence of homosexuals in Hollywood, it now takes a real maverick with proven box-office credentials, such as Mel Gibson, to buck the tide and affirm traditional values. And even Gibson felt compelled to meet very publicly with a group of homosexual writers, directors, and producers to explain that he was not "homophobic" for featuring the murder by the king of an undesirable homosexual who had been seducing the king's son in the Oscar-winning film *Braveheart*.

ACTIVISM AS A WAY OF LIFE

The homosexual movement's use of television is in keeping with the wider liberal agenda that has dominated television since the 1970s. In a 1983 study of the views of more than a hundred of the top television producers, 66 percent agreed with the statement "TV should promote social reform."[31] In 1992, "Murphy Brown" producer Diane English told the Associated Press that "Murphy expresses a quite liberal point of view. It's also my point of view . . . [Murphy's] a dyed in the wool Democratic liberal."[32] Don Reo, creator of "Blossom," which features a single father, acknowledged of such shows, "Most of them are created by guys who are divorced. The reason they do them must be wish-fulfillment. They're subliminally trying to kill their ex-wives."[33]

Sometimes, Hollywood personalities attempt to directly influence the political process beyond the content of their shows. Fundraisers are often held for Democratic Party candidates, such as Bill Clinton, who has raised millions of dollars in Hollywood. A list of Clinton contributors reads like a Who's Who of Hollywood, from Disney Chairman Michael Eisner to director Steven Spielberg. The Hollywood Women's Political Caucus had been a major fundraiser for the liberal wing of the Democratic Party for more than a decade before it folded in 1997. Sometimes, Hollywood personalities even go out on the stump for various causes and candidates.

In 1988, Representative Pat Schroeder (D-CO) organized the "Great American Family Tour," which featured Harvard pediatrics professor T. Berry Brazelton, Diana Meehan of the Institute for the Study of Women and Men at the University of Southern California, and Gary David Goldberg, creator and executive producer of the eighties sitcom "Family Ties." Goldberg frankly acknowledged that his intent was to generate support for legislation that he said would help families. But the list of items was a feminist shopping list, not a pro-family agenda. At the top was government-subsidized child care and a whole range of redistributionist policies favored by liberal Democrats. Goldberg wrote off the traditional family altogether, saying that his own show, which featured a mother and a father, was an anachronism. "This is not about parents. This is about children," he said. "They're here and we can't pretend that they're not and wish for a return to a different time, or wish that people would stop having children; they're not going to . . . [I]t's just that the American family looks different now. It's usually a single-parent family or a divorced family . . ."[34]

At the same time that liberal "messages" were being planted in what had been merely an entertainment medium, daytime television talk shows began echoing the themes and mainstreaming deviancy through repetition. Phil Donahue, Sally Jesse Raphael, Geraldo Rivera, Oprah Winfrey, Jerry Springer, Rikki Lake, Rolonda and Canada's "The Shirley Show" became forums for an unending parade of weirdos—and a few people who defended the moral order. (For the record, I appeared on "Jerry Springer," "Oprah," and "The Shirley Show" as the token conservative against an army of pansexual advocates. The shows and the audiences were packed with homosexual activists who screamed things like, "Hey Bob. You're a bigot, Bob! Get over it, Bob!").

As early as 1990, even Geraldo had had enough of trafficking in abnormality. Before moving on to a more serious interview show on CNBC , he told the *Los Angeles Times* that competing with "Oprah" made him schedule shows such as the one on "Debbie Duz Donuts," about a topless donut shop in Colorado, and "battered lesbians."

"I went too far," Rivera said. "I think in November, I used up my quota on deviant behavior." As the *Times* relates: "Another watershed point came last fall, when Rivera discovered that there weren't enough deviants to go around. He and Phil Donahue unwittingly booked the same deviant: a former Los Angeles police officer who had become a prostitute. Geraldo's topic: 'Men Who Marry Prostitutes.' Donahue's topic: 'Prostitutes and Gigolos.' Embarrassingly enough, both shows aired on the same day in New York. 'There were no normal people on any of the three shows ["Geraldo," "The Oprah Winfrey Show," "Donahue"],' Rivera observed."[35]

Oprah, too, felt compelled to clean up her act and eventually acquired a reputation for airing the most thoughtful afternoon talk show. Her only blind spot continued to be homosexuality, which she to promoted with a single-minded vengeance, going so far as to play a psychologist who helps Ellen Degeneres realize her lesbian identity in the heavily hyped "Ellen" "coming out" episode.

Meanwhile, the amount of sex and violence on "entertainment" television rose to unprecedented levels.

6

Television Sex and Violence: The Jading Game

Unable to dismiss the increasingly unequivocal evidence of the negative impact of brutal media images, apologists for the entertainment industry resort to shrugs of the shoulders, knowing smiles, and the accurate but irrelevant argument that complaints about bloodshed on screen represent nothing new.[1]

Michael Medved

IN 1981, cable television entrepreneur Ted Turner appeared in Washington before a House subcommittee to give his comments about network programming. As a cable tycoon seeking government help in breaking the networks' hegemony, he stood personally to benefit from criticism of broadcasters. Nonetheless, his remarks were hailed widely as expressing what many Americans were thinking: "A large portion of our population is sick and the major culprits are the tremendous television networks and the motion picture companies that are turning our young people into a society of lawbreakers, murderers, drug addicts, and perverts."[2]

CBS, NBC, and ABC, Turner said, were producing a steady

stream of imagery designed to elicit the worst reactions from viewers: "They glorify violence, illicit sex, reckless driving, materialism, and just plain stupidity. Their entertainment programs make a mockery of all our institutions that have made our Nation the greatest, freest, best governed, most prosperous, and most generous the world has ever seen. For at least the last ten years their programming has become antifamily, antireligion, antilaw, antieducation, antibusiness, and antigovernment."[3]

Over the years, television moved away from being a wholesome, if unrealistic, mirror of the best in American society. Gradually, dysfunction became the theme of most shows and made-for-TV movies. The good guys still won, but the good guys were no longer so . . . good. Like a pusher who gradually increases the dose of his victim, the television barons fed higher doses of sex, foul language, and violence to a jaded public.

In 1974, NBC crossed a line when it broadcast the movie *Born Innocent*. Featuring actress Linda Blair of *Exorcist* fame, the film graphically portrayed Miss Blair being raped with a broom handle in a reform school. The outrage was quick and sustained. NBC received more than three thousand letters, most of them denouncing the violence.[4] Parents of a girl who was similarly raped in San Francisco days after the broadcast filed a lawsuit against NBC, and Congress began pressuring the Federal Communications Commission to put pressure on the networks. In September 1975, the New York–based advocacy group Morality in Media presented the FCC with a one hundred thousand–name petition calling for hearings into television's portrayals of sex and violence.[5]

The House Communications Subcommittee held hearings, and experts flayed the networks, suggesting that self-policing had not worked. Brandishing a surgeon general's report on television violence issued in 1972, reformers secured an agreement by the National Association of Broadcasters for a "family viewing hour" between 7:00 and 9:00 PM. But viewers continued to see objectionable material and threatened to boycott program sponsors.

The National Citizens Committee for Broadcasting, a private group formed in 1969, hired George Gerbner, Dean of the Annenberg School of Communications at the University of Pennsylvania, to monitor programming. Gerbner had already begun documenting television violence in the late 1960s. His periodic reports document what most viewers know: television has lots of violence, which has stayed steady over the past twenty-five years.

Since 1975, the public and Congress sporadically have become incensed over violence on television, with the latest volley being fired in 1990, when Senator Paul Simon (D-ILL) secured passage of the Television Violence Act of 1990. That legislation, which has since been extended, exempted the networks for three years from antitrust law so they could meet together to find ways to reduce television violence.

By the time the 1993–1994 viewing season began, the public—and Congress—were demanding results. During the 1993–94 session of Congress, at least six bills were introduced regarding television violence. At that point, the four networks (ABC, CBS, NBC, and Fox) agreed to run advisories before violence-prone shows that say: "Due to some violent content, parental discretion advised."

The National Cable Television Association, representing such networks as Showtime, USA Networks, Home Box Office, and Nickelodeon, also agreed to run the advisories. The networks also promised to reduce violence, especially gratuitous portrayals. There is some evidence that this has occurred. A list of children's top ten prime-time shows in 1982–1983 contained four violent action-type shows, such as "The A-Team." In 1993–1994, the top ten list for children consisted solely of situation comedies.[6]

According to a 1994 study by the Center for Media and Public Affairs (CMPA) that compared the premiere episodes of 1992 prime-time shows with those of 1993, network television violence was reduced.[7] Although the total amount of violence rose slightly, from 338 to 361 scenes, the scenes of "serious violence" (physical assaults that go beyond a single punch, slap, or push) dropped by 28 percent (from 119 to ninety-three) and dropped by 50 percent in promotional spots. Gunplay dropped even more, by 58 percent (from fifty-seven to twenty-four scenes).

Eight syndicated series (independently produced, non-network shows) continued to emphasize violence, accounting for 33 percent more serious violence than all seventy-four network series in 1993. Six of the ten most violent shows were syndicated, as were seven of the top ten for "serious violence."

"The networks really have taken steps to reduce violence," said S. Robert Lichter, codirector of CMPA. But Dr. Lichter noted that Washington's recent focus on network programming has "bypassed the most violence-prone part of prime time," syndicated programs.

By 1996, however, Lichter and company reported that the networks had slipped back into their old ways, particularly with lurid promotional spots.

Once again, Congress summoned Hollywood's television moguls for flailing and even passed a law dictating that all new television sets be equipped with a "v-chip" (V is for violence) within two years. The chip allows a parent to block programs, each of which is equipped with a signal by the broadcaster. The law also called for establishment of a government ratings system if Hollywood did not solve the problem.

In spring of 1997, Jack Valenti, whose Motion Picture Association of America (MPAA) ratings system helped give movies a free pass for inclusion of sex, violence, and foul language, unveiled an industry-concocted ratings system that divided television shows by age appropriateness. TV-Y and TV-G were for all ages, TV-7 was for children seven and above, PG was okay for children up to age thirteen, TV-14 was for fourteen and older, and TV-M was for mature audiences. The public yawned. Polls showed overwhelming lack of trust in either Hollywood or the federal government in determining what is suitable for children. The networks shot themselves in the tube by issuing absurdly inappropriate ratings. Shows like "Friends," "Melrose Place," and even "Beverly Hills 90210," heavy on sex, foul language, and homosexual themes, were given PG or TV-14 ratings. This meant that Hollywood thought that fourteen-year-olds should surf in a television lagoon full of nonstop sexual promiscuity and crude vernacular. In a survey done by a Aragon Consulting of St. Louis, nearly 80 percent of parents said they were unhappy with the ratings and preferred more information. Asked to rate a couple of dozen shows, the parents consistently chose TV-14 or TV-M for programs that the industry had pegged at PG.

Chastened by Congress and pounded by the polls, the television industry decided to enhance the age-based ratings with content information. "S" was for sexual content, "V" for violence, "L" for profane or obscene language, and "D" for suggestive dialogue. Valenti, who doggedly fought the content system, insisted that there was no way that program raters could differentiate between a chaste kiss on "Dr. Quinn, Medicine Woman," and the R-rated film *Basic Instinct*.[8] Many observers concurred. Leaving the kids in the care of Hollywood, they said, would be like entrusting them to the misfits cruising Santa Monica Boulevard.

Since television sets began flickering cathode-ray imagery into America's living rooms in the late 1940s, scientists have tried to answer the question: How does television affect viewers?

Nobody reputable contends that television has zero effect; that view would not pass the "straight-face test," much like the tobacco companies' insistence that smoking has no effect whatever on health. It would also be news to advertisers who spend billions of dollars each year to influence viewers' behavior.

Research conducted in the mid-nineties indicates that violence has declined somewhat, at least on the major networks. Most hit television shows, for example, are situation comedies or info–news documentaries, such as "Sixty Minutes." But violence has increased on news programs. While crime rates leveled off from 1992 to

1993, crime news doubled and coverage of murder tripled in 1993.[9] And cable television continues to traffic in explicit sex and violence because programming standards are looser and more uncut films are shown. Cable operators argue that they should have greater flexibility since their product is available only to people who want to pay for it, unlike broadcasters, who transmit universally.

Behind all the interest in television violence is a spectacular rise in crime since television's inception and a growing body of scientific evidence that television violence plays some part in viewers' aggressive behavior. Statistics compiled in "Big World, Small Screen," a 1992 report from the American Psychological Association, are now almost numbingly familiar: A child who watches an average of two to four hours of television a day will have witnessed eight thousand homicides and one hundred thousand other acts of violence by the time he reaches junior high school. He will have seen twenty thousand homicides by the time he graduates from high school. The report concludes: "Television can cause aggressive behavior and can cultivate values favoring the use of aggression."[10]

The onslaught of real and televised violence even has some Hollywood executives worried about what kind of culture their children are inheriting. ABC executive Ted Harbert told the *New Yorker* why he has joined the ranks of those concerned: "[Three-year-old] Emily's entrance into the world totally changed the way I look at television. I have a massive problem . . . now with violence on television."[11]

A 1972 report by the Surgeon General concluded that children who are predisposed toward aggression become more violent after watching television violence. In 1982, an update of the report extended the findings to include nonaggressive children and even adults. In other words, viewing television violence is said to affect everybody, and especially those who are already aggressive.

Some of the documented effects, as summarized by psychologist Brian L. Wilcox, are:[12]

- *Copycat violence.* Some children directly imitate aggressive behavior on television.

- *Removal of inhibitions.* Viewing television violence can remove or reduce inhibitions that children might have that normally preclude aggressive behavior.

- *Desensitization.* The most firmly established effect is on attitudes and values. Children who watch repeated acts of violence on television are less horrified by it in real life. Some people develop a "bystander" mentality, in which real violence is viewed as unreal because it is all part of a video event. One study (Liebert & Sprafkin, 1988) found that a steady consumption of television violence spawns antisocial values and attitudes, with violence being seen as a primary or first-resort way to solve problems. The research indicates that this holds true for adults as well as children.

- *Exaggerated fears.* People who watch lots of television violence feel the world around them is a more dangerous place than those who don't watch much television.

THE GOVERNMENT'S ROLE

Since 1934, when the Federal Communications Commission (FCC) was created, the government has prohibited the airing of obscenity in broadcast media, but has not addressed violence. Because of the First Amendment's guarantee of freedom of speech, lawmakers have resisted the urge to regulate most programming content.

In 1992, the FCC enacted a twenty-four-hour ban on indecent programming after Congress ordered the agency to target material that falls short of obscene or pornographic but is considered "contrary to standards for broadcast medium." Following guidelines set in the 1973 Supreme Court case *Miller v. California*, the FCC defined indecent materials as "depicting sexual or excretory activities or organs" in terms "patently offensive as measured by contemporary community standards for the broadcast medium." Shortly thereafter, the U. S. Court of Appeals for the District of Columbia struck down the twenty-four-hour ban as unconstitutional. Congress next ordered the FCC to restrict programming between midnight and 6:00 a.m., and the same court struck this down also, saying that the FCC had not adequately considered the rights of adults over those of children. "We can locate no evidence in the record," the court said, "that the government has taken the First Amendment interests of adults into account in advancing its compelling interest in the protection of children."[13]

The National Association of Broadcasters used to have its own standards for television programming based on FCC guidelines, but these were struck down in 1984 by a federal court, which ruled that the FCC rules were an unconstitutional restraint of trade.[14] The Television Violence Act of 1990 exempted the networks from the ruling so they could meet to discuss how to curb television violence.

In December 1992, the three major networks issued a pact regarding television violence which states that "conflict and strife are the essence of drama, and conflict often results in physical or psychological violence. However, all depictions of violence should be relevant and necessary to the development of character, or the advancement of theme or plot."[15] The pact condemns "gratuitous or excessive depictions of violence," the depiction of violence as "glamorous" or "as an acceptable solution to human conflict." The networks also agreed to take special care in situations involving children and to provide "realistic" portrayals "in human terms, the consequences of that violence to its victims and its perpetrators."

In August 1993, Paul Simon convened hearings around the impending expiration of his 1990 Television Violence Act. In February 1994, the networks promised to hire an independent television monitor to be in operation by the beginning of the 1994–

1995 season in September. They also agreed to issue annual reports on television violence.[16]

The cable television industry, target of the most severe criticism, runs much more violent programming than the networks and uses more syndicated programming (non-network, independent shows) such as "The Highlander," which has more violence than most network shows. In the face of congressional pressure, The National Cable Television Association also has promised to hire an independent monitor.[17]

Broadcasters, for their part, have acknowledged that the public is concerned over violence, but reject the conclusions of most of the research. "We stopped arguing the research a long time ago," says CBS Program Practices chief Beth Bressan, who contends that CBS has recognized that "there is a problem and that we are dealing with it."[18] She noted that the 1993–1994 CBS program lineup was "much less violent than it was ten years ago."

In a 1993 poll, 74 percent of television station managers said there was too much needless violence on television.[19] At ABC, Program Practices head Christine Hikawa said that public comment is having an impact: "I think the general public is very angry with TV, and I think that some of it is earned."[20] Hikawa says that ABC has "edited out the worst violence on our shows," and opposes any governmentally imposed rating system. In children's programming, she says, ABC tries to discriminate between "fantastic" violence and "anything imitable" because "we all agree that children imitate the actions they see on television . . . We didn't accept the Ninja Turtles because they kick and punch, and kids do those things." ABC runs the "Roadrunner" cartoons, which contain prolific amounts of slapstick violence, such as the hapless Wile E. Coyote falling down a mile-high canyon—onto a rocket that blasts him skyward.

"The coyote is out in the desert," explains Hikawa. "And he uses big rockets that he gets from [fictitious mail-order firm] ACME. Kids don't have ACME. In 'Roadrunner,' nobody is stabbing anyone with a fork, because kids could stab each other with a fork. One reason I don't object to 'X-Men' [another cartoon] is that it is very fantastic, with them zapping each other with lasers. 'Tom and Jerry' (the vintage cartoon slapstick team) worry me because they hit each other a lot."

According to Senator Simon, his staff has "discovered nearly 3,000 scholarly articles and studies on the harmful effects of television violence on children and adults."[21] Although some experts point out that much of the research is about the effects of television in general and does not specifically target violence, most agree that at least two hundred studies are available that show a link between television violence and greater aggressiveness in children.

Here is a summary of the major studies, as reproduced from "Cultural Pollution," a Family Research Council *Family Policy* paper from which much of the information on television violence in this chapter was extracted:[22]

- In 1956, two dozen four-year-olds were split into groups. One group watched a violence-laden "Woody Woodpecker" cartoon. The other watched a peaceful cartoon, "The Little Red Hen." Afterward, researchers observed that the "Woody Woodpecker" children were more prone to get into fights and arguments with other children, to break toys, and be disruptive and destructive.

- In 1960, Leonard Eron and L. Rowell Huesmann, University of Illinois psychologists, conducted a survey of 875 third-graders and their parents in a semirural New York county. After ten years, Eron found a high correlation between boys who had viewed violent television at age eight and their aggressiveness at nineteen. He also found that boys who had ranked low on aggression ten years before, but watched violent television, had higher rates of aggression than boys who had originally ranked high on aggression but had not

watched violent elevision . In 1990, Eron revisited the
subjects, who were now age thirty. He found "no relation
to what they were watching at age nineteen, or at age thirty.
But there was a strong relation between what they watched
at age eight and their aggressive behavior at age nineteen
and at age thirty."[23]

- In 1967, George Gerbner of the University of Pennsylvania
began documenting the amount of violence on television
and studying the effects on viewers. The measures included
frequency of violence, rate of violence per program per hour,
and the role that the main character played as perpetrator/
victim of violence. The researchers produced a Violence
Index and concluded that "heavy viewers of violence,
especially children and youth, tended to be more concerned
about their personal safety and more likely to perceive the
real world as being dangerous and frightening than those
persons who watched very little television."[24] Further,
Gerbner contended that the evidence shows that exposure
to television violence desensitizes the viewer to acts of
violence and sometimes incites viewers to violence.

- In 1972, the Surgeon General released "Television and
Growing Up: The Impact of Televised Violence," a report
that included five volumes of research collected by the
National Institute of Mental Health (NIMH) entitled
"Television and Social Behavior." The report concluded
that there is a causal relationship between children's viewing
of violent programs and subsequent aggressive behavior.
The report stressed, however, that this applies only to children
who are predisposed toward aggression.[25]

- In 1975, the South African government began to permit
television broadcasting, years after other Western countries

had it. Researcher Brandon S. Centerwall of the University of Washington compared white homicide rates in South Africa and the United States and Canada (97 percent white in 1951). After introduction of television into the U.S., the annual white homicide rate increased by 93 percent from 1945 to 1974; in South Africa, where television was banned, the white homicide rate fell by 7.2 percent during the same period; and in Canada, the homicide rate increased by 92 percent after television was introduced during the same period. For Canada and the United States, there was a lag of ten to fifteen years between television introduction and a doubling of the homicide rate. In South Africa, by 1987, white homicides had increased by 130 percent.

- In 1978, television came to a remote Canadian town called "Notel" by the researchers, who used a double-blind design to compare forty-five first- and second-grade students in "Notel" and two communities that had already had television. Rates of physical aggression (hitting, shoving, and biting) did not significantly change in the communities that already had television, but "Notel" children increased their aggressive activities by 160 percent within two years.[26]

- In 1982, NIMH released an update of the 1972 Surgeon General's report entitled "Television and Behavior: Ten Years of Scientific Progress and Implication for the Eighties." This compilation of research focused only on entertainment television, corroborating the 1972 findings and extending them to conclude that viewing television violence causes aggressive behavior in children and youth regardless of predisposition. The only significant criticism of this finding came from a study funded by NBC, which found that "these short-term effects found experimentally do not lead to stable patterns of aggression."[27]

- In 1990, G. Comstock and H. Paik did a meta-analysis of two hundred previous studies, looking at the relationship between violent programming and aggressive behavior, including criminal activity. Overall, they found a significant, causative correlation between viewing and behavior.[28]

Regarding the hefty body of evidence on television violence, CBS spokeswoman Beth Bressan says, "A lot of this has become folklore, not fact." She declined to name any studies that CBS might find persuasive, adding, "I'm not sure there are any reliable studies." Lack of differentiation between types of violence and context are major problems, she asserts, noting that according to typically indiscriminate criteria, the twenty-fifth anniversary reunion show of the comedy program "Laugh-in" was rated the most violent program in 1993.

Marcy Kelly of Mediascope, a Los Angeles-based research organization, notes that "car crashes, for example, shown in the film (about the founding of Mothers Against Drunk Driving) would be counted as violent acts."[29]

Researcher George Gerbner acknowledges that he counts all violence in his studies, defining it as "overt physical demonstration of power that hurts or kills. Whether it is done in a so-called serious way or a so-called humorous way has no functional significance."[30] But he says that extreme examples such as an often-cited story about his recording of someone slipping on a banana peel as a violent act "was invented by an NBC executive twenty-five years ago."[31]

At the May 1993 Senate hearings on television violence, Fox executive George Vradenburg III pledged that his network would "portray any antisocial violent act as unacceptable; tries to associate antisocial violent acts with real consequences for its victims and its perpetrators; associates antisocial violence with wrongdoing, with punishment, and with pain."[32]

Amid the debate, a key element is in danger of being ignored, or at least undervalued. And that is the moral content of the scenes involving violence. In storytelling, all violence is not equal, and sheer quantity of violence, while being a problem in and of itself, should not be the only concern, contends media critic Laurence Jarvik: "The issue is not violence; the issue is morality. Social engineers never want to accept the notion of individual responsibility. Everyone's a robot. Nobody makes a moral choice. It's TV's fault. It's society's fault. I'm not saying TV doesn't have an effect; of course it does. But its influence is being overblown as part of a larger agenda. It's all part of social engineering. The bottom line, is, bureaucrats want to control the media, and this is a useful stick."[33]

Gerbner, however, argues that any form of violence, even cartoon violence, has an impact and is therefore worth measuring: "Violence is a social relationship, a demonstration of power," he told *Congressional Research Quarterly*. "It's who can do what to whom and get away with it. Cartoons are the most controversial and effective demonstrations of power, with humor as the sugar-coating pill."[34]

While condemning "abuse" of violence in programming, Fox's George Vradenburg sees a positive role for violence "as a creative device to dramatize human emotions and behaviors—conflict and confrontation, jeopardy, and danger, revenge and retribution. The device is as old as storytelling itself—it is as essential to the story of the exodus of the Jews from Egypt as it is to . . . [the] Academy Award–winning picture *Unforgiven* (1994)."[35]

Jarvik says that although everyone, including him, is against "gratuitous violence," he believes that many of the studies make no distinction between "necessary" violence and "unnecessary" violence: "If you look at the shows they hate, it's the ones that have a clear conflict between good and evil, like westerns. Not only don't they want to resolve the conflict through violence; they want only nonviolent conflict resolution. They want the guy in the white hat and the guy in the black hat to go into therapy. It's essentially a pacifist message."

In 1991, the most violent show on television was "The Young Riders," with an average of fifty-five incidents of violence per hour. In syndication on The Family Channel, "The Young Riders" is considered by that network to be good family fare because of its clear moral context and lack of "gratuitous" violence. Without the moral consideration, the program would be condemned outright by children's advocates. Part of the reason for this is the research itself. Many studies are flawed because they make little distinction between Elmer Fudd getting bopped on the head with a carrot and the Terminator graphically blowing away human beings. The Lichter study is one exception, specifically seeking to avoid that problem by concentrating on "serious" violence and "scenes" of violence, instead of individual punches or gunshots. Zeroing in solely on quantity eliminates the moral factor, on which it is far more difficult to find a consensus in the Age of Consent.

The debate over television violence is being conducted in a way similar to the gun control issue. When the moral context is eliminated, the issue is framed entirely around the sheer number of guns, whether they belong to Joe Q. Law-Abiding Family Man or to a hoodlum. In the same way, all television violence, whatever the moral context, is seized upon by some as inherently wrong. In both cases, individual accountability is devalued, and government stands to gain more control at the expense of individual freedom.

Recent research on crime indicates that the single most reliable indicator is not how much or how early children watch violence on television (with the exception of the Eron studies), but the number of fatherless families in a given area. The breakdown of families and communities, along with the erosion of a moral consensus about behavior and the liberalization of criminal law have combined to create lawless enclaves in large cities and a higher incidence of crime across America.

A question often asked in the debate over television violence is: Does television merely reflect the violence in society or does it cause it? This is a strawman proposition in which neither answer is satisfactory. The most reasonable conclusion is that television violence does reflect violence in society but is also playing some part in the creation of a violent culture.

The most dangerous doses of television violence occur when sexuality and violence are intertwined. In their 1984 book *Pornography and Sexual Aggression,* Drs. Neil Malamuth and Edward Donnerstein observed young men watching violent pornography and concluded that: "There can be relatively long-term, antisocial effects of movies that portray sexual violence as having positive consequences" (such as women indicating enjoyment of rape).[36]

Donnerstein summed up the problem this way for a 1993 television industry conference: "If you take normal males and expose them to graphic violence against women in R-rated films, the research doesn't show that they'll commit acts of violence against women. It doesn't say they will go out and commit rape. But it does demonstrate that they become desensitized to violence against women, they have less sympathy for rape victims, and their perceptions and attitudes and values about violence change. Does that mean they're going to commit violent acts? Not necessarily. But should we be concerned about those effects? Certainly yes."[37]

Dr. Victor B. Cline, author of several books on media violence and pornography, notes: "The literature on aggressive pornography is rather impressive in its consistency in suggesting a variety of harms or possibility of antisocial outcomes to this material. This should not be surprising after forty years of research on film and TV violence arriving essentially at the same conclusion."[38]

"Slasher" films, which combine sex with violence, are aimed at the market of teenaged boys and are showing up more frequently on television, mostly on cable. Often, the low-budget films depict a young woman either naked or in various stages of undress, just before she is brutally murdered or maimed.

In her 1991 book *Soft Porn Plays Hardball,* media analyst Dr.

Judith Reisman explains that slasher films actually provoke bodily responses such as a mixture of adrenaline and sexual arousal that can permanently mark a viewer. In other words, if a young man becomes sexually excited while watching a young woman, and that young woman is then brutally attacked, the attack becomes part of the erotic repertoire in the young man's imagination.[39]

The growing sexualization of the medium is mostly ignored in the discussion over television standards. Some media observers have commented, however. When liberal newspaper columnist Richard Reeves returned to the United States after spending several years in Europe, he was shocked that American television was "awash" in sexuality, with double entendres, near-nudity, and constant sexual allusions in most prime-time programs. Not to mention the violence. While there is bipartisan agreement that television violence is harmful, there are few lawmakers on either side of the political spectrum that have drawn a link between media-aided relaxation of sexual morality, the subsequent breakdown in family life, and the emergence of unsocialized, violent young men who prey on others.

So any discussion of the link between television violence and real violence is incomplete without reference to the rise in sexual imagery, and particularly sexual imagery that involves violence.

The First Amendment protects broadcasters from unreasonable restrictions on content, barring only obscene speech, which is unprotected. Court decisions over the years generally have upheld the FCC's authority to regulate indecent programming, especially when children are most likely to be watching. But the FCC's twenty-four-hour ban on indecent programming was struck down by a federal court in 1993.[40]

Stung by criticism that the industry doesn't care about its effect on children, or adults for that matter, television executives have tried a two-fold strategy. First, they deny that watching television has any impact on anybody. Then they blame it on the culture.

The perverse sex and gore, they say, is merely a reflection of society, not a causative factor.

The first position is made ridiculous by two powerful facts: advertisers are spending billions to buy precious seconds of television time to affect people's behavior. And research overwhelmingly indicates that people are influenced by what they watch. Furthermore, the networks themselves have been putting out rhetoric since the forties espousing the "good" effects of television for the nation.

In March 1992, MPAA chief Jack Valenti took part in a panel discussion at the American Enterprise Institute. Valenti declared that he had examined social research and "[had not] found anybody who has said that movies cause anybody to do anything." But another view has been given by screenwriter and actor Ben Stein, author of the book *The View from Sunset Boulevard* (1980), which chronicles the gap between middle American values and Hollywood.

Stein sees the people in Hollywood as believing "themselves to be part of a working class distinctly at odds with the exploiting classes . . ." Of all the producers and writers he interviewed for his book, "all thought of themselves as politically 'progressive.'"[41] This means dispensing with traditional religion and embracing relativism. As one interviewee put it, the church "has been narrow-minded. It hasn't grown with the times. It's been lumbering along, and hasn't taken cognizance of what's going on in the world. It hasn't made the changes it's got to make. The church brought us up to believe that things were the way they made them out to be. As we've become wiser and more educated, we've started to challenge these implanted beliefs."[42]

One could not ask for a more revealing statement of not only Hollywood's view, but that of an entire relativistic culture that sees truth as an evolving concept and "wisdom" as the rejection of biblical morality. For contrast, here is Romans 1:21–24: "[Men] became vain in their imaginations, and their foolish heart was darkened.

Professing themselves to be wise, they became fools, and changed the glory of the uncorruptible God into an image made like to corruptible man . . . Wherefore God also gave them up to uncleanness through the lusts of their own hearts, to dishonour their own bodies between themselves."[43]

Given their prejudice against anything "old," television producers have turned out a steady diet of shows that depict small-town life as cramped and retrograde and religion as a stumbling block from another era, when it is addressed at all. Most of the time that clergy are on television, it is in the course of a funeral, a wedding, or for a quick bit of advice from a major character. On television, there is almost no sense that religion plays a part in anyone's life. It is not so much that television bashes religion, but that it ignores it and thereby declares it unimportant.

In the absence of any substantial spiritual content, the combination of mood-inducing advertising and cynical programming invites the viewer into a relativistic world where people make up right and wrong as they go along.

As Stein summarizes, "TV culture is at war with the folk culture . . . It is over life styles . . . On television, life is lived in the fast lane. The motto is to live it up, right now. Forget about quiet living. There is no wisdom in one's elders, and the past offers no guides to the present. That is the lesson of TV situation comedies and adventure shows . . . Old-fashioned people are not to be trusted. The life to live, on television, is the life of Los Angeles."[44]

And what is Los Angeles but a polyglot of cultural relativism that is so ethically "diverse" that a judge in an early nineties pornography case declared that standards based on "community values" were useless in LA because nobody could possibly determine them. By the time O. J. Simpson had been acquitted and punks from the riots had been given a slap on the wrist, many people began to feel as if they were living in a state of anarchy.

On a larger level, in America, the steady diet of scandal, amorality, and betrayal found among business people on television series has a direct link to a decrease in business ethics. "You can see the effect in the insider trading scandals on Wall Street," Stein told an interviewer. "The people involved are mostly young guys, influenced in large part by television's ethics and mores. The mores you now see at Goldman, Sachs, and Salomon Brothers are the mores of 'Dallas' and 'Dynasty.' It's not just coincidence . . . Television doesn't make people adverse to being business people. It isn't showing business as a profession without rewards. It's simply saying that you have to be a thief to get them . . . you have to be an unscrupulous creep."[45]

Few researchers would contend that a single show or movie "causes" someone to do something, although there are isolated instances in which teens or children committed "copycat" crimes patterned directly on what they just saw on television. In October 1993, for instance, a little girl was burned to death in a mobile home fire, set by her five-year-old brother who had just watched Beavis and Butthead set fires on their MTV show. And a total of twenty-six deaths by Russian roulette were attributed to the television showing of *The Deer Hunter*, in which a major character blows his own brains out during a gambling session.

Common sense, and research, indicate that television has become one of the most pervasive influences in the culture. Hollywood perennially uses the straw man argument that particular shows do not directly *cause* criminal behavior. But they ignore the obvious implication that a steady diet of sex and violence can *encourage* antisocial behavior. As Michael Medved observes, "I never stress the pernicious power of one movie or TV show, or one hit song; what concerns me is the accumulated impact of irresponsible messages that are repeated hour after hour, year after year."[46]

Although the sheer repetition of the liberal message may be having an impact on viewers, many have tired of the propaganda and are tuning out. The decline of television integrity and quality clearly has taken its toll. In 1974, a Gallup Poll showed that 46 percent of Americans felt that watching television was their favorite way to spend an evening. In 1990, well after the advent of cable, satellite transmissions, and vcRs, that percentage had dropped to 24 percent. More, the viewers seemed to be saying, is less.

7

Television Families: Relativizing the Relatives

By and large, television programming reflects the antifamily side of America's cultural civil war. In fact, for years the intact family has been a TV *oddity.*[1]

Gary Bauer

ECAUSE TELEVISION REACHES MORE PEOPLE, more powerfully than any other communications medium, debates often center on whether television creates societal change or whether it just reflects society. The answer is a qualified "both." Television affects society, or people would not fight over what's on it and sponsors would disappear.

The society shown on the tube may not be the American culture in general but a subculture with more than its share of pathologies, excesses, and hubris. The "community" that cranks out America's movies and television is very small. Centered in Los Angeles, this community seems to think the rest of America is inhabited by pitchfork-wielding villagers prone to violence over any challenge to their sexist, racist, Christocentric culture.

While family dysfunction has been a growing problem around the nation for the past three decades as well as a literary focus for thousands of years, the Hollywood crowd has always been ahead of the curve in America. For them, monogamous marriage for a lifetime in the Age of Consent is an unattainable goal, with serial polygamy the norm. Well-behaved children exist only in fantasies because Hollywood is full of precocious, cynical, foul-mouthed brats (aren't all children like this?). All teens are "doing it," and those few who aren't are probably being kept in detention pens by the dreaded fundamentalist Christians. Nobody believes in religion anymore, since people are all evolving past that stage. Everybody is also swearing. And they are all drinking to excess and doing drugs, which breed their own disjointed view of reality. Between "Beverly Hills 90210," "Melrose Place," "Friends," "Central Park West," "Frasier," "Cybil," "Caroline in the City," and MTV, a world has been created of young adults consumed with casual sex, money, drugs, and autonomous lifestyles. Missing entirely are a sense of generational continuity, community ties, religion, and family. All of these require deferred gratification, which does not lend itself to sensational television.

As one television historian puts it, "If one accepted the full litany of television content as isomorphic with the depiction of life, the ensuing beliefs and social expectations would be so distorted as to be laughable, pitied, or scorned."[2]

The product on television has less to do with reality than it does with the concepts floating around in the minds of a handful of people sporting sunglasses and extravagant tastes. As Ben Stein has remarked, "Television is not creating a world that reflects a composite of the American experience. Nor is the TV world the result of random chance. Television is what comes out of the Los Angeles TV community's heads, and since Los Angeles is what goes into their heads, Los Angeles is what comes out."[3]

And what is Los Angeles? Not exactly white-picket-fence

America, which is busy gobbling up L.A.'s pathologies and wondering why nobody respects traditional notions of right and wrong anymore. But in LA, crudity is equated with sophistication, just as pornography made for immature minds is labeled "adult" material.

Listen to *Los Angeles Daily News* television critic Ray Richmond make fun of parents who object to the increasing vulgarity on television: "Thinking adults are hardly going to turn into a heaping pile of gelatin because they hear the word 'ass' on the air. I don't see this 'vulgarity' as a loosening of standards, but rather as a reflection of the reality around us."[4]

A perfect politically correct stance in the Age of Consent. Since television has already gotten crude and its viewers jaded, they deserve to be shocked some more. If they are still shocked, then they just haven't watched enough television. But television has no effect, you understand. It is merely reflecting "the reality around us."

Particularly hard-hit by this attitude has been the family, or at least the notion of the family as a nuclear unit of dad, mom, and children, with extended relatives such as grandpa and grandma.

In the 1950s and 1960s, television families largely consisted of this model. Series such as "The Honeymooners," "Leave It to Beaver," "Father Knows Best," "The Adventures of Ozzie and Harriet," the "Real McCoys," the "Donna Reed Show," "I Love Lucy," "The Patty Duke Show," "Dennis the Menace," "Rin Tin Tin," "Lassie," and many others give the impression that families begin with marriage and continue with children (even when the star is a dog). Or when mom is absent. "My Three Sons" is about a once-intact family whose mom died, leaving the dad to raise his boys. Even the fifties action show "Superman," which revolves around the staff of The Daily Planet newspaper, is fueled by the subplot of Lois Lane's wish to eventually marry her man.

Throughout the television world, few successful shows have either a real family or at least a pseudo-family. As social critic Carl Traynor Williams remarks, "Beneath 'comedy' and 'drama,' and other forms, what really generates television's form and content—the genre beneath the genre—is the structure of the American family . . ."[5]

The western, which flourished in the fifties and early sixties, often had a loner or wandering hero, but was preoccupied with law and order so that families could flourish. Roy Rogers and Dale Evans made a rare modern-day western in the fifties based on a marriage that mirrors their own. In the Old West, even the exceptions proved the rule. Chuck Connors's "The Rifleman," with its widower father raising a son, often made clear that the absence of a mother was no small thing. And "The Rifleman," like all good westerns, taught that right and wrong are not relative. (Even the James Bond–inspired "Wild, Wild West" never left any doubt as to who the good guys were.)

On "Bonanza," widower Ben Cartwright sometimes recalled his sons' mother. There was no indication that Ben might have contemplated getting rid of her so he could have a "trophy wife." Many families, too, figured into the "Bonanza" subplots. The Lone Ranger and Tonto, the Cisco Kid, and Hopalong Cassidy also often aided besieged families, and some of the plots involved bringing estranged fathers back into the fold.

There were several shows, however, that pioneered the "nonblood family," in which ensembles were formed in the workplace or the military. "The Dick van Dyke Show" mixed the two genres, with sketches based on van Dyke's family life or with his nonblood family of comedy writers. Phil Silvers as "Sgt. Bilko" was the paterfamilias of a "family" of con-men GIs. Ernest Borgnine's "McHale's Navy" did the same for a PT-boat crew. "Hogan's Heroes" revolved around an American colonel who led a camp of World War II American and British prisoners of war to numerous victories, large and small, over their oafish and preposterously stupid Nazi captors.

"Gilligan's Island" featured a somewhat befuddled "Skipper" and his idiot "son" overseeing an unlikely group of castaways. "Star

Trek," whose brief run (1967–1969) triggered an enormous boom in science fiction, was the quintessential nonblood family, with William Shatner's Captain Kirk presiding over quarreling "siblings" Mr. Spock and Dr. McCoy, with faithful sons Scotty and Sulu, and faithful daughter Uhuru helping the *Enterprise* stay on keel. "The Mod Squad," with its young, interracial heroes, displayed generational bonding in the face of a corrupt world.

The nonblood family has certain advantages, most notably the infinite romantic possibilities of its adult characters. It is easier to invent new "types" of potential partners than it is to develop character over a long period of time. For some reason, Hollywood finds it difficult, if not impossible, to keep the "spark" going between a husband and a wife. Part of the reason for this is that conflict and novelty are easier to conjure up for characters that are dysfunctional to begin with. As Tolstoy observed, happy families are all alike, but unhappy families are each miserable in their own way. And the audience is probably grateful that their own lives are not as calamitous or bizarre.

Major exceptions to the dysfunctional rule include "The Cosby Show" in the eighties and "Mad About You," "Dave's World," "Family Matters," "Home Improvement," "Newhart," "Seventh Heaven," "Step by Step," and "Promised Land" in the nineties. "Dr. Quinn, Medicine Woman," has aired many pro-family messages, but it also has a record of promoting enough liberal causes to earn it the sobriquet "PC on the Prairie." The show shocked many family viewers in April 1997 when it used the occasion of a visit by poet Walt Whitman to cast homosexuality in a positive light.

Notwithstanding the huge success of "All in the Family," which debuted in 1971, a boom in the nonblood family "ensembles" came in the 1970s, 1980s, and 1990s, with "M*A*S*H," "Mary Tyler Moore," and "Murphy Brown" leading the way. Children are virtually nonexistent in these adult vehicles, with plot lines revolving around egos, rivalries, office politics, and the full range of human frailties.

Nonblood families are portrayed in varied settings, including the police station ("Murder One," "NYPD Blue," "Barney Miller," "Hill Street Blues"), the courts ("Law & Order," "Courthouse"), an Alaskan town ("Northern Exposure"), a newspaper ("Lou Grant"), a cab company ("Taxi"), a restaurant ("Alice"), a radio station ("WKRP in Cincinnati"), an apartment complex ("Bob Newhart," "Three's Company"), a governor's staff ("Benson"), a mayor's staff ("Spin City"), an inner city high school ("Welcome Back, Kotter"), a business office ("9 to 5"), a high school for the performing arts ("Fame"), a basement bar ("Cheers"), a hospital ("ER," "Chicago Hope," "St. Elsewhere"), a beer plant ("Laverne & Shirley"), a law office ("Law and Order," "L.A. Law"), a retirement community ("Golden Girls"), and a small-town airport ("Wings").

Action shows with "ensemble" surrogate families include "Star Trek" and its various spin-offs, "Knight Rider" (a *car* is part of the family, though the comedy "My Mother the Car" actually pioneered the concept years earlier), "S.W.A.T." (the team that crunches terrorists together), "The A-Team" (Mr. T: "I pity the fool" who messes with me and my ensemble buddies), "Hawaii Five-O" ("Book'im, Danno"), "Starsky and Hutch" (blond and dark lawmen clean up San Francisco, sort of), "Kojak" (hair-free law enforcement), "Airwolf" (familyesque ties in the skies), and "The Dukes of Hazzard" (car chases and Southern stereotypes, such as inbred sheriffs).

Actual families have had representation, but they constitute a minority presence. Children have figured prominently in such shows as "Family Matters," "Head of the Class," "Silver Spoons," "Growing Pains," "Family Ties," "Good Times," "Brotherly Love," and "Who's the Boss?", but were all but ignored in "Fantasy Island" and "The Love Boat," as well as adult comedies such as "Bosom Buddies." Three prominent exceptions to the trend were "Little House on the Prairie," "Family," and "The Waltons," which featured intact, loving families who bond while solving myriad problems.

Some liberal observers were threatened even by the handful of family shows that still featured two parents. Speaking at a conference on television families, critic and author Ella Taylor stated flatly: "[T]here are all kinds of families, but there is no such thing as *the* family, the nuclear family . . . I am quite worried about the impact of shows like 'The Cosby Show,' 'Growing Pains,' and to some degree 'Family Ties,' which give us these extraordinary families that approximate nobody's life."[6]

Taylor preferred the nonblood families such as those on "Barney Miller" or "Mary Tyler Moore," a format which "suggests to a career-oriented generation that the family can no longer provide the emotional supports they expect from it and that if there is any place where they can find these supports, it's in the workplace."[7]

She was particularly annoyed by "The Cosby Show's" depiction of parents as wise counselors: "[T]here seems to be no public life outside the family and the easy parental authority, and the parents seem to know the difference between right and wrong very conveniently and very easily, and I find that troubling in a world that is highly ambiguous."

Taylor finished her remarks by denouncing "Cosby" as "an autocratic show, patriarchal in the extreme," and then prefaced a few more remarks with the comment, "I'm not a parent, but I have many friends who are parents . . ."[8] It would be interesting to find those parents and ask them if they were upset by portrayals of in-charge parents or whether they preferred that their children watch incompetent adults who are the butt of children's jokes.

A different view was given by social critic David Blankenhorn, who told an interviewer that "The Cosby Show," while admittedly an "idealized" family, was an antidote to earlier programs that pictured families as "oppressive and inept . . . Would the critics' frustration be assuaged if we just showed everybody unhappy all the time and depicted family life as a cauldron of conflict? Would that make people feel better? I'm baffled at why it's a bad idea to have some shows that present families in a good way."[9]

Portrayals of black families during the 1960s and 1970s were comparatively rare and distinctive. A 1980 study found that "one could see a regularly appearing black family on four or five shows. Most typically, that family would have a single parent; a complete family of two parents plus children was a rarity, *averaging one a season.*"[10] As usual, Hollywood is ahead of the curve in conveying, and perhaps facilitating, dysfunction. Although illegitimacy has become epidemic among American blacks, it was by no means the norm in the 1960s and 1970s. It took a couple of decades of destructive Great Society welfare—and lowered cultural expectations—to do the job on the black family. The situation improved somewhat in the eighties and nineties with "Family Matters," "The Fresh Prince of Bel-Air," "Hangin' with Mr. Cooper," and "The Wayans Brothers."

Daytime serials, another distinctive television category, center around mostly adulterous relationships. The "soap opera"—named for the producers of detergents, soaps, and other cleansing products that sponsor them—has made an art of family dysfunction. Watched by millions of housewives, college students, and those women whose jobs permit it, the soap operas have created a world of sexual adventurism. They also, like the rest of television, have grown increasingly steamy, bordering on the pornographic. When groups such as Terry Rakolta's complained about the sex and violence on prime-time television, liberal critics shot back, not without cause, saying that Christian family types were hypocritical because they were absorbing the guilty pleasures of the scandalous afternoon soaps. Rakolta denied skipping the soaps in her concerns and blasted them for their antifamily plots.

With the advent of "Dallas" (1979), the prime-time family drama made a comeback. "Dallas's" success quickly prompted other family-business series such as "Falconcrest," "Dynasty," "Knot's Landing," "The Colbys," "Flamingo Road," and others. Murder, intrigue, and family dysfunction were at the heart of the nighttime soaps.

In 1984, "The Cosby Show" struck a blow for intact marriage, fatherly authority, and clean comedy, triggering a wave of commentary about the return of the television family. The show, which topped the ratings for several years, features a doctor father and a mother who is a lawyer. Plots often concern the children's ill-fated attempts to get around their older and wiser parents, which they never do. As television historian J. Fred MacDonald writes of "Cosby," "The long-overdue model worked, becoming the leading program throughout the last half of the decade, sparking a renaissance of the sitcom genre and precipitating a business turnaround that soon made N B C the premier operation in national television."[11]

Some critics complained that the well-to-do Huxtables were anything but a typical black family, while others applauded the breaking of racial stereotypes. All too often, blacks had been portrayed as victims or as foible-free paragons by guilty Hollywood liberals who did the programming. A show about blacks who came across as real people without an obvious racial context was considered revolutionary. And especially one about black parents who demanded respect from their offspring. In many sitcoms, the children run circles around the duller adults who are not "with it" because they are captives of older times and values.

Bill Cosby himself said that the show's roaring success was due in no small part to the public's hunger, especially children's, to see the parents in charge again. The fact that the family was black was secondary. As Cosby told Larry King in 1990, "It's real simple. The parent wins. Look at all the other sitcoms; the kids get the best lines."[12]

"Cosby" spawned a number of spin-offs and other black-oriented shows, including "A Different World," "Growing Pains," "Charlie & Co.," "Amen!," "227," "The Robert Guillaume Show," "Webster," "Family Matters," the short-lived but critically acclaimed "dramedy", "Frank's Place," and the "Fresh Prince of Bel-Air." "Family Matters" most conspicuously continued the Cosby legacy with its wholesome portrait of a black, intact, middle-class Chicago family headed by a strong father figure.

Whether it was cause or effect, black households are watching more television. By 1988, black households tuned in to television an average of 10.6 daily hours, compared with 7.3 hours per day for the total population.[13]

While many of these shows contain clean comedy or drama, more and more television during the early evening hours in the 1970s began addressing adult themes. Under pressure from Congress, the FCC, and viewers, the networks agreed in 1975 to establish the "family viewing hour" between 8:00 and 9:00 PM (eastern standard time) for audiences of all ages. Although a federal court struck down the Family Hour in 1976, the networks operated as if it were still in effect, up until the 1990s. By 1995, the Family Hour was as good as dead. Sex, violence, foul language, and mature themes had become commonplace for shows as early as 8:00 PM.

The comedy "Roseanne," which aired at 9:00 PM during the early 1990s, began as a clean, innovative show about a blue-collar family that loved each other despite their disrespectful banter and griping. Buoyed by high ratings, "Roseanne" began to take liberties with its mixed-age audience, introducing them to such topics as condoms, premarital sex, and homosexuality. The show's star, Roseanne Barr, frankly admitted that she wanted to use the program to promote her "progressive" views. A lesbian screenwriter for "Roseanne" told a homosexual magazine that she tried to inject feminist and lesbian themes whenever she could. Accordingly, a recurring lesbian character (played by lesbian comedienne Sandra Bernhard) was added, a male homosexual marriage was performed, and Roseanne herself experienced a kiss from a lesbian in a gay bar.

In 1995, "Roseanne" was moved to the 8:00 PM slot, prompting *USA Weekend* to declare that "a cultural Rubicon of sorts was crossed."[14] Soon, adult and young-adult series such as "Mad About You," "Martin," "Melrose Place," and "Beverly Hills 90210" replaced such family-friendly, Family Hour series as "Blossom" and "Full House," which went off the air. "Roseanne" itself finally went off the air in 1997, a victim of slipping ratings.

Monitoring five evenings of prime-time television in 1995, students from American University noted 370 incidents of crude language or sexual situations, an average of one every 8.9 minutes. The real news, however, was that more than half—208—occurred during the Family Hour.[15] "Melrose Place" totaled twenty-five incidents, while "Roseanne" had twenty-one. These Family Hour shows totaled more even than the raunchy-by-design "NYPD Blue." As "Roseanne" producer James Anderson remarked, "The face of TV is going to be seriously redefined over the next couple of years. I mean, 'Melrose Place' is on at 8:00, and they have way more T&A [tits and ass] than 'Roseanne' does."[16] This comment reflects a couple of things. First, it shows the cavalier attitude that some Hollywood people take toward children—and teenagers—many of whom are watching at that hour and cannot be monitored by their parents every moment. Second, it is a classic dodge—we're not so bad because someone else is worse. Comparing evil to a greater evil— instead of to the good—is the devil's favorite debating ploy.

But Hollywood's abandonment of the family hour has more to do with marketing than its very real ideological war on family values. Advertisers covet the eighteen to forty-nine audience of consumers, and Fox had captured a significant share of this market before the other networks caved in. It is not just the enormous amount of discretionary income that this group has; early identification with a particular product often results in a lifelong brand loyalty. McDonald's understood this early. The burger maker hooked an entire generation of baby boomers by aggressively marketing the Golden Arches to children. Many adults who long ago eschewed fast food for healthier fare still make a stop at McDonald's every so often for a "comfort" burger that tastes remarkably like the first one they had thirty years ago.

The fragmentation of families into self-seeking individuals is another reason that television has lost its ability to make shows that appeal to everyone.

"We are a victim of the multiset household," explains ABC

Entertainment President Ted Harbert. "If Mom wants to let little Jimmy stay in the living room and watch 'Full House,' she can go into the bedroom and watch [NBC's more adult] 'Wings.' We don't have much of an intention of letting that continue, where we become an electronic baby-sitter. We need to deliver adults to the advertising people (who) pay all of our salaries out here in Hollywood."[17]

Driven by calculated merchandising, as well as the biases of the Hollywood community, the concept of "family" has been redefined almost continually on television since the 1970s.

When the hour-long drama "thirtysomething" became a hit in 1988 among the young and upwardly mobile, the periodical *Television & Families* interviewed a Yuppie couple from Los Angeles in 1988 to discuss the show. The man was an art gallery owner and the woman was an entrepreneur with a line of gourmet condiments. They were living in Sherman Oaks and "discussing whether or not to have a child." The couple identified with the group of Yuppies on the show. In addition to the show's portrayal of the angst of affluent modern life, the man said he liked the fact that "the characters constitute a family. I think you're born into a family and it's the luck of the draw, but the friends that you choose are the people who are with you long after family members drop off. That's the family that 'thirtysomething' celebrates." As for the woman, she found "thirtysomething" a refreshing change from earlier family shows: "The television shows we grew up on represented family in an unreal and unattainable way: Ozzie and Harriet. The characters on this show ['thirtysomething'] are real characters . . ."[18] This, from a couple that is discussing not *when* to have a child, but *if*. Talk about making family unattainable. But "thirtysomething" was about to guarantee its own mortality. When the show began promoting homosexuality by showing two men in bed, sponsors bolted, costing the program more than five hundred thousand dollars.

In the late eighties, an episode of "L.A. Law" championed the right of the law firm's retarded office clerk, Benny, to adopt a teenage boy. Although the show ostensibly was about the rights of the retarded, it was a stalking-horse for the dismantlement of the traditional notion of the family as the best place for children. By advancing the notion that emotions are paramount ("love—not a mom and a dad—makes a family"), the show paved the way for homosexual marriage and adoption.

In 1992, "Murphy Brown" struck the same chord when Candice Bergen's title character, pregnant out of wedlock, ponders whether to start a fatherless family or have an abortion. The cavalier way in which Murphy's "choice" is presented drew a brief comment in a speech by Vice President Dan Quayle, who was campaigning for re-election. Quayle's remark, and his defense of the two-parent family, caused near-hysteria in Hollywood and throughout liberal ranks and became the shorthand reference to the "family values" debate that is at the heart of the Age of Consent.

In 1991, CBS broke a language barrier on the comedy "Uncle Buck" when a youngster yelled, "You suck." By 1995, numerous "family" shows such as "The Simpsons" featured mild profanities and innuendo. On "Wings," which aired at 8:00 PM in most markets, one character snapped "That rat bastard." Prime-time television in the mid-nineties became quite comfortable with not only "bastard," but "bitch," "ass," "suck," "piss," and other vulgarities, including variations on the "f-word." Combined with an almost nonstop focus on sex, almost all of it outside marriage, television had turned into a medium that appeared to have been written by a gang of bisexual, overcharged adolescent boys. Most egregious was the Fox sitcom "Married With Children," with its sex-starved, cynical mother, corrupt and ineffective father, sexpot daughter, and masturbation-crazed son. It's family life as a nightmare, the kind of stuff that pansexual activists think of as a great inside joke.

During the fall of 1995, the Media Research Center conducted a four-week survey of family-hour programming on the broadcast networks, including ABC, CBS, NBC, Fox, UPN, and WB. The researchers measured the use of vulgarities, "adult" topics, and suitability for children. They found that a sea change had occurred: "In NBC's powerhouse Thursday lineup of a decade ago, the 8:30 program, 'Family Ties,' featured an intact, nuclear family and contained virtually no sexual content; it was followed at nine o'clock by 'Cheers,' which was populated by unmarried adults and was a font of innuendo. The boundaries were not always so clear, but there was a sense of what material was appropriate for children and what wasn't, and there was a general understanding that the latter would not air before nine o'clock. This understanding began to crumble a few years back and is now largely in ruins."[19]

As family hour fell, the later hours became even seedier places to visit, featuring plots laced heavily with masturbation, homosexuality, condoms, defecation, and barnyard epithets. ABC's "NYPD Blue" brought outright profanity and nudity to primetime. The hit sitcom "Friends" promoted premarital sex and homosexual parenting and even included a lesbian wedding in a 1996 episode in which the "straight" characters at the reception wistfully regretted not being gay themselves. On the other side of the ledger, CBS's "Promised Land" featured a family that not only stayed together but prayed together, and a few other clean shows such as "Family Matters" continued to pull in large audiences.

Overall, however, moral relativism pervaded the network offerings, with the only real sin being intolerance of anything— except Judeo-Christian values. The creed of relativism is quite rigid on this latter point, and with few exceptions, the relativistic creed of Hollywood "family values" dictates that the mom-and-dad variety be portrayed as only one of many family forms. As for religion itself, television mostly ignores, trivializes, or distorts the beliefs of millions of Americans.

8

Whose Beliefs?
Television vs. God

> *Christians are the only group Hollywood can offend with impunity, the only creed it actually goes out of its way to insult. Clerics, from fundamentalist preachers to Catholic monks, are routinely represented as hypocrites, hucksters, sadists, and lechers. The tenets of Christianity are regularly held up to ridicule.*[1]
>
> Don Feder

ANDY SIPOWICZ was treading in deep waters. The police detective played by actor Dennis Franz in ABC's "NYPD Blue" was paralyzed with grief over the shooting death of his son. In a mystical sequence set in a diner, he encounters Andy Jr., along with Jesus Christ, portrayed as a truck driver. As related by executive producer David Milch: "In the dreams, Christ speaks in Sipowicz's language, using some obscene words as he tells Sipowicz, 'I told you what to do: Speak through me.' Christ is the part of Sipowicz's consciousness that tells him that, in forgiving himself, he will find the ability to part with his son."[2]

Jesus here is a plot device, and a crude one at that. By contrast, the Jesus of the Bible is "Lord of Lords" and "King of Kings," creator and inhabitant of heaven, where no sin exists. A depiction of Jesus as anything less than divine is an extreme insult to Christians and an attack on the entire premise of Christianity.

Milch's explanation reveals a modernist perspective of unbelief characteristic of the Age of Consent: Jesus is a Jungian archetype hidden within Sipowicz's soul, a figment of his own imagination. It doesn't matter whether Jesus is real; it only matters that Sipowicz believes it. Truth is self-generated. Reality and fantasy are equally valid.

A 1997 survey commissioned by *TV Guide* showed that three-quarters of those polled believe that prime time has become a less moral, spiritual, and religious place over the preceding five years. Two-thirds wanted to see more prime-time spirituality.[3]

Given Hollywood's New Age leanings, asking television to take on more spiritual themes is a little like asking the town prostitute to come up with a primer on how to raise a little girl to be a lady. There may be worse things than being ignored.

As television tackles "religion," it often reflects the New Age trends that are coursing through the theological world. In much of modern theology, religion is considered something that evolves with the times, or not. If it does, it remains "relevant." If it doesn't, as in traditional Catholicism, orthodox Protestantism, Eastern Orthodoxy, Orthodox Judaism, or orthodox Islam, it is a dark force, holding back progress. It does so mainly by keeping alive the idea of sin. This annoys the Age of Consent relativist, who believes that right and wrong are peculiar to individuals, cultures, and religions, and therefore should not be taken too seriously. In a "Babylon 5" episode, an alien floats upward in one scene, glowing like an angel. A group of witnesses each interprets him differently, thus illustrating how subjective religion is in the New Age.

George Sim Johnston notes of relativist theologians, "The only absolutes they believe in are plurality (i.e. the absolute relativity of the absolute) and freedom of expression—as long as certain liberal taboos aren't violated . . . They seldom attack religion directly, but seek rather to create a soft, undermining atmosphere in which it becomes finally unintelligible."[4]

The same goes for television. It is not so much that television shows attack religion as they ignore it or trivialize it. "God on prime-time television is like God in American culture: submerged most of the time, emerging only as a guest star whose appearance is rarely announced," observes author and critic Jack Miles.[5] Television creates the impression that religion is either something that is not too important, or at the least, something that can be gotten around with a bit of imagination.

How about clerical vows of chastity, for instance? In 1983, CBS premiered *The Thorn Birds*, adapted from Colleen McCullough's best-selling novel about a Catholic priest in Australia played by Richard Chamberlain, who beds Meggie, a married woman played by Rachel Ward. In 1996, CBS produced a sequel, *The Thorn Birds: The Missing Years,* in which Richard Chamberlain again beds Meggie, who this time is played by Amanda Donohoe. The theme of both made-for-television films is that passion is its own justification for breaking the rules—especially church rules about sexual morality. Casting could not have been more appropriate in the form of Miss Donohoe, who blazed trails on "L.A. Law" as the lesbian lawyer C. J. Lamb. Donohoe, who has openly attacked Christianity and the church in interviews, said she enjoyed playing Meggie because of the character's feminism: "She was a woman ahead of her time with her independence, her sheer willfulness, the desire to have what she wanted when she wanted it . . . all those things. It brings her pain and misery, but what I love about her is that she's a woman in a world where there are no men anymore, because they've all gone off to fight in a war."[6]

Most of the time, church morality is not so openly attacked. Television's sin is to make religion seem unimportant. In 1993, a survey revealed that of eighteen thousand evening news stories, only 212 were about religion, and of more than twenty-four thousand morning news segments, only 197 had religious content. In 1994, coverage of religion actually fell, with only 225 religion stories appearing on the network evening news programs and only 151 on the morning shows.[7] Significantly, although the Roman Catholic Church led with the most references, New Age spirituality was featured in more stories than all of the Protestant denominations combined.

In entertainment television, clergy rarely appear, and when they do, it is usually to perform a wedding, a funeral, or to hear a quick confession. Mentions of God usually come in the form of expressions such as "Thank God!" or by taking God's name in vain.

Of more than a thousand hours of new, prime-time television programming introduced each year, very little is dedicated to religious content of any kind, positive or negative. A study released in 1992 showed that of 1,462 speaking characters on one-hundred hours of network television during November 1990, only eighty-one had an identifiable religious affiliation. This means that 94.5 percent of all speaking characters on television during that time had no discernible religion.[8]

A 1994 Media Research Center study found that in 1993, only 116 depictions of religion occurred during prime time, with 42 percent being negative, 30 percent "mixed or neutral" and 28 percent positive.[9] Of the major networks, only ABC had more positive portrayals of religion than negative. Of NBC's portrayals, 56 percent were negative, followed by CBS (45 percent) and Fox (43 percent). A prime example of negative programming is an episode of Fox's "Martin," in which a pimp-turned-minister continues to act like a pimp, saying things like, "God does provide. God provides like a son of a bitch." In a later episode, the minister bamboozles his congregation and harasses a woman. On CBS, a made-for-television movie, "Judgment Day," featured a devout Lutheran who terrorizes his family for being insufficiently pious. He finally kills his mother, wife, and children. On NBC's "John Larroquette Show," a prostitute talks about a customer "who could someday be Pope," and on NBC's "Nurses," a character laments her Catholic upbringing, saying of a nun, "Her kind smacked the compassion out of me in the fourth grade."[10] On NBC's "Sisters," the Christmas episode in December 1995 was largely about a woman who tries to talk her husband into donating sperm to artificially inseminate a lesbian friend. How's that for Christmas spirit!

But television is not entirely without its spiritual side. Television celebrities speak for God every now and then, usually to bash the idea of "judgment," as if God, in extending grace, no longer believes in the morality that he created in the first place. An outright contempt for anything smacking of fundamentalism or orthodox Catholicism is obvious in some programs. As columnist Don Feder remarks of traditionalist Christians, "No other group is so consistently maligned on prime-time television. These defamatory portrayals betray a deep-seated hostility."[11]

Television's tendency to promote New Age concepts can be seen in numerous episodes of the various "Star Trek" series, particularly the loopy observations of the mystical barkeep played by Whoopi Goldberg in "Star Trek: The Next Generation." Like the show's official shrink, Counsellor Troi, the Whoopi character urges all comers to let their feelings be their guide. It is all reminiscent of the Jungian rantings of the New Age puppet Yoda in Part II of the Star Wars trilogy, *The Empire Strikes Back*. The only difference is that Whoopi doesn't back into her sentences the way Yoda does or try to levitate her intergalactic booze bottles.

In 1995, NBC boasted of creating a new show that was supposed to appeal to religious viewers. "Amazing Grace," starring Patty Duke, turned out to be a lukewarm series about a feminist minister who avoids references to either God or Jesus and buries the Christian gospel in a fog of relativism. Dan Lauria, who played an attorney on the series, explains the show's real mission while taking a shot at conservative Christians: "I shouldn't say this, but I think the right wing out there is so narrow-minded and so anti-religious. I think the minister Patty plays is an example of how to take in all the different points of moral view and make a decision based on that. And it's not this narrow-minded blindness that we see."[12]

As for Duke, her eclectic approach to religion does not include traditional manifestations. She told television critics, "to suggest that one must spout Moses, or Jesus, or Buddha, or chant like Tibetan monks in order to be religious, I believe, is not to walk in the path of Christ." Later, she declared that she does not want to be seen as "the leader of the family values" group on television, noting that, "We rarely use the word G-O-D."[13] The show bombed, quickly disappearing in an unholy fashion.

Television's effort to water down, distort, or actually misrepresent Christian theology sometimes turns up in unlikely places. Even the pro-religion, pro-family seventies show "The Waltons," an island of sanity amid the wasteland, waded into New Age waters in its episode entitled "The Sermon." John-Boy Walton, the writer in the family, is conscripted to give a sermon at the local church. Instead of consulting the Bible, he spends most of the episode looking anywhere but the Bible, finally coming under the sway of his nature-loving (some would say nature-worshipping) grandfather. Fortified by a day on the mountain communing with nature, John-Boy gets into the pulpit the next day to distort the Gospel into a pantheistic celebration of "different" ways of communing with God. It is so broad that his agnostic father grins in surprised appreciation that he must not have wandered into a Baptist church after all and won't have to deal with whether or not Jesus Christ is who he says he is. In fact, Jesus is notably absent from the sermon. John-Boy gives a nod to his devoutly Baptist grandmother by noting that even she is okay in "her" way, that is, seeking fidelity to the scriptures. But a straight reading of the Bible is just one of many ways to regard it, none of which is better than any other as long as the pilgrim is sincere in his quest.

Only Hollywood could have placed a relativistic screed like this in a Bible-believing Baptist church of the 1930s in rural Virginia and have the congregation sit there glowing with received illumination. (In relating this, I am fully aware that I am opening myself up to easy ridicule: "He's even picking on 'The Waltons,' for crying out loud!" or "Even 'The Waltons' are too radical for him!" or "Who's next, the dastardly Mother Teresa?" Such is our sound-bite culture that a discussion of thematic integrity can be easily distorted.)

Television's hostility toward orthodox religion is not surprising given the makeup of the creative folks who make the programs. In one poll of television leaders, 93 percent said "they seldom or never attend religious services," and 45 percent "claimed no religious affiliation whatever."[14]

Veteran television producer John Prizer acknowledges that the "lack of religious commitment on the part of people in Hollywood is quite astonishing. I can't think of a director or actor or writer under forty-five who goes to church or synagogue."[15] Given Hollywood's animus against religion and Christians in particular, there are some people who are active in churches but prefer not to let it be known. Some have even adopted pseudonyms outside Hollywood so that their cover won't be blown and their career ended. A few actors have been open about their faiths and their moral standards, and it has cost them. One actress estimates that she has passed up 75 percent of the roles offered to her because they involved nudity or lewdness.

AND NOW FOR SOME GOOD NEWS

In the mid-1990s, commensurate with the baby boomers' resurgent interest in spiritual matters, religion began making a comeback on television. Well, not really a comeback, since it never was a very strong force even in the Golden Age. But several shows began featuring Christian characters and treating religion with respect. And ABC appointed an openly Christian reporter, Peggy Wehmeyer, to a newly created religion beat for "World News Tonight."

On August 10, 1995, Wehmeyer's influence became clear in a special report on the Christian conversion of Norma McCorvey, the Jane Roe whose case resulted in the 1973 Supreme Court decision striking down all abortion laws in the United States. McCorvey, who had been a feminist symbol of freedom, was shown being baptized in a swimming pool by Operation Rescue director "Flip" Benham. She explained on camera that her turnabout came from the love and acceptance she had experienced from Benham and other Operation Rescue staffers who had set up offices next to the abortion clinic at which she was working. She also said that one day, while walking near a playground, she saw a set of empty swings and began to wonder what had happened to all the children. When she realized that many of them had been aborted, she began to cry and reassess her values. The ABC segment showed an empty swing set while McCorvey related her emotional awakening. Later, the segment featured McCorvey talking bitterly about being exploited by the abortion movement, then featured a clip of National Abortion Rights Action League leader Kate Michelman worrying that the pro-life crowd would exploit poor Norma. The effect was devastating. And it would not have happened had ABC not begun taking religion and the pro-life movement seriously by hiring people like Wehmeyer.

Other signs that the networks were beginning to thaw out from their icy hostility toward Western religion: In 1994, "L.A. Law," which was losing ratings as it steadily declined into predictably liberal plots, added an evangelical Christian attorney, Jane Halliday, to the firm. Although critics braced for this graduate of Bob Jones University to be a foil for her more sophisticated colleagues, the Halliday character got the upper hand. This new open-mindedness on the part of NBC was not enough to save the show, however, and "L.A. Law" was canceled at the end of the season.

In 1992, CBS premiered "Dr. Quinn, Medicine Woman." Despite its frequent feminist and environmental subthemes, "Dr. Quinn" has depicted religion in a positive light. All main characters attend church regularly, and the preacher is an educated, well-respected man. The series hit a low in 1997, however, when it introduced children to the topic of homosexuality through a visit by an openly gay Walt Whitman.

Even quirky shows like "Picket Fences" included segments that portrayed religion as an important element. One of the top-rated shows in the mid-nineties was "Home Improvement," starring comedian Tim Allen. The sitcom features an intact family, strong marriage, and a Christian background, with one of the boys singing in the church choir in a Christmas episode. Even "Beverly Hills 90210" had two characters attend a Christmas Eve service in a December 1995 show, with one saying afterward, "Every year, my first impulse is to avoid going [to church], but then you go and you let it all sink in and you end up feeling that everything is all right with the world."[16] On ABC's often-cynical "My So-Called Life," an angel leads a family to church on Christmas Eve.

Even Fox Television, which consistently produced more raunchy shows than the other networks, chimed in with such offerings as "Living Single," starring Queen Latifah. The cast reportedly prays together before every taping. In one 1997 episode, Latifah's character Khadijah attends a church service nervously for the first time in two years. Producer Yvette Lee Bowser told *TV Guide* that she hoped the episode "encouraged some people to get back to the church. After all, it doesn't matter how often you go, but that you keep God at the center of your life."[17]

In 1995, CBS broke new ground with "Touched by an Angel" and "Christy." "Angel," in which a heavenly being helps someone through difficulties, is openly pro-God and has achieved impressive ratings, reaching the top five by 1997 and hitting the number-one spot for dramas. "Angel" spun off another successful series, "Promised Land," "in 1996, starring Gerald McRainey ("Major Dad") as the father of a God-fearing family living on the road, encountering people in spiritual need. Assisted by periodic appearances from "Touched by an Angel's" heavenly cast, "Promised Land" was climbing steadily in the ratings in 1997. Warner Brothers, whose parent company Time-Warner had been blistered for its production of anti-family and obscene rap music, also entered the pro-God market with "Seventh Heaven," a program about a minister and his family.

"Christy," which brought to the screen the heroine of Catherine Marshall's novel about a young missionary to Appalachia, was a critical and ratings success, yet still was canceled by CBS. According to "Christy" producer Ken Wales, more than 1.5 million letters were sent to CBS by people asking that the show be kept on, double the previous record. The network explained that sponsors want shows that appeal to the prime audience of young people and that "Christy" was drawing only older, poorer, and less urban viewers. This was not reflected in the Nielsen ratings, according to Wales. But it did not seem to matter. CBS canceled anyway. Picked up by cable television's Family Channel, the show gained audiences and critical plaudits. Created by veteran producer Wales, one of the few openly Christian principal figures in Hollywood, "Christy" took seventeen years to become a television reality. Turned down by countless studios, Wales finally struck gold when television moguls Barney Rosenzweig and Aaron Spelling liked what they saw. Given that the novel *Christy* has sold more than eight million copies since 1967, it should not have been hard to persuade Hollywood that there was an audience for this sort of thing. But hostility within CBS to "Christy's" openly Christian message made the difference in the decision to cancel, Wales told a conference on Religion and Prime Time Television in June 1995.

The conference itself, held in Santa Monica, was a sign that Hollywood was waking up to the reality that it had been ignoring the religious nature of its audiences at its own peril. Heavyweight television people such as Leslie Moonves, head of Warner Brothers television productions and soon-to-be head of CBS entertainment programming, attended, as did Ted Harbert, president of ABC-TV's entertainment division, and Danny Goldberg of Warner Brothers Records, plus writers and producers from "Roseanne," "Christy," and other shows. They frankly discussed television's treatment of religion with orthodox Jews such as Rabbi Daniel Lapin and Michael Medved, and Catholic and Protestant attendees, including Focus on the Family Vice President Tom Minnery and the Rev. Don Wildmon, who became the lightning rod because of his successful boycotts over television content. At one point, Harbert complained bitterly that ABC had wanted to do some programs in which young women chose to have abortions, but that this was impossible because of "people like" Wildmon.

The conference could not have been held at a more propitious time. The day before, Senator Bob Dole, who was running for President, came to Los Angeles to blast the entertainment industry for its role in the trashing of American values. The Dole speech became the touchstone of the conference, even though Twentieth Century Fox emeritus George Vrandenburg dismissed the Dole comments early on. He noted that Dole's staff had called various people in Hollywood and warned them it was coming and not to worry about it; it was just politics, after all.

Perhaps Hollywood's newfound interest in religion is not all that surprising. The baby boomers, who once believed that they were unique in all of history, began finding out that the old verities were indispensable. Shedding the Marxian conceit that they could begin history anew, creating a just society out of the ashes of (and somehow funded by) the old society, they began reclaiming their heritage. Just as St. Augustine observed sixteen hundred years ago, the boomers learned that "we were made for thee, O God, and our hearts are restless until they rest in thee."[18] Many boomers are burning out from material pleasures in the Age of Consent that no longer satisfy and ersatz religion that doesn't touch the heart, and they are returning to the churches and synagogues.

Capitalism has provided unheard-of wealth to the largest number of people ever, but it has also tempted people to adopt a relativistic outlook. As George Sim Johnston notes, "What the money did for baby boomers was to multiply the possible substitutes for the Almighty."[19] With cable, satellites, and the Internet, more information than ever is coursing through people's brains, a nonstop distraction. This is all to the good, the relativist says, because knowledge in and of itself is useful, whatever the source. That is why relativists (read: liberals) almost invariably offer "education" in place of "morality" as the solution to the latest disaster created by earlier errors. The New Age liberal thinks that lack of information is the problem, not lack of morality. It never seems to dawn on them that pagan Nazi Germany was one of the most well-educated nations in the world in the 1930s.

9

Hollywood Films:
The Real Plot

The cultural elite and its values control the "high ground" in Hollywood. From that perch they are able to constantly promote the values they believe in—secularism, modernity, sexual liberation, radical feminism—and they denigrate the values they reject—religious faith, tradition, family, and patriotism.[1]

Gary Bauer

WHEN WINSTON CHURCHILL was touring California in 1929 as the guest of publisher William Randolph Hearst, he spent several days in Hollywood. One evening, he dined with Hearst and sixty guests—including Charlie Chaplin. Churchill suggested that if Chaplin would consider playing the young Napoleon, then Churchill would write a script. Chaplin, however, had grander plans. He wanted to play Christ. Churchill thought for a moment and asked: "Have you cleared the rights?"[2]

Given the current, secular atmosphere in Hollywood, it is hard to imagine very many people there worrying about, much less wondering about, what God might think of what they are doing.

Back in 1973, *Los Angeles Times* film critic Charles Champlain described the movies' "trendy moral anarchy." Filmmakers, he said, were "letting the bad guys win . . . [T]he pendulum has swung so far (and frozen there) that now the surprise is when the good guys win, virtue triumphs, and when something is understood to be right or wrong."[3]

Hollywood's plunge into moral relativism was swift and far-reaching. In 1965, the Best Picture award went to *The Sound of Music*, a sweet story of love, music, and triumph of good over evil. A mere four years later, in 1969, the Best Picture Oscar was awarded to *Midnight Cowboy*, a raunchy tale of male prostitution. Movie-goers eventually voted at the box office, with weekly attendance dropping from forty-four million in 1965 to seventeen million in 1969. As film critic Michael Medved explains, "the values of the entertainment industry changed, and audiences fled from the theaters in horror and disgust."

For several decades, Hollywood had been restrained by the Hays Office, which issued a self-monitoring industry Production Code in 1930 that restricted sex, foul language, violence, ridicule of religion, ethnic insults, and the portrayal of drug usage. The code was a response to an alarm sounded by churches and social commentators in the early 1930s, as coarse elements began creeping into Hollywood's products. In 1966, Jack Valenti became president of the Motion Picture Association of America. Twenty-five years later, he boasted that "The first thing I did . . . was to junk the Hays Production Code, which was an anachronistic piece of censorship that we never should have put into place."[4]

Instead, Valenti fashioned the industry-controlled ratings system, which gave a G, P G, R, or X rating to films. The general idea was to warn patrons about what was in the films. If the system worked at all, it succeeded in making films coarser, more violent, and more sexually explicit.

The ratings were uneven from the start and became progressively unreliable. As Christian film critic Ted Baehr points out, two 1989 films, *Honey, I Shrunk the Kids* and *Ghostbusters II* inexplicably received P G ratings. *Honey* is family entertainment with a moral premise, marred by a gratuitous reference to a "French kiss." *Ghostbusters II*, however, "is over-flowing with child sacrifice, idolatry, profanity, obscenity, blasphemy, spiritism, occultism, and demonic activity. This film is evil. It presents the triumph of man through the use of occultic powers: the essence of the New Age movement and Satanism."[5]

Over the years, the ratings were stretched to reflect the coarsening. What would have received an R rating in 1969 would get merely a P G in the 1980s. To accommodate this trend, the Motion Picture Association created a new category, P G-13, as a sort of buffer between P G and R. Then, in 1989, Valenti tried to eliminate the stigma of the x rating by creating a new category, N C-17 (no one admitted under 17 with or without a parent or guardian). The first N C-17 film, *Henry and June* (1989), bombed at the box office, as have all N C-17 titles since. In 1995, Hollywood tried again to mainstream pornography with the release of *Showgirls*. Costing eighty million dollars to make and promote, the film sold only about four million tickets and quickly faded from theaters. What was more alarming to its producers was the news that the giant Blockbuster video chain announced that it would refuse to carry *Showgirls* just as it has refused to carry any N C-17 rated films. By 1996, however, a toned-down version of *Showgirls*, still loaded with nudity, was ready for the video market. Likewise, *Striptease*, in which actress Demi Moore bared her breasts for a record twelve million–dollar salary, was a 1996 box-office bomb. Voted worst movie of the year by many critics, *Striptease* nonetheless recouped its losses at the video counter and in foreign sales.

Besides the change in movie content, other factors have contributed to the theater drain, which continued through the seventies and eighties into the nineties despite record turnout for such blockbusters as *E. T.*, the *Star Wars* trilogy (including its re-release in 1997), *Jurassic Park* (1993) and *The Lost World* (1997), the Indiana Jones trilogy—*Raiders of the Lost Ark* (1981), *Indiana Jones and the Temple of Doom* (1984), and *Indiana Jones and the Last Crusade* (1989), and *Independence Day* (1996), the latter of which racked up more than four hundred million dollars—before video sales began. To make up for declining numbers, theaters kept raising the price of tickets and reducing the size of the screens to offer a broader selection. Fewer adults felt good about ponying up six or seven dollars a ticket (or nine dollars and fifty cents in Manhattan), plus skyrocketing fees for babysitters, just to cram into a tiny theater where they would frequently be confronted by a loud, abusive contingent of teenagers who talked and joked during the film. The aging of an increasingly jaded baby boom generation in the Age of Consent is another reason. What haven't they seen by now?

Another factor is technology. With the advent of the Video Cassette Recorder (vcr) people could rent movies to watch in the privacy of their own homes, at their own pace, and for less money than going out. This was a disaster for theater owners, but a bonanza for filmmakers, who would see their products recycled to an entirely new market. In 1982, only 4 percent of American homes had vcrs. By 1988, the number had jumped to 60 percent.

Despite the innovation of the vcr, and partly because of it, film quality continued to decline. Producers did not have to hit a home run at the theaters to earn a return for their investors. The expanding overseas market and the steady appetite for videos meant that even stinkers like *Striptease* could make money. Because humor and subtle cultural satire does not lend itself easily to translation for foreign markets, many producers stopped worrying about making films with meaning and concentrated on cheap thrills. Sylvester Stallone, Jean-Claude van Damme, Steven Segal, and Arnold Schwarzenegger all became instant stars overseas. Sex and violence are quick and easy to film and they sell all over the world.

Consequently, while other nations show no signs of slowing down in importing American films and television shows, resentment is growing against America for being the source of cultural pollution. In Japan, Europe, and the Middle East, for instance, wholesome shows such as "Bonanza" and the "FBI," which gave a positive view of American values, are giving way to sleazy soap operas, ultra-violent films such as the *Die Hard* series (1988–1995), the *Robocop* series (1987 and 1994), *Terminator I* and *II* (1984 and 1991), *Eraser* (1996), and a flood of soft- and hard-core pornography such as *Basic Instinct* (1992), *Color of Night* (1994), *Crash* (1995), *Showgirls* (1995), and *Striptease* (1996). *Crash*, which won a Special Jury prize at the Cannes Film Festival, in particular stretched the limits. The film consists of a series of perverse sex scenes linked to fatal auto accidents and mangled bodies.

In an interview with political talk show host John McLaughlin, Valenti was asked about the American trend of marketing sex and violence to audiences in other countries, with these revealing responses:

> McLAUGHLIN: Europeans and Canadians complain that they're becoming too Americanized. Surely, you can appreciate the validity of that concern, Jack Valenti?

> VALENTI: Well, that's a decision that's taken by the citizens of that country. I mean, who's wise enough to say to the people of France or Germany or Great Britain, You should watch this and not watch that? These are free countries. And so if they're becoming " too Americanized" it's not anything that's being foisted on them by America. It's the people of that country making their own decisions about what they want to watch. I find that reasonable.

> McLAUGHLIN: You want to help them to be able to reject their own culture? Is that what you want to do?

> VALENTI: No, no. I want them to be able to be free to choose

whatever they want. If anyone's culture is so flimsily anchored that a television show is going to cause them to rupture their connection to culture, it probably wasn't as deeply rooted as it should have been.[6]

Again, Valenti raises the straw man of "a" single television show radically altering behavior and neatly sidesteps the drumbeat effect of a long-term, steady diet of American-style sex, sleaze, and violence. In his indifference to the medium's effects, he takes on the tone of a date rapist, who informs his victim after the fact, "Well, if this one incident alters your view of life, don't blame me. You must not have cared very much for your virginity in the first place." It should hardly be surprising that the tide of anti-Americanism raised by Muslim zealots in Iran is resonating elsewhere. If our products resemble something out of Satan's studio, we should not be puzzled when God-fearing people in traditionalist cultures call America "the Great Satan"—they've got plenty of evidence to back it up.

Oscar-winning director Frank Capra, who compiled an unequaled record of best-loved American films, including *It's a Wonderful Life* (1946) and other classics, told an interviewer during the early 1970s that he could not make the kind of "harsh and pessimistic" films then in vogue. "Movies," said Capra, "should be a positive expression that there is hope, love, mercy, justice, and charity . . . It is the [filmmaker's] responsibility to emphasize the positive qualities of humanity by showing the triumph of the individual over adversities."[7]

Producers who find such sentiments quaint often do not have a clue as to what will work. Many try different formulas almost at random, looking for a hit. This reflects what Oscar-winning screenwriter William Goldman (*Butch Cassidy and the Sundance Kid* [1969] and *All the President's Men* [1976]) calls, "the single most important fact, perhaps, of the entire movie industry: NOBODY KNOWS ANYTHING."[8]

Goldman means that nobody in Hollywood has a monopoly on what will work "out there," where the tickets are bought. What often seems a sure thing can become a monumental flop, such as *Heaven's Gate* in 1982 or *Ishtar* in 1987. But a few filmmakers have had an almost unblemished string of successes. *Star Wars* and Indiana Jones trilogy filmmakers George Lucas and Steven Spielberg have had only a couple of duds (*Howard the Duck* [1986] and *1941* [1979], respectively). When Frank Capra was at Columbia Pictures, he had probably the best batting average in movies, producing thirty-six feature films between 1926 and 1964, including *It Happened One Night* (1934), *Mr. Deeds Goes to Town* (1936), *You Can't Take it With You* (1938), *Mr. Smith Goes to Washington* (1939), *Meet John Doe* (1941), *Arsenic and Old Lace* (1941), *Pocketful of Miracles* (1961), and *It's a Wonderful Life*, arguably America's best-loved movie.

Bob Thomas, biographer of Columbia Pictures mogul Harry Cohn, explains how Capra and Cohn, who produced many of Capra's pictures, managed hit after hit: "Other studios tried to duplicate their success, but they generally failed for lack of the important ingredient. The formula was profound, yet simple: you can explore any cosmic possibility as long as your characters remain human beings. Capra alternated scenes of pure comedy with others that delineated character."[9]

Moral relativism was simply not part of Capra's ideological makeup.

Stanford humanities scholar Raymond Carney put it this way in his 1986 book on Capra: "It is impossible to say whether the political philosophy of *Mr. Deeds Goes to Town*, *Mr. Smith Goes to Washington*, or *Meet John Doe* is fundamentally Republican or Democratic, New Deal or anti-New Deal, populist or elitist. That is not because the films are muddled ideologically but because they are engaged in an analysis of human experience deeper than that described by ideology, an analysis that is fundamentally anti-ideological."[10]

In his autobiography, published in 1971, Capra bitterly summed up the Hollywood ethos that took hold in the 1960s:

The winds of change blew through the dream factories of make-believe, tore at its crinoline tatters. . . The hedonists, the homosexuals, the hemophilic bleeding hearts, the God-haters, the quick-buck artists who substituted shock for talent, all cried: 'Shake 'em! Rattle 'em! God is dead. Long live pleasure! Nudity? Yea! Wife-swapping? Yea! Liberate the world from prudery. Emancipate our films from morality!'

There was dancing in the streets among the disciples of lewdness and violence. Sentiment was dead, they cried. And so was Capra, its aging missionary. *Viva* hard core brutality; *Arriba* barnyard sex! *Arriba SHOCK!* Topless-shock! Bottomless-shock! Mass intercourse, mass rape, mass murder, kill for thrill—shock! Shock! To hell with the good in man. Dredge up his evil—shock! Shock![11]

Film reviewer Leslie Halliwell, noted for his massive *Halliwell's Film Guide,* which lists more than 16,000 mini-reviews of movies, wrote an essay in 1978, updated in 1987, in which he lamented the takeover in Hollywood by a generation of filmmakers who are acting like ungrateful heirs to a great legacy: "Steeped in the history of Hollywood's golden age, they have no idea what made it work so well, and as soon as they become successful they begin to despise their audiences and are concerned only to overspend enormous budgets while putting across some garbled self-satisfying message which is usually anti-establishment, anti-law-and-order, and anti-entertainment."[12]

In 1989, on the fiftieth anniversary of the release of *Mr. Smith Goes to Washington,* a group of Hollywood activists under the banner of the Creative Coalition lobbied Congress to renew funding for the National Endowment for the Arts. Led by actor and coalition founder Ron Silver, the group included Alec Baldwin, Christopher Reeve, and Susan Sarandon. Baldwin later turned up in 1997 as the chief Hollywood shill for the NEA, testifying at congressional hearings and employing his star power to overwhelm news coverage of the issue.

Other actors have fortified their left-wing repertoire of ideas by attending weekly seminars at Network, a California think tank founded by Jane Fonda and Tom Hayden. The alumni include actors Rob Lowe, Daphne Zuniga, Judd Nelson, Esai Morales, and Helen Slater, who publicly voiced support for Marxist governments in Nicaragua and Cuba and criticized U.S. involvement.

The trend toward leftist ideological filmmaking began with the granddaddy of them all, *Mission to Moscow* (1943), an overt attempt to paint Stalin's Soviet Union as America's warm, fuzzy ally. In retrospect, studio chief Jack Warner said he regretted ever having let it be made. Author James Agee described *Mission to Moscow* as: "A mishmash of Stalinism with New Dealism with Hollywoodism with opportunism with shaky experimentalism with mesmerism with onanism, all mosaicked into a remarkable portrait of what the makers of the film think the Soviet Union is like—a great glad two-million dollar bowl of canned borscht . . ."[13]

In the 1950s and 1960s, filmmakers lost interest in making stories about larger-than-life figures and, as Halliwell notes, "showed an alarming tendency not merely to make heroes of 'people like us' but to rub our noses firmly in the gutter by devising stories whose leading characters had few redeeming features." In 1966, the release of the film version of homosexual writer Edward Albee's bitter, obscenity-filled caricature of marriage, *Who's Afraid of Virginia Woolf*, opened the doors to more crude fare. *The Texas Chainsaw Massacre* (1974) did for violence what Virginia Woolf did for foul language, unleashing the "slasher film" genre in which attractive young people, mostly women, are dispatched in grisly ways. As Halliwell notes, popularity does not excuse the filmmaker from responsibility: "It is all very well to say in defense of such films that large numbers of people flock to see them; so they did once to bear-baiting and public executions and witch hunts, but the human race long ago prided itself on having passed that stage."[14]

As with modern art, the critics played a pivotal role in the evolution of the movies into nihilism, gore, and pornography. "The new cinema journalism simply encouraged the worst motives of the new breed of filmmaker, who came to know that whatever idiocy he perpetrated would be staunchly defended, researched, and psychoanalyzed by one of these mercenaries in search of a cause."[15]

In 1990, *The Cook, the Thief, His Wife, and Her Lover* was released to critical acclaim. The film contains mutilated corpses, sex amid garbage, bloody violence, and in the words of Michael Medved, "the most graphic scene of cannibalism ever portrayed in motion pictures. There is, in short, unrelieved ugliness, horror, and depravity at every turn. Naturally, the critics loved it."[16] *The Cook* set the stage for the next year's Oscar winner, *The Silence of the Lambs*. Cannibalism, a la Jeffrey Dahmer, was suddenly in vogue.

Medved was particularly revolted by *The Cook* because he took his wife to it on the advice of a friend who told him that it was "a very dark comedy, but it's lots of fun—terribly witty and terribly sexy. I really think your wife will enjoy it." Mrs. Medved was horrified, but the reviewers were not. Caryn James of the *New York Times* wrote that *The Cook* was "something profound and extremely rare: a work so intelligent and powerful that it evokes our best emotions . . . The Cook has nothing sensational, pornographic, or disreputable about it."

Time magazine's Richard Corliss called the film "exemplary, exciting, extraordinary," and Siskel and Ebert gave it their "Two Thumbs Up" endorsement, calling it "provocative."

As for Medved, he reluctantly agreed to review the film on his "Sneak Previews" show on PBS, calling it "loathsome," an assessment shared by his colleague Jeffrey Lyons. Later, in his book *Hollywood vs. America,* Medved described *The Cook* as "a putrid, pointless, and pretentious piece of filth." His comments unleashed a firestorm of complaint, in which friends and viewers accused him of "right-winged bigotry" and being "a Jesse Helms clone."

It is not surprising that mere criticism of a filthy film should earn a respected critic such politicized disapprobation. Films have been instruments of ideology since Vladimir Lenin announced, "Of all the arts, for us cinema is the most important." One of the Left's great goals has been to destroy the family by undermining sexual morality. As such, anything or anyone who slows down this process is correctly identified as an ideological enemy of the Left. Just as architects from the Bauhaus imported their left-wing ideology when they fled Nazi Germany, left-leaning writers such as novelist Thomas Mann and playwright Bertolt Brecht brought their ideological biases to America in the 1940s. As social critic and author Richard Grenier remarks, most of the pro-communist intellectuals preferred life in the United States even while they made a living condemning it. He writes that "Bertolt Brecht, although steadfast in his theoretical support of Communism, never put his theories to the test by staying in the world's first 'workers' state,' but, fleeing the Nazis, crossed the USSR like a shot and passed World War II amidst the capitalist rot of Pacific Palisades, California."[17]

While Brecht was cozy in California, his former interest, East Berlin's workers, staged riots—the first uprising against communism in the Soviet Bloc. Brecht dismissed the rioters as "fascist, war-mongering rabble" and praised the Soviet tanks and troops for their "swift and accurate intervention."[18]

Over the years, leftist sentiments in Hollywood were kept in check by hard-nosed, patriotic, pro-American studio owners such as Sam Goldwyn and Louis Mayer. Goldwyn in particular had no time for political nonsense, or any nonsense. Commenting on the growing popularity of psychoanalysis, Goldwyn famously remarked, "Anybody who goes to see a psychiatrist ought to have his head examined."

Hollywood's worst tendencies were also curbed by the reality of having the Roman Catholic Church's film office, as well as the Protestant Film Office review scripts from 1933 to 1966. The reviewers made sure a film met the requirements of the Motion Picture Code promulgated by the Hays Office before issuing the Motion Picture Code Seal. Theaters would not screen films without the seal.

According to George Heimrich, director of the National Council of Churches' West Coast Film Office, the NCC "killed the Motion Picture Code" in 1966 when it declined to recommend for an Academy Award *The Greatest Story Ever Told*, while recommending awards for other films depicting nudity and blasphemy.[19] The NCC's actions, he said, "completely pulled the legs out from under" the studios that were adhering to the code.[20]

It was like losing a nagging but benevolent parent. As Christian Film and Television Commission President Ted Baehr explains, "Hollywood studios enjoyed having the Churches to blame for clean, moral movies and appreciated having a director or producer tell them they had gone far enough. The studio heads could then sympathize with the director or producer and claim they had to bow to the moral nit-picking of the Churches, thus guarding the Christian family audience."[21]

The churches' capitulation paved the way for Valenti's bold move to scrap the Motion Picture Code altogether and usher in a floodtide of depravity passing for entertainment or "art." The studios also felt free to be more openly ideological. Although the current wisdom is that Hollywood is just in it for the buck, that does not explain Hollywood's persistent love affair with anti-American, pro-communist movies and the near-absence of anti-communist themes.

Richard Grenier notes that after a few patriotic, pro-military films were released in 1982 such as *Firefox*, *An Officer and a Gentleman*, and *First Blood*, the studios in 1983 cranked out a string of hard-left movies, all of which bombed: *The Book of Daniel*, an apologia for Julius and Ethel Rosenberg, the spies who were executed for giving nuclear secrets to Stalin's Soviet Union; *Hannah K.*, an anti-Israel, pro-Palestinian tale; *Beyond the Limit*, a sympathetic story of Latin American terrorists who kidnap a U.S. ambassador; *The*

Deal of the Century, which blames Third World wars on American and Israeli arms sales; *Under Fire*, which applauds American journalists' deliberate falsification of news to assist the Sandinistas in taking over Nicaragua; and *Testament*, an anti-nuke war-to-end-all-wars saga.[22] *Testament*, incidentally, was produced with grants from the National Endowment for the Arts, which Jane Alexander later chaired during the Clinton Administration.

Apart from Oliver Stone's persistently hard left, anti-American films, such as *Born on the Fourth of July* (1989), *The Doors* (1991), *JFK* (1991), *Nixon* (1995), *Natural Born Killers* (1996), and *The People vs. Larry Flynt*, which Stone produced in 1996 but didn't direct (leaving that to Milos Forman) Hollywood has turned mostly to what Grenier calls "soft-left" themes. "The Soft Left is far more woolly than the hard, its members floating lightheadedly from one notion to the next, often without any clear idea that these various political belief systems have clear-cut precepts, sometimes quite incompatible. The defining element of the Soft Left, in my view, is a kind of persistent utopianism, in the name of which some shining social ideal or other, no matter how unworkable, will always be honored."[23]

The Big Chill (1983) is a prime example of this mushy, relativistic mindset. A more ambitious version of the low-budget John Sayles 1980 film *The Return of the Secaucus Seven*, Lawrence Kasdan's *Big Chill* laments the loss of idealism in the midst of real life and finds solace in the smashing of sexual mores. A single woman who is a real estate lawyer wants to have a baby, so her friend graciously offers the services of her husband. Adultery? No big deal. Share and share alike, just like passing a joint! Fatherless family by design? No big deal. We're just paving the way for Murphy Brown and a thousand lesbian couples, each of whom seems to have a personal reporter promoting their story in the mainstream press.

When it wasn't amusingly portraying baby boomer ex-radicals as whiners, *Big Chill* was pushing the feminist agenda—hard. Who needs families anyway? Not when you have "the extended commune, extending from Atlanta to Los Angeles," as Grenier puts it.[24]

In 1996, Hillary Clinton toured the nation promoting her book *It Takes a Village (to Raise a Child)*. Her dictum that "there is no such thing as other people's children" is right out of the spirit of *The Big Chill*. The only part of *Chill* she might have had a hard time swallowing is the idea of sharing her husband sexually. And who could blame her? By all indications, she's already given more in that department than any wife, even a New Age baby boomer, could be expected to.

Of all the targets of the Hollywood Left, from the American South, to Big Business, to the oppressively small-minded small towns, nothing has secured more negative attention in the Age of Consent than religion, particularly Christianity.

As surveys have shown, few of the movers and shakers in Hollywood are religious, and those who are tend to favor the New Age flavors. Most are unfamiliar with the basic doctrines of Judaism, Christianity, and Islam either personally or even by association. After Richard Nixon's landslide victory in the 1972 presidential race over George McGovern, *New Yorker* film critic Pauline Kael made a remark that epitomizes the situation. Kael said she could not believe Nixon had really won because "nobody I know voted for him." The same goes for religion in Hollywood. As Michael Medved notes, "Hollywood's writers and directors are far more familiar with Jimmy Swaggart than they are with any of the working clergy in their local communities." Medved recalls one producer saying that he disbelieved the polls showing that nearly half the American people attend religious services each week: "If all those people really go to church, then how come I don't know a single one of them?"[25]

More often than not, religion in movies is either ignored, as on television, or cast in a negative fashion through portrayals of bizarre characters. Gone are positive characters such as the priests played by Bing Crosby in *Going My Way* (1944), *Bells of St. Mary's*

(1945), and *Say One for Me* (1959), or Pat O'Brien in *Angels With Dirty Faces* (1938), or Spencer Tracy in *Boys Town* (1938). Instead, we find priests at the heart of financial scandal (Christopher Reeve in *Monsignor* [1982], in homosexual relationships, *Priest* [1994], from the Walt Disney Company's Miramax division), or as a Leer-type fool (the Pope as portrayed in the Chevy Chase–Goldie Hawn comedy *Foul Play* [1978]). If Catholics get the short end, evangelical Protestants fare even worse. Beginning with *Crimes of Passion* (1984), the perverse porn flick with Kathleen Turner as a hooker and Anthony Perkins (*Psycho*) as a sex-crazed street preacher, born-again Christians turn up as swindlers in *Salvation!* (1987), *Pass the Ammo* (1988), and *Leap of Faith* (1992); hypocritical missionaries in *At Play in the Fields of the Lord* (1991); homicidal cranks in *Misery* (1990), *The Rapture* (1991), and *Guilty as Charged* (1992); as perverse villains in *Light of Day* (1987); as totalitarians in *The Vision* (1987) and *The Handmaid's Tale* (1990); as hostile zealots in *Edward Scissorhands* (1990); and even as supernatural fiends, as in *Children of the Corn* (1984), *Poltergeist II* (1986), and *The Blob* (1988). In the 1991 remake of *Cape Fear*, Robert DeNiro plays a killer whose back is carved with biblical verses and who quotes Scripture just before raping and killing. In *Misery*, for which Kathy Bates won the Best Actress Oscar as a sadistic misfit who tortures a prisoner for weeks on end, special care was taken to highlight the character's Christian affiliation. Michael Medved explains: "Perhaps in the hope of giving this slick and empty horror picture some deeper significance as a piece of social commentary, director Rob Reiner focuses repeatedly on the tiny gold cross that Ms. Bates wears around her neck; it often catches the light and flashes out at the camera, particularly on those occasions when her behavior is most menacing and bizarre. The character also makes several references to God, Jesus, church, and the Bible that are clearly meant to make her all the more terrifying to the audience."[26]

In the 1930s, before the Nazi Party achieved total power in

Germany and began rounding up the Jews for shipment to the death camps, the party's artists, cartoonists, and filmmakers began demonizing Jews. The Greedy Jew, the Sadistic Jew, the Molester Jew found their way into the media until the Jews as a people became identified as a threat to Germany's moral and fiscal health.

In order to communicate the "danger" posed by Jews and provide a rationale for actions taken against them, several media campaigns were mounted. For example, World War II political cartoons characterized Jews as everything from pickpockets to corpulent oppressors of the German lower middle class and small merchants. Although later films took a hard-line view of Jews, for example making them responsible for the fragmentation of German society, two 1939 films *Robert und Bertram* and *Leinen aus Irland* softly vilified Jews through comedy. In the 1941 film *Heimkehr*, the Jews prompt the Poles to commit atrocities against the German minority in Poland.[27]

For students of political correctness, it might be interesting to note that propaganda minister Joseph Goebbels in 1939 forbade the term "anti-Semitic" and replaced it with "defense against Jews" or "opposition to Jews." In May 1940, Goebbels informed all filmmakers and critics: "Films in which Jews appear are not to be labeled as anti-Jewish. We want it to be made perfectly clear that such films are not determined by any tendentious consideration, but reflect historical facts as they are."[28]

Building on such propaganda, Hitler was able, without opposition, to enact laws banning Jews from owning newspapers, publishing houses, broadcasting and film studios, teaching at universities, or engaging in any profession in which values were transmitted.[29]

Although it is nowhere near official (and with notable exceptions, such as *Independence Day*, which contains a Jewish father who rediscovers his faith, and the imperfect but overtly Christian-themed Disney film *The Preacher's Wife* [1996]), the same sort of exclusion is now aimed at religious people in America, whose works are vetoed daily by large publishing houses and film studios dominated by leftover Marxists and pansexual secularists. It is far easier to get a film made about a demonic Christian than to get one made about a sane Christian. It is far easier to sell a script that makes fun of Jewish beliefs (see Woody Allen's films) than it is to sell one that presents those beliefs as normal, important, and at the heart of Jewish family life. Given the near-absence of Christians in the television and film industries, mainstream publishing houses, and major art institutions, it should come as no surprise that Christian values are not at the top of the list of themes that make it into the mainstream arts. The same goes for orthodox Jews, who are appalled by the Age of Consent's ubiquitous relativism.

Hollywood's tendency to vulgarize noble topics was epitomized in Stephen Spielberg's *Schindler's List* (1993), a landmark film about the Holocaust. Despite its extraordinarily powerful message, the Oscar-winning film was severely criticized by the Rabbinical Alliance of America and other Orthodox Jewish groups because it contains foul language and gratuitous sex and nudity. In 1997, NBC televised *Schindler's List*, uncut, during what used to be the "family hour." It was the first time that the f-word and full frontal nudity had invaded network television. When Representative Tom Coburn (R-OK) protested NBC's decision to air the most explicit sequences between 7:00 and 9:00 PM when many children are watching television, he was actually accused of anti-Semitism and prudishness. It did not seem to matter that he had prefaced his remarks with overall praise for the film's excellence and importance. Smuggling sex and profanity into otherwise laudable films is Hollywood's curious habit.

In 1998, *Titanic* (PG-13) snagged eleven Academy Awards, including Best Picture and Best Director. Although James Cameron's epic did not win any acting or writing awards, it tied *Ben-Hur*'s record for the highest number of Oscars. Anything but a disaster at the box office, the film grossed nearly five hundred million dollars *before* the Academy Awards were announced. Multitudes of teen-aged girls flocked to see a soggy story about doomed lovers amid class warfare aboard the "unsinkable" ship. Boys came to see the big boat go down, along with Kate Winslet's modesty. *Titanic*'s popularity unleashed a tidal wave of peer pressure that only the hardiest parents could withstand. Along with nifty special effects, *Titanic* offered romantic fornication, along with honest-to-Hefner soft-core pornography. Millions of America's children were treated to their first view of movie-screen-sized naked breasts and a couple who "do it" in the back seat of a car after knowing each other for two days. As *Titanic* was sailing into box office history, the real-life Ship of State, captained by the President of the United States, was sinking into a spectacularly sordid sex scandal. Bill Clinton's handlers could hardly be blamed if they took comfort in America's indifference to *Titanic*'s glorification of quickie sex. Hollywood's staple theme—The Old Rules No Longer Apply (even in the past)—had apparently penetrated middle America.

The Age of Consent demands entertainment that pushes the boundaries of taste, in order to free the audience from all those taboos. Often, it is done so subtly that it goes largely unnoticed. In Disney's *Honey, I Blew Up the Kid* (1992), which a major movie anthology describes as "a charming and funny film that's fit for the whole family," the special effects and family-friendly theme mask a large-scale advertisement for Las Vegas. In *Honey*, the glittering casinos are as wholesome as apple pie, each playing a part in the rescue of a child who is accidentally giantized by his father's invention. The viewer is left with the feeling that the Vegas strip, a place built on greed, prostitution, and other vices, is a great place to take the kids!

In 1997, Disney skipped the theaters, quietly releasing *Honey, We Blew Up Ourselves!* as a video, which was a wise move. This turkey, which was technically innovative, fell horribly short in characterization. The film is about a quartet of parents whose kids hold a wild party while the parents, unbeknownst to the kids, are helplessly looking on, shrunk to less than an inch tall. The kids think the parents have gone off on a car trip after having left strict rules about no parties. Despite open disobedience, the teens are never disciplined at the end of the film. During the party, one girl deftly puts down the advances of an uninvited punk party crasher, not knowing that her mother and father are watching every move. After the parents are re-sized to normalcy, the mother gives her daughter a hug and tells her in effect that she done good. The message: obedience is no big deal, and parents should lighten up because kids can make their own decisions. Traditionalists are supposed to be content that the daughter did not consent to have sex with a stranger.

In *Pretty Woman* (1990), Disney turned prostitution into a cinderella tale, with Julia Roberts nonchalantly performing oral sex on clients before falling in love with a businessman played by Richard Gere. The prostitute, naturally, shows the cold businessman how to really be a human being. Hollywood has always loved prostitutes, who almost always have hearts of gold. From Belle's girls in *Gone With the Wind* (1939), to Barbra Streisand's lovable eccentric in *The Owl and the Pussycat* (1970), to Dolly Parton's spirited trollops in *The Best Little Whorehouse in Texas* (1982), to Robin Wright's winsome, persistent *Moll Flanders* (1996), prostitutes display far more character than the "church ladies" who look down on them. More than three hundred full-length films involve the topic of prostitution, which is not surprising when you consider that Hollywood is prime territory for real-life hookers. When he was caught having sex with a street hooker in Los Angeles in 1996, heartthrob Hugh Grant (*Four Weddings and a Funeral*) was momentarily embarrassed. But he soon went on to make more movies. As the tabloids worked overtime to bring this breaking story to the rest of America, Hollywood yawned. The question seemed not to center on Grant's lack of morals but on the surprising fact that, as one of the world's top film stars, he would have to pay for sex.

Given the palpable hostility in the film industry toward Judaic-Christian values, one answer would be to create a religious subculture with its own publishing houses, film studios, and television shows. Under the auspices of the Family Channel, several films have been made for television with explicitly Christian world views. The Family Channel's success in marketing family-friendly fare finally caught the eye of media baron Rupert Murdoch, who outbid other suitors to bring the Family Channel out of founder Pat Robertson's domain and under the Fox umbrella. Whether Fox will leave the channel alone or turn it into a clone of Fox's vile "Married With Children" is anyone's guess.

The Family Channel's success still does not solve the problem of the mass brainwashing against religion that continues in major media. For religious people, the solution is the same as it was for Gramsci's Marxists, but the stakes are even higher. Gramsci wanted to use the media to change the world. Religious folks want to keep a hostile media at bay.

A Jewish fable relates that a man stood at the gates of Sodom and cried out against sin. He implored men to repent and change their ways. As things got progressively worse, he continued to cry out his warning. When it looked absolutely hopeless, a passerby asked him why he still bothered. He answered, "I used to cry out so that men would change their ways. Now I cry out so that they won't change me!"

It is necessary for God-fearing people to capture the culture, or at least to be a part of it, if only to keep the culture from demonizing the devout.

10

Whatever Happened to Art?

. . . [I]n the substitution of masks for personalized faces . . .
Picasso adopted this latter device as a means of detaching
himself emotionally from the figures as human beings and
from such considerations as beauty or ugliness (which then
as now he always refused to recognize).[1]

Douglas Cooper

CRITIC AND PIANIST Samuel Lipman once told about the
time he did a recital for some inner-city teens. They listened
politely at first, then got completely out of hand, laughing,
talking, and leaving their seats. Lipman looked out on the audience
and then thundered out the opening chord from Beethoven's Fifth.
As he put it, "Beethoven spoke out across the centuries to say 'I am
HERE.'" The children listened raptly and gave Lipman a standing
ovation at the end. It was the most satisfying recital he ever gave
and the clearest proof to him that great art is universal.

Culture is not something isolated in a museum or concert hall
or on a CD but is defined by the realm of meaning and value and
the actual ways in which these values are carried out in everyday

life. A culture that embraces the concept that life is random and meaningless will become a culture that does not respect life. A culture that elevates the senses to an undeserved status is a culture that will not be able to discern between fads and timeless truths. A culture that confuses relativism for healthy skepticism will erase the important distinctions that help keep us a free people. Without these distinctions, based on traditional morality, it has become easy to substitute coercion for compassion, to mistake hedonism for the quest for knowledge, and to undermine the cause—and guarantors—of human freedom.

"Music is the measure for heaven and earth, the principle of balance and harmony," Confucius wrote in the fifth century BC.[2] In the Book of Genesis, Laban rebukes Jacob for fleeing by noting what he had missed: "Why didn't you tell me, so I could send you away with joy and singing to the music of tambourines and harp?"[3]

In the Book of Chronicles, King David appoints a large contingent of musicians to perform at the tabernacle where the Ark of the Covenant is housed. The Book of Psalms is named after the word used by the Greeks to denote stringed instruments such as harp, lyre, and lute.

Although affected and shaped by culture, art is not culturally bound. The elements of art are found in all cultures, just as natural moral laws are found in all cultures. No society rewards cowardice, for example, nor fails to appreciate honor. Marriage and family are cultivated all over the world, and murder and theft are discouraged by law. Similarly, art and music may have vastly differing styles in different cultures, but essential harmony of design or sound is apparent everywhere.

As historian Edith Borroff writes, "All ancient peoples of whom we have knowledge gave music a place of honor; they considered it a potent religious and moral force, intimately related to the most formal, as well as the most informal, aspects of life . . . It is difficult to find universal materials if one looks for an entire language or grammar, but certain idioms and predilections pervade music on a worldwide basis. All cultures have cultivated the lyrical song, and many cultures throughout the world put the voice to work as an improvising instrument as well as a lyrical one."[4]

The only art that conflicts with this universal principle is the Western modern art born of relativism in the past one hundred years, when men decided to free themselves from the boundaries imposed by nature. As one critic notes approvingly, "The shift from a static world view [God's natural order] to the present dynamic view of the universe, which began with Copernicus and Galileo, has swept all before it . . . This relative world, moreover, is populated by men who see themselves in multiple images and express themselves in a multiplicity of styles . . . Modern art as the mirror of this relativistic world thus assumes many shapes to reflect a multiplicity of human images."[5]

Great art is a mirror of specific cultural beliefs, customs, and traditions, but it can touch the human heart from any culture. The modern tendency to appropriate and distort art from other cultures and earlier periods to illustrate a progressively modern theme works against the truths implicit in the original works. In recent years, Shakespeare has been the most prominent victim of this ideological kidnapping. As social critic and Shakespeare scholar Joseph Sobran points out, the Bard has suffered mightily through interpretation during the past several decades. Laurence Olivier's *Hamlet* (1948) focused heavily on an "Oedipus complex—not in homage to Sophocles, but in deference to Freud . . . The camera focused on him kissing his mother with unseemly passion . . . the real action was in the images, not the words. Thus was Shakespeare brought into harmony with what then seemed the latest in modern science."[6]

Later productions have kept the Shakespearean text but created a powerful subtext through which the camera "can easily upstage the verse . . . and the subtext isn't a deeper version of the text; it's always a misreading superimposed *on* the text." In 1970, Peter Brook filmed "his bleak, bleak 'existentialist' rendition of *King Lear*, starring Paul Scofield, apparently on the theory that not only life is meaningless but Shakespeare, too. It was a tale told by an idiot. The film looked as if it had been shot within the Arctic Circle in prehistoric times, and the characters all appeared to be in a catatonic stupor."[7] Other productions have placed *Richard III* in the 1930s as a fascist dictator. And Orson Welles's Mercury Theater production of *Julius Caesar* in the 1930s was staged as a modern, anti-fascist drama.

A more honest appropriation of a Shakespearean theme came in the early 1960s, when the musical *West Side Story* was produced as a Broadway play, then a movie. The story about doomed lovers on opposite sides of warring gangs in New York's west side of Manhattan worked because only the basic premise of *Romeo and Juliet* was borrowed. *West Side's* dialogue and characters were fresh and appropriate for the modern setting. The writers wisely avoided trying to import Shakespearean dialogue into the banter of the Sharks and Jets. And they even satirized some modern notions, as when the Jets sing a song ("Officer Krupke") mocking the prevailing theories about the causes of juvenile delinquency. The point was made not by bombarding the audience with noise and heavy-handed lyrics but by the persuasive power of art.

So-called "art" that is dissonant to the moral order is not art at all but a form of "aesthetic terrorism," a term coined by author Carl Raschke to describe the destructive trends in rock 'n' roll.[8] Writing two centuries earlier, Ludwig von Beethoven wrote that his form of art had a source transcending his own talent: "Like all the arts, music is founded upon the exalted symbols of the moral sense . . . To submit to these inscrutable laws, and by means of these laws to tame and guide one's own mind so that the manifestations of art may pour out: this is the isolating principle of art . . . So always art represents the divine, and the relationship of men towards art is religion; what we obtain from art comes from

God, is divine inspiration, which appoints an aim for human faculties that we cannot attain."[9]

By contrast, the late rock musician Jim Morrison of the Doors was quite candid in his musical aims: "Erotic politicians, that's what we are. We're interested in everything about revolt, disorder, and all activity that appears to have no meaning."[10]

Great art speaks to the universal heart and soul, shining a light into the human soul. Unfortunately, bad art works the heart and soul over in reverse. It can get attention not by being well executed or touching what is great and good in us, but by consciously seeking to offend. This kind of art is much easier to produce; it is always easier to destroy than to create. Aristotle (ca. 384–322 B C) warned of the power of music to be a force for evil if used improperly: "And the music will correspond to their minds, for as their minds are perverted from the natural state, so there are perverted modes and highly strung and unnaturally colored melodies. A man receives pleasure from what is natural to him . . ."[11]

The redefinition of art as a wholly relative concept to each individual is part of a larger sociopolitical movement of relativism. Masked in the rhetoric of equality, the modern drive toward meaninglessness is the antithesis of genuine tolerance and diversity because it eliminates the important universal distinctions that transcend all other human groupings. Those distinctions, as expressed in art, are craftsmanship, a sense of order and design, and the themes of grace, beauty, heroism, intelligence, and honesty, tempered by discernment.

If you accept the proposition that we live in a moral universe, art that is simply elegant or beautiful is not morally neutral—whether it is overtly utilitarian or not. Art is good because it mirrors the creation itself and adds to the quality of life or an understanding of life. A Christian perspective, as explained by C. S. Lewis, is that Creation—that is, the material world—is itself good. As Lewis said, God likes matter; that is why he made so much of it.

If the creation is abused or misused, it can become the handmaiden of evil. Lewis's definition of evil was that of something that begins as good but is perversely twisted. A craftsman can carve a beautiful wooden mallet, but in the wrong hands it can become a murder weapon. The object itself contains no intrinsic evil, but can be used for evil purposes. The same can be said about art.

An older definition of art, one that goes back to the Greeks and Romans, holds that art is that which instills virtue, not merely that which adds to human understanding. This view is supported by the idea that there is a hierarchy of knowledge—some things are worth knowing more than other things. But the Greco-Roman concept of virtue is in some ways antithetical to the Judeo-Christian view. To the Greeks, mortal sin was not so much the state of being separated from God due to sinning against God's moral order but from a lack of knowledge. In Euripides' *The Bacchants*, the tragic heroine Agave murders her own son after surrendering her reason to an irrational cult. She is so far gone in bacchanalian revelry that she actually takes her son Pentheus's head to show off as a trophy of sorts, thinking it is the head of an animal. Pentheus, for his part, loses his chance to be crowned king (and literally loses his head) because he does not bring enough reason to bear on the insanity unfolding around him. By failing to appreciate the circumstances, he proves that he is ultimately unfit to be a ruler.

Likewise, in Sophocles' *Oedipus the King*, Oedipus's offense is that he is so ignorant that he does not realize he is carrying on with his own mother and murdering his own father.

As author William Fleming notes, "The entire Greek philosophical tradition concurred in the assumption that, without the knowledge and the free exercise of the faculty of reason, there is no ultimate happiness for mankind."[12]

Defenders of obscene works militate against the very idea of the hierarchy of knowledge. They praise such works as Robert

Mapplethorpe's sadomasochistic photos, Sally Mann's nude photos of her children performing bodily functions, or Andres Serrano's photos of crucifixes and other religious icons immersed in vats of the artist's urine. These artworks, they say, have value because they represent a part of life that does exist. Mere examination of phenomena does not mean the artist is promoting any particular idea, they insist.

During the 1980s, when I worked as a news editor for the *Los Angeles Times*, a pop music critic took this stance in an article that examined the seventies-era rock group Black Sabbath. Even though the group's albums were festooned with satanic symbols and their songs littered with references to Satan, the critic took a benign view of the material. When I asked him about it, he told me that Black Sabbath wasn't "promoting" Satanism, just "merely examining it." A gifted writer and committed liberal, this critic's idea of objectivity prevented him from acknowledging the obvious, since it invited a judgment between good and evil.

Much ugly and evil "art" has been justified on the grounds that it merely reflects reality. In Great Britain, a controversy erupted at the national gallery in the 1960s when a pile of soiled diapers was put on display. You can't get much more real than that. In recent years, modernists have nearly demolished the old view of art as embodying virtue. The quest for knowledge—any knowledge—subordinates moral concerns. In fact, moral concerns are relegated to the realm of the merely utilitarian. This is unfortunate for two reasons. First, it cheapens the artist's quest; he does not have to shoot very high. Secondly, it cheapens our culture for the same reason. As virtue becomes merely one element on the infinite menu of moral relativism, art loses its unique claim and thus its ability to inspire.

All around us, we can hear the modern mantras. Who is to say what is good? What may be art to you may not be art to me. Art is anything anyone wants to say it is.

By the time you arrive at this point, art can easily be seen as just another form of human expression, of no more value than any other form of human expression. This was the essence of the Dada movement earlier this century, the first concerted movement to embrace meaninglessness as a totem. The name of the movement was aptly chosen as an expression of its intent: someone put his finger in a French dictionary at random and landed on "dada," which means rocking chair. It has no meaning other than that, and that is precisely the point. Dada is anti-art because it is anti-everything.

But the movement itself had a very real goal which mirrored the declared goal of the socialists: to eradicate all standards and institutions and thus pave the way for the creation of the New Man. As socialism required the burying of the old moral order, so the Dadaists tried to bury the old artistic order as a way to bury the moral order. Propelled into the public eye by publicity stunts and gullible critics, the Dadaists helped confine art to a smaller circle of adherents based in the universities and the art world itself. Art began to be seen as the private province of the mystical few who were empowered to truly understand it—or as a fool's paradise. Many people dispensed with art that they could no longer enjoy or appreciate. The term "modern art," in popular usage, has become an exclusionary description or a term of derision. But to progressive critics, it is the highest form art can take because it knows no limits.

"Historical relativism has provided the modern artist with an unparalleled number of choices of styles and techniques from the past as well as the present," writes critic William Fleming, to which he adds, "Most twentieth-century ideas and problems are variations on old themes that have bothered men ever since the fifth century BC. Those that in the past led to sharp dissonances have never been resolved; instead, they have become outmoded, outgrown, temporarily forgotten, or they are bypassed, circumvented in one way or another, or assume new shapes and forms."[13] One of the ways to "bypass" ideas is to ignore them entirely. Although Judaism's world view has been around for perhaps five thousand years, Fleming pegs the inception of meaningful Western ideas to the fifth century B C, when pagan philosophies began to take shape. As a celebrator of modern art, Fleming correctly identifies many of the driving forces beneath the art:

> In [modern art] can be found Marx's proletarian man, speaking in some form of social protest and bent on bringing about the ultimate triumph of the working classes and masses. Darwin's jungle man is there, beating on his neoprimitive tom-toms and discoursing in existentialist vocabularies on the survival of the fittest. Nietzsche's superman, determined to impose his mighty will on an unwilling world, has been thwarted in two world wars. The voice of Freud's psychological man is heard coming from couches and canvases as he tries to share his surrealistic nightmares with the world at large. Mechanical man, the spawn of the Industrial Revolution and the Machine Age, walks robotlike at large, thinking mechanistic thoughts in his electronic brain and expressing futuristic principles in his mechanical style. There, too, is Einstein's scientific man of relativity, drawing abstract pictures of this space-time world in slashing angular lines organized by the multifocus perspective of cubism. *Modern art as the mirror of this relativistic world thus assumes many shapes to reflect a multiplicity of human images.*[14]

Indeed. Modern art, in other words, reflects man's flight from natural order of all kinds, the singular feature of the twentieth century. Much of contemporary art is, in Walt Whitman's words, a "barbaric yawp" over the rooftops of the world.

II

From the Sublime
to the Incomprehensible

By the mid-1930s, Modern Art was already so chic that corporations held it aloft like a flag to show that they were both up-to-date and enlightened, a force in Culture as well as commerce. The Dole Pineapple Company sent Georgia O'Keefe and Asamu Noguchi to Hawaii to record their impressions, and the Container Corporation of America was commissioning abstract work by Fernand Leger, Henry Moore, and others.[1]

Tom Wolfe

ALTHOUGH THERE HAS BEEN a revival of realistic art in the latter part of the twentieth century, much of the visual arts world is mired in the ruins of modernism.

Major museums such as New York's Whitney and Guggenheim, or Washington, D.C.'s, Hirschorn, along with many lesser galleries, regularly present what many members of the bewildered and disgusted public call "My kid could do better than that" exhibits.

To illustrate the extent to which critics have played a part in fostering artistic lunacy, I will quote at length from the beginning of a 1995 essay by artist Frederick Turner, who finds some amusement in it all:

> Recently one of the most fashionable contemporary galleries in Dallas mounted an exhibit of New York artists. The reader will, I hope, forgive me if I quote from a review of it published in Dallas's leading newspaper, focusing on what the reviewer evidently regarded as the centerpiece of the show:
>
> "What at first glance appears to be a wooden box from which a work of art has been removed is revealed by the materials information on the checklist to consist of 'human feces on white cube.'
>
> "So when you look again you see it, about the size of a roach dropping, dead center on its pedestal. Actually, it's pretty easy to see the first time around, but because it's only 5 millimeters in diameter, it's also pretty easy to dismiss, until you know what it is.
>
> "Here is a work of art tailor-made for criticism. It enters into the discourse on 'baseness'—a gleaming white 'base' supports a speck of the world's basest material. It is a metaphor for creativity—'Mommy, look what I did!' 'That's nice.'
>
> "In the form-vs.-content department, the object vigorously wages a debate that belies its minute proportions. The same could be said for its 'presence,' one of those attributes that works of art are hardly expected to have anymore. This one's presence, however, permeates the gallery, despite its antiseptic presentation."
>
> The reader must take my word for it that this article is not a spoof or a parody. It is a glowing and serious review of an art exhibit; it is tongue-in-cheek not about the work of art itself but about the double-take of the wretched viewer of it. Comment on it would obviously be superfluous. Sometimes the would-be satirist must simply take his hat off to a reality that transcends the art of satire. It is precious and perfect as it is.[2]

How did we get here, to a completely relativistic world of art, from the rich tradition that produced the likes of Michelangelo, Titian, Rembrandt, Durer, Vermeer, El Greco, Rubens, Renoir, Gainsborough, Winslow Homer, Edward Hopper, Andrew Wyeth, and Norman Rockwell?

It didn't happen overnight. Western art evolved over the centuries as artists sought out new ways of reflecting nature. But the greatest break in tradition, the one that led to the eventual abandonment of representation, was spawned during the French Revolution. Unlike the American Revolution, which was fought to reassert the traditional rights of Englishmen in America, the French Revolution was a revolt against the entire established order. Christianity was attacked as anti-progress, and the "Reign of Virtue and Reason" was proclaimed. Robespierre, the "spiritual" father of the Revolution, went so far as to invade Notre Dame Cathedral to symbolically crown a woman as "the Goddess Reason."

The French revolutionaries saw themselves akin to pagan visionaries, and revolutionary artists began to reassert Greek and Roman themes in their paintings. Seeking to replace Christianity, some philosophers turned to the Greek mathematician Pythagoras, who, as historian James H. Billington writes, "became a kind of patron saint for romantic revolutionaries, who needed new symbols of secular sanctity . . . An undercurrent of fascination with Pythagorean thought in the High Renaissance and Enlightenment came to the surface during the French Revolution."[3]

Along with Pythagoras came the influence of the occultic, egalitarian Masons, whose membership formed a revolutionary underground in Paris and other European cities. The twin emphasis on equality of man and the methodical unlocking of the secrets of the universe apart from Scriptural references fueled the flight from hierarchical authority of all kinds, including artistic standards. The revolutionary painter Phillipe-Auguste Jeanron abandoned classical themes to portray the proletariat in revolutionary scenes. As director of the Louvre during 1848–1850, Jeanron attacked the official art of the institute, which he called "the Bastille of artists" after the infamous prison, but also neoclassical themes in general, which he called "the old regime in art."[4]

Among artists, the choice of topics became more varied, as the class structure that had supported the official arts was toppled (beheaded is probably more apt, given the bloody predilections of the Jacobins). The spirit of revolution transcended the political upheaval, because the Enlightenment had already unleashed forces that challenged the existing order. Rationalism began to replace theology as the study of the enlightened. Francis Bacon and René Descartes elevated the power of the human mind to an all-encompassing authority, reducing God to an abstract concept. Unimpeded by the Judeo-Christian view of man's imperfection, Bacon declared humanity's purpose as being not to worship and serve God but to "extend the power and dominion of the human race itself over the universe."[5]

Man became the measure of all things, and the focus of artists did not necessarily have to deal with the Creation as God made it. Increasingly, each man's own vision gained more importance. As the nineteenth century approached the midway point, the Industrial Revolution created a vast middle class with purchasing power and a variety of mass-produced goods, including art. As historian E. H. Gombrich notes, public taste deteriorated in the mid-nineteenth century, a development also noted by French writer Alexis de Tocqueville. In his classic study, *Democracy in America,* Tocqueville lamented the loss of excellence: "Something analogous to what I have already pointed out in the useful arts then takes place in the fine arts; the productions of artists are more numerous, but the merit of each production is diminished . . . In aristocracies, a few great pictures are produced; in democratic countries, a vast number of insignificant ones. In the former, statues are raised of bronze; in the latter, they are modelled in plaster."[6]

Because of the cheapening of art, many artists became prima

donnas in response. The relations between patrons and artists became more strained, as artists became more apt to create their own visions, while the patrons had their own, usually more conservative, visions of what they wanted to buy. For many artists, "it became an acknowledged pastime to 'shock the burghers' out of their complacency and to leave them bewildered and bemused. Artists began to see themselves as a race apart, they grew long hair and beards, they dressed in velvet or corduroy, wore broad-brimmed hats and loose ties, and generally stressed their contempt for the conventions of the 'respectable.'"[7]

They also began to experiment more and more. Eugene Delacroix (1799–1863) pioneered the superiority of color and impression over draftsmanship and explored more themes integral to French life and history.

During the period of the Revolution of 1848, when socialists attempted to seize power in France, a group of artists formed the Realism movement, which stressed mundane themes instead of the typical scenes of grandeur or beauty found in previous paintings. Gustave Courbet (1819–1877), who coined the term "Le Realisme," portrayed himself striving for artistic purity. In a letter he wrote: "I hope always to earn my living by my art without having ever deviated by even a hair's breadth from my principles, without having lied to my conscience for a single moment, without painting even as much as can be covered by a hand only to please anyone or to sell more easily."[8]

While this stance may seem heroic, it also contains the seeds of arrogance that helped bring art to its knees—disdain for any other viewer of the art, including patrons and the public. Courbet could get away with this because he was a gifted artist. But legions of no-talent "artists" have covered their lack of skill with a misplaced surfeit of pride. The idea of artist as revolutionary with no one to please but himself echoed eighty years later in the writings of Ayn Rand (1905–1982). In her most famous work, *The Fountainhead*

(1943), Rand depicts a visionary, atheistic architect named Howard Roark and his quest to build only for his own pleasure. Patrons who ask for classical forms on their buildings are dismissed as fools, with Roark telling them what is good for them. *The Fountainhead*'s theme is that human greatness depends on those who break the rules, since the human ego is the fountainhead of progress. Innovation results only from ignoring all standards and conventions—especially religion. Rand, who did an admirable job dissecting the fallacies of socialism and communism, fell prey to the opposite temptation— self-absorption, which has become the creed of our relativistic times.

As for Courbet, it took another few decades before his attitude became predominant among artists, and, meanwhile, much innovation occurred, some of it quite good. Edouard Manet (1832– 1883) began to portray natural settings as bright splashes of color, with less detail. Other Impressionists, such as Claude Monet (1840– 1926), Auguste Renoir (1841–1919), Camille Pissaro (1830–1903), Vincent Van Gogh (1853–1890), Paul Gaugin (1848–1903), Paul Cézanne (1839–1906), and Georges Seurat (1859–1891) created distinctive styles, breaking up traditional forms and evoking moods by forcing the eye to reassess what it had taken for granted. Many of these artists were influenced by the importation of cheap Japanese prints, often used to wrap packages shipped from Tokyo to Paris. The colorful prints emphasized simple, everyday themes, and inspired French artists to do likewise. The movement picked up the name "The Impressionists" as a term of ridicule from a critic who reviewed an 1874 exhibition of landscape painters, which included Monet's painting of a harbor in morning mists, "Impression: Sunrise." Monet had a strong effect on American artists as well, hosting the likes of Mary Cassat (1845–1926) and John Singer Sargent (1856–1925) at his compound in Giverny, where a small American museum stands today.

One major American artist, James McNeill Whistler (1834– 1903), shared the major European Impressionists' talent and also shared their less attractive trait—contempt for the public's interest in traditional themes. For Whistler, form mattered more than substance. Nowhere did he illustrate this view more obviously than when he named an 1871 painting of his mother "Arrangement in grey and black." An appreciative public, which clung to the idea that people are more important than artistic pretentions, renamed the painting "Whistler's Mother."

At the turn of the century, a group of artists in Paris began to ignore even more conventions of style and use colorful objects to create decorative patterns. Henri Matisse (1869–1954) was the most prominent of Les Fauves ("the savages"), who seem tame by comparison with what was to come. Although all of the above-mentioned artists broke new ground, they remained within the representational school; people could recognize what the paintings were about without an explanatory note attached by a gallery.

This was about to change with the arrival of a Spanish painter, Pablo Picasso (1881–1973), founder of the "cubist" style. As the saying goes, the sins of one generation are multiplied in the next. Widely regarded as the most influential artist of the twentieth century, Picasso helped usher in abstract art, surrealism, Dadaism, and other modern styles. Cubism consists of breaking up familiar objects (such as a violin) and presenting various aspects of the object in layers of imagery that consist of geometric shapes.

As a young artist, Picasso asked for assistance from Paul Cézanne, who in a letter advised him to look at nature in terms of geometric shapes, such as spheres, cones, and cylinders.[9] Cézanne probably meant that artists should look to natural configurations to help them organize their compositions, but Picasso apparently took him literally, breaking up reality into overlaying geometric shapes.

In 1907, Picasso unveiled his ground-breaking painting of prostitutes in a Spanish bordello. Titled *Les Demoiselles d'Avignon* (Avignon is a French city that was the site of the papacy for a time) the picture consisted of five nude women in variously misshapen form, with an overall sense of casual exhibitionism. Generally regarded as the first cubist painting of note, or at least the first to use cubist elements, *Les Demoiselles* was painted while Picasso was undergoing a crisis with a model who had become his lover. In *Degenerate Moderns: Modernity as Rationalized Sexual Misbehavior* (1993), E. Michael Jones traces the destructive tendencies of modernism to a longing for freedom from sexual constraints. Picasso, who hated the church and was a professed communist, painted women as disjointed objects, often in an intentionally ugly fashion. His abstractions were painted during the collapses of his various affairs. As Jones illustrates by chronologically displaying plates of Picasso's works, the artist reverted to a realistic style each time he fell in love. As the relationship with his lovers worsened, the paintings of the female lovers became increasingly abstract and even threatening. For example, in 1918, Picasso painted attractive realistic portraits of his wife, Olga. By 1925, as their marriage disintegrated, he began painting cubist mutilations of the female form. *Tete d'une femme*, a 1929 painting of a woman's head, consists of a "series of angular, dismembered female forms in which the mouth is turned ninety degrees into a threatening *vagina dentata* [a vagina with teeth] . . . By 1930, Picasso was portraying women as having a female form with a preying mantis head."[10]

The violence done to women and to form in Picasso's art was no isolated development. It represented a larger embrace of relativism in which the Judeo-Christian worldview of each life having an eternal soul and eternal significance was cast aside. As with Whistler's cavalier treatment of his mother, Picasso used women as objects to demonstrate his own allegiance to form over substance. In the same way, pornographers deliberately "objectify" women by emphasizing their bodies over their other attributes, creating objects of lust. This perversion of sexual energy depends on the male users being kept ignorant of the women's real lives. It is not so easy to cultivate uninhibited lust when the viewer truly knows the woman in the picture as a daughter or mother or someone's sister. *Playboy* magazine's mini-biographies of their centerfolds are designed to give a minimum of knowledge about the model and convey a sense of wholesomeness about portraying her in the nude. Any more than a few lines would spoil the illusion, however. It is enough to know that she is just the "girl next door," the kind young males fantasize about.

Picasso himself admitted that his true aim was to smash traditional values in his paintings. As a dedicated communist and sexual revolutionary, he used his art to shock and scandalize, which have become the main aim of many a modern artist.

"I want to give it a form which has some connection with the visible world even if it is only to wage war on that world," he once said. " . . . I want that internal surge . . . to propose itself to the viewer in the form of traditional painting violated."[11] He might just as well have added that he wanted to violate women, too, but perhaps that is too obvious. Near the end of his career, Picasso "became a master of the crotch shot. But it was porn a la Picasso. The crotches were drawn in the minutest realistic detail, but the faces remained Cubist masks."[12]

After Picasso began violating form and subject matter, his visual anarchy was taken to its logical conclusion by other artists. Georges Braque (1881–1963) was the other great cubist innovator, who began incorporating cubist motifs right after viewing *Les Demoiselles* at Picasso's studio. Instead of attempting to paint a particular woman, he tried to convey the *idea* of woman. He said, "I want to expose the Absolute, and not merely the factitious woman."[13] Hence, models lost their own identities and became merely a source for archetypal forms, thus dehumanizing the women in the pictures. The idea of the individual was gradually being lost in the search for the universal. Since great art depends on a grasp of the specific as well as the universal, this relativistic doctrine pushed artists further away from an appreciation of people as eternal souls created to be uniquely individual by an all-powerful God.

Even cubism depends on enough realism so the viewer can appreciate what is being ripped apart and reconstructed. People and commonplace objects are the prime subjects, as they are in "surrealism," in which familiar forms are placed in situations that create illusions of continuity, such as in the paintings of Salvador Dali (1904–1989), the most famous of which have melting clock faces that drip over landscapes. Many cubist and surrealistic paintings show considerable skill and a sophisticated sense of color and design, particularly the earlier ones. But as the field grew crowded, many artists gave the viewer less and less to behold.

The realistic aspect was dispensed with altogether in the work of Russian painter Wassily Kandinsky (1866–1944), who ushered in the "abstract" school. Living in Munich, Germany, surrounded by fellow painters who revolted against material progress, Kandinsky railed against his culture's advance in technology and science. Professing a mysticism of the natural, Kandinsky tried to create an art of pure "inwardness," without acknowledgment of nature, people or any recognizable forms. In other words, instead of reflecting God's creation, or even man-made objects, the artist creates something entirely subjective, born of his own imagination. This is the ultimate in relativistic art, with the artist serving as master of nothing but his own inner world, much like children who are unaware of the disciplines necessary for representative art. If no one else understands or appreciates it, that's tough.

Kandinsky was followed by other abstractionists such as Swiss painter and musician Paul Klee (1879–1940), who included realistic elements in his paintings to create an entirely new perspective. Like other painters of his time, Klee rejected the "slavish" fealty to realism and instead sought to allow nature, through him, to create as he went along. The Dutchman Piet Mondrian (1872–1944) was also a mystic who sought to overcome the subjective appearance of the real world and create something new. His paintings of straight lines and primary colors inspired many artists to abandon representation for pure form. Going still further, American artist

Jackson Pollock (1912–1956) dispensed with form and placed his canvases on the floor, dripping, pouring, or throwing paint on them. His mishmashes of interconnecting lines and swirls, which gave birth to the "abstract expressionism" movement, allowed many unskilled people the hope that they no longer had to know how to draw to be considered artists.

In 1913, the first major exhibition of avant-garde art in America was held at the Armory Show in New York. The public recoiled at the sight of the disembodied figures, hastily done images, and sheer ugliness. But the elites who dominated major institutions flocked to Postimpressionism. One British arts observer marveled fifty years later at how times had changed. "In 1914, when he was referred to indiscriminately as 'cubist,' 'futurist' or 'modernist,' the post-Impressionist artist was regarded as a crank or a charlatan. The painters and sculptors whom the public knew and admired were bitterly opposed to radical innovations. The money, the influence, and the patronage were all on their side. Today [1964], it is almost true to say that the situation is reversed. Public Bodies such as the Arts Council and the British Council and Broadcasting house, Big Business, the Press, the Churches, the Cinema, and the advertisers are all on the side of what, to use a misnomer, is called nonconformist art . . . there is no form of pictorial eccentricity which can provoke or even astonish the critics . . ."[14]

In America, much the same phenomenon had occurred. In 1939, the Museum of Modern Art in New York staged an exhibit called "Art in Our Time." During the opening, MOMA board trustees posed for a photo with the exhibit's major attraction—Picasso's *Les Demoiselles d'Avignon* (1907).[15] Among them were Ford Motor Company heir Edsel Ford and Rockefeller empire heir Nelson Rockefeller. Unintentionally, but fittingly, the photo shows Rockefeller standing close to the painting, his finger pointing directly at a prostitute's crotch. With very public help from elites like Rockefeller, Ford, and other major corporate donors, Postimpressionistic art eventually took over the American art scene.

In 1964, modern art champion Harold Rosenberg, writing in the *New Yorker* magazine coined the term "Vanguard Audience" to describe how a segment of society had radically altered the art world: "[T]he Vanguard Audience is open to anything. Its eager representatives—curators, museum directors, art educators, dealers—rush to organize exhibitions and provide explanatory labels before the paint has dried on the canvas or the plastic has hardened. Co-operating critics comb the studios like big-league scouts, prepared to spot the art of the future and to take lead in establishing reputations. Art historians stand ready with cameras and notebooks to make sure every novel detail is safe for the record. The tradition of the new has reduced all other traditions to triviality . . ."[16]

Since art could no longer be understood by the average viewer, the critic became as important—in many cases more important—than the art itself. Social critic Tom Wolfe described this process as the production of "the painted word," and wrote a book by the same title in which he explains: "Modern Art has become completely literary: the paintings and other works exist only to illustrate the text." Meaning, if there is any, is subject to the interpretation of the beholder, the critic who can foist his explanation upon a hapless public. Unlike other disciplines such as film, music, and literature, art became separated from the public, with new stars crowned and dethroned before the public even became aware of them. Unlike market-driven products, art was critic-driven, with arts publications proclaiming the trends and the fleeced benefactors gaining sanctification through their support of the latest angels. As art culture became entirely separated from the Judeo-Christian world view, it became a religion unto itself, as explained by Wolfe: "The arts have always been a doorway into Society, and in the largest cities today the arts—the museum boards, arts councils, fund drives, openings, parties, committee meetings—have completely replaced the churches in this respect."[17]

Politics and art came together in the 1960s as Wolfe has chronicled in his various books dealing with "radical chic." Unable or unwilling to find immortality through worship of God, many heirs and heiresses, corporate leaders, and other monied members of the society set placed art at the center of their spiritual lives. Sunday brunch replaced church-going, and bequests to churches gave way to windfalls for art galleries and museums. The critics became the high priests of this new secular culture, which could not be understood apart from their guidance. In addition to the satisfaction of giving to a quasi-spiritual cause, the benefactors gained something else—another way to set themselves apart from the despised middle American. By supporting whatever is trendy in art, the benefactor gains "the feeling that he may be from the middle classes but he is no longer in it . . . the feeling that he is a fellow soldier, or at least an aide-de-camp or an honorary cong guerrilla in the vanguard march through the land of the philistines. This is a peculiarly modern need and a peculiarly modern kind of salvation (from the sin of Too Much Money) and something quite common among the well-to-do all over the West, in Rome and Milan, as well as New York . . . Avant-garde art, more than any other, takes the Mammon and the Moloch out of money, puts Levi's, turtlenecks, muttonchops, and other mantles and laurels of bohemian grace upon it."[18]

During the 1950s and 1960s the Vanguard Audience crowned Dutch expatriate Willem de Kooning (1904–1997) as its star. Although de Kooning, like Picasso, was capable of producing realistic portraits and landscapes (he had spent eight years at the Rotterdam Academy of Fine Arts and Techniques), he secured his fame by painting wildly colorful and messy abstractions. Some of his most famous works were bizarre pictures of women, with eyes and breasts and hair suggesting human figures within a chaos of color. In 1974, the National Gallery of Australia paid $850,000 for *Woman V*, an oil and charcoal on canvas done in 1952–1953 that features a woman with gigantic eyes and breasts amid garish splashes of red, blue, and pink. The woman has choppy blonde hair and a cartoonish grotesquery. Describing one painting, de Kooning explained in an interview that he was very ambivalent about painting women in the first place: "I might as well stick to the idea that it's got two eyes, a nose and mouth and neck. I got to the anatomy and I felt myself almost getting flustered. I really could never get a hold of it. . . . A lot of people paint a figure because, since they're human beings themselves, they feel they ought to make another one, a substitute. I haven't got that interest at all. I really think it's sort of silly to do it. But the moment you take this attitude it's just as silly not to do it."[19]

Art historian Harry Gaugh notes that de Kooning changed his style radically in 1964, painting "frolicking, fertile muses" instead of the more somber women of his earlier works. One critic said that these "recent wenches must come across as fundamental as a belch."[20] Indeed, as Gaugh notes, "in *Woman, Sag Harbor* [oil on wood, 1964], and other figures of the 1960s—male as well as female— de Kooning vigorously exposes and probes their sexuality. Women are repeatedly opened up, legs lifted, and spread frog-fashion. Such splayed poses and well-lubricated genitalia are also features of de Kooning's sculpture."[21] So de Kooning, like Picasso, began with realism, plunged into abstraction, and wound up painting and sculpting lewd views of women's sexual organs.

To critics such as Clement Greenberg, the sheer grotesquery of much modern art qualified it to be art. "All profoundly original art looks ugly at first," Greenberg proclaimed during his campaign to promote Jackson Pollock's drip art.[22]

Likewise, critic Harold Rosenberg coined the term "Action Art" in his campaign to make de Kooning the darling of the New York art scene. "At a certain moment the canvas began to appear to one American painter after another as an arena in which to act," said Rosenberg. "What was to go on the canvas was not a picture but an event."[23]

Although many artists were still slopping out abstract expressionist art in the late 1990s, a reaction of sorts took place in the late 1950s and 1960s, when "Pop Art" was ushered in by Jasper Johns and Robert Rauschenberg, and later Andy Warhol and Roy Lichtenstein. Johns kicked off the revolt against abstraction with an exhibit in 1958 that featured paintings of American flags, alphabet letters, rows of numbers, and archery targets. Warhol painted Campbell's soup cans and giant portraits of pop icons such as Marilyn Monroe. Lichtenstein created cartoon panels complete with dialog and a campy sense of romance. As Wolfe notes, "Pop Art absolutely rejuvenated the New York art scene. It did for the galleries, the collectors, the gallery-goers, the art-minded press, and the artists' incomes about what the Beatles did for the music business at about the same time. It was the thaw! It was spring again! The press embraced Pop Art with priapic delight."[24]

By the late 1960s, Op Art and Psychedelic art reflected the influence of the drug-soaked counterculture. "Op Art" consists of hundreds or thousands of lines arranged in a pattern that force the eye to keep refocusing. "Psychedelic" art is less structured and contains distorted or exaggerated realistic elements to be distorted further by the viewer's own hallucinatory mind. Peter Max's primary-color cartoonlike posters with dizzying detail were perfect for the hallucinogenic reveries celebrated by the Beatles, the Rolling Stones, Cream, and other rock groups during the late 1960s and 1970s. And the Op Art visual mazes could keep a stoned partygoer glued to the same spot for minutes on end until another distraction came along.

Inside the official art world, "Minimalism" began making waves in the mid-sixties, with some artists dispensing with canvases altogether and hanging only frames, or placing an empty box on the floor or a pile of bricks. Museums were full of such Dada-esque stunts, giving the pop art even greater appeal by comparison.

Outside the official art world, most Americans continued to buy and display works by realists. Prints by the European impressionists or by Americans Winslow Homer, Edward Hopper, and Andrew Wyeth were and are still found in homes and offices across the nation. Norman Rockwell (1894–1978), whose brilliant illustrations for the *Saturday Evening Post* in the nineteen-thirties, forties, and fifties, became an enduring chronicle of small-town American life, was the artist that the critics hated and the people loved. In the future, when de Kooning's tortured scrawls are unearthed someday by art historians merely to track the collapse of art in the modern era, prints of Rockwell's pictures will continue to be bought and hung by the millions.

12

The Perils of
Government Sponsorship

*The way an artist is paid profoundly affects his product.
At one extreme, he sells what he has already made. At the
other, he is paid in full before he starts to make anything.
An artist in that position is relieved of the pressure to please
the public, the audience, and is free to court the approval of
an inner circle of colleagues, critics, and experts—to be self-
indulgent . . . [T]he effect of public subsidy has been to keep
art turned away from the public, instead of bringing it to
the public. It has damaged the very people it was designed
to benefit—not the least, the artist himself, or herself.*[1]

Sir Kingsley Amis

I N THE 1920S AND 1930S, Italian Marxist Antonio Gramsci urged
his fellow socialists to forsake traditional warfare and instead
"capture the culture." Gramsci meant that Marxists could
rise to power by commandeering the vital institutions that transmit
values—the arts, schools, universities, government agencies, even
the churches, and not merely use those institutions to discredit
the old values but to supplant them with new ones, based on entirely
materialistic concepts.

The way the National Endowment for the Arts (NEA) has promoted the destruction of artistic standards is proof that Gramsci's goal has at least been partially met. Another is the success of MTV (music television), pop singer-actress Madonna, and various rock and rap groups that peddle nihilism, drugs, perverse sex, and violence against women.

Since the eighteenth century, and until recently, art was more specifically defined. The term "art" for most people meant the fine arts—painting, sculpture, dance, music, and literature. Arts writer Louis Torres defines the fine arts as "the major forms of art that exist solely for the contemplation of the beholder, rather than for any utilitarian purpose."

Recently, art has been redefined to mean anything anyone wants it to mean. Often, this means making it a vehicle for a political agenda. To some, this is a natural outcome of a general drift toward tolerance and diversity and is to be applauded, encouraged, and whenever possible, sponsored by public monies.

Beginning in 1989 and continuing into the late 1990s, the principal topic of conversation in the arts has been less about artistic style than the role of government funding. There are two issues here. One, public funding, deals solely with the question of sponsorship. It is not a matter of censorship. That is the other issue, and it is far more complex.

Lovers of real art might well be leery of government sponsorship, especially on the federal level. It puts some people in the position of using tax money to tell the rest of the populace what is art and what is not. Even with the best of intentions, government sponsorship invites the specter of official art. In a federal case involving NEA regulations, U.S. District Judge John G. Davies noted the enormous power wielded by the arts agency across the market: "If an artist chooses not to be bound by the NEA's obscenity restriction, he will not be able to obtain private funding."[2] In other words, without an NEA grant, an artist won't be considered an artist.

In undemocratic countries, the state absolutely dictates artistic style. Artists who don't submit are jailed or killed. Even great artists find themselves co-opted by governments. In the Soviet Union, Dmitri Shostakovich was forced by Josef Stalin to stop creating symphonies and to compose chorale works instead, on the grounds that the communal nature of choruses better reflected Communist Party ideals. Later, the poet Yevtushenko was forced to add a stanza to his poem *Babi Yar* that falsely exonerated the Soviet Union of anti-Semitism. He had little choice, since the government was the only one paying the bills. And it had all the guns.

In America, artists are not forced to be under the government's thumb. Many of them seek government subsidy simply to get official sanction for their work. A single government dollar gives a project the stamp of approval of the United States Government, no small sponsor.

Decades before the birth of the NEA, the federal government under the New Deal sponsored artists in a variety of ways from 1933 to 1943. Thousands of musicians, actors, writers, painters, sculptors, dancers, and photographers received federal paychecks. Not surprisingly, many returned the favor by creating works that supported Franklin Roosevelt's philosophy of big government. A brochure for a 1997–1998 exhibit at the National Archives entitled "A New Deal for the Arts," describes why Roosevelt's critics found the program threatening: "Many politically active artists worked for the New Deal projects. United by a desire to use art to promote social change, these artists sympathized with the labor movement and exhibited an affinity for left-wing politics ranging from New Deal liberalism to socialism to communism. In the extreme, their art became a crude weapon aimed only at exposing capitalism's abuses and exalting the struggles of the working class."[3]

Even in a more financially stable era, artists continue to seek government sponsorship to validate their ideology, but also to raise money in the private sector. As former NEA director John Frohnmayer said, "Our grantees state unequivocally that fund-raising is substantially easier because of an Endowment grant. It is an endorsement—a mark of quality and achievement."[4]

In February 1994, at the NEA-funded Walker Art Center in Minneapolis, a performance artist named Ron Athey pushed NEA tolerance to the limit. Athey, who is HIV-positive, sliced into another man's back with a knife, soaked up the blood on towels and sent them winging over the horrified audience on clotheslines. He also had two female assistant "artists" puncture his scalp with needles, and he pierced the women's cheeks with steel spikes.[5] Asked by a reporter what she thought of the performance, NEA chairman Jane Alexander had this reply: "Not all art is for everybody . . . Americans are certainly not used to seeing bloodletting, except in films, and when it happens in person, it must be surprising . . ." Alexander noted that she understood that "all appropriate precautions" had been taken by the artist to ensure that there be no risk of HIV infection to the audience. "So what are we left with that is controversial? The sacrification [sic], the ritual-like aspect? Is it that the man is homosexual?"[6]

In short, Alexander saw nothing wrong with using tax dollars to support ritual bloodletting by a homosexual activist with the AIDS virus. And why should she? She made her agenda clear in an interview with a homosexual magazine, where she said that she intended to use the tax-funded NEA to "introduce people gently to gay themes all across the country. And I mean gently, because if you start with a kind of very overt thing, people get scared . . . You gently bring in gay people and introduce them to the world through art."[7] Besides having difficulty with the word "art," it seems Miss Alexander also might be at odds with the public concerning the definition of the word "gentle."

On a larger level, it is unlikely that the founders had this sort of thing in mind when they wrote the Constitution. Even if the

NEA did nothing but fund the best art, it would still be an abrogation of the limits on federal power contained in the Constitution. Over the years, the NEA has funded much art that would be considered by nearly everyone to be "quality" art—major symphonies, dance companies, opera, ballet, and theaters and museums all over the nation, albeit not geographically equal. The arts money goes where the artists are—New York, California, Minnesota—where the art world (artists, critics, publications, and major stages) hold sway. As relativistic modernism coursed through the art world, the taxpayer money has followed, with enough going to the "traditional" arts to create a broad-based arts constituency. Just as Franklin Roosevelt and Lyndon Johnson bought support for the welfare state by hooking the middle class on entitlements, the NEA has ensured its growth by doling out money to groups large and small in communities all over the Unites States.

When reformers have tried to reign in the NEA, they have run into resistance from the rear—Republicans who sit on the many small arts boards that have a stake in keeping the grant money flowing. The artists groups such as the American Arts Alliance make the most noise whenever the NEA gravy train is threatened with derailment, but it is the wives of political contributors who mount the most effective pressure. Many a "conservative" politician has begun bravely to bring the NEA to heel, only to be brought to earth himself by a spouse who becomes distraught at the static she receives at arts soirées. In a media-driven culture in which status is granted according to progressive tastes, many otherwise conservative folks are only too eager to participate in local arts groups as a hedge against being called philistines. Some take a real interest in art, even apart from the social aspects, such as the wine and Brie parties at new galleries or at symphony openings. Their husbands are supportive, according to one arts insider, because the men that the wives encounter are predominantly homosexual and pose no threat to the marriage. Many arts sponsors and board members have a genuine interest in art, understand it well, and do a creditable job pursuing excellence. But many, also, are cowed by the arts elite and fail to raise objections when the arts degenerate toward "the cutting edge."

Since the National Endowment for the Arts was established in 1965, it has increasingly fostered an Official Art, one that champions novelty over excellence, avant-garde, "cutting edge" works over those of traditional art forms, and the hegemony of an artistic elite whose values are, shall we put it delicately, somewhat at variance with those of most Americans who are footing the bill. As NEA Visual Arts Program Director Susan Lubowsky told the *Washington Post*, "Art is always on the cutting edge, and anything on the cutting edge is going to offend someone."[8] This means that traditional forms of art, such as representative paintings or sculpture, do not qualify as art *unless they offend.*

Webster's Third New International defines "avant-garde" as "those who create, produce, or apply new, original, or experimental ideas, designs, and techniques . . . *sometimes* such a group that is extremist, bizarre, or arty and affected."[9] The NEA seems to have taken to heart the latter part of the definition. The artist, we are told, is not truly an artist unless he is standing outside his society and slamming it. Wearing nothing but a strategically placed bullwhip, the late Robert Mapplethorpe registered his disapproval of societal norms in a photo included in an NEA-funded traveling exhibition.[10]

Actually, by "performance art" standards, Mapplethorpe may have been overdressed. In 1994, veteran NEA grant recipient Tim Miller won critical acclaim while touring NEA-funded theaters on both coasts in his "My Queer Body" revue, in which the artist stood naked before the audience describing his homosexual encounters. He climbed into the lap of a man in the audience, and finally masturbated in the finale.[11] Miller's performance art theater in California, Highways, which features acts such as lesbians fantasizing about having sex with House Speaker Newt Gingrich's mother, continued to receive NEA funding into 1995–1996. Confronted with such examples, NEA defenders are quick to point out that much "cutting edge" art in the past was rejected at first, so lighten up, folks, especially you whining taxpayers.

The idea that art has to be "cutting edge" is chronologically provincial, a fairly recent aberration. Historically, artists have striven to represent the best in their cultures. The romantic view of the artist as a heroic outsider creating his own standards began in the late nineteenth century but came to full force in the twentieth century. As critic Joseph Epstein quipped in a PBS debate over arts funding, the avant-garde is now telling Americans, "We're the cutting edge; you buy the scissors."[12]

What avant-gardists spurn as censorious strictures and hampering standards in fact have spurred production of the greatest art. Certainly it produced the greatest literature. Shakespeare was forced to conjure up Iago's description of a couple engaged in sexual intercourse as "making the beast with two backs." Today's artist does not have to be so imaginative. This is why much twentieth century art is useless, artless, and uninspired. Without strictures and standards, imagination and skills wane. The NEA should be defunded, first, because it is an unconstitutional expansion of federal power, and second, because it has worked to undermine artistic standards. If artists—and their friends on the peer review panels—are the only authorities over whether the work has value—the public be damned—then standards are flexible to the point of meaningless.

The ultimate in relativistic art standards is Dada, which is the idea that all standards must be mocked, including art. Dada is anti-art just as relativism is anti-truth. Our current Dadaists are the more bizarre performance artists, who call whatever they do art and often insist that the public pay for it. One such "artist" gained fame in California in the seventies by shooting himself in the arm with a gun. Others who operate in the spirit, if not the name, of Dada are the legions of abstract artists who are pulling a massive hoax on the gullible. When they convince some publicity-seeking heir to a great fortune to pay fifty thousand dollars for a canvas that has two or three squiggly lines on it, they are doing more than defrauding that particular buyer, who, it could be argued, is getting exactly what he wants. They are participating in a lowering of standards and fostering a general contempt for art. When a private buyer does this, it is unfortunate. When the federal government does this, it is a waste of taxpayers' money and a betrayal of taxpayers' faith in their ability to govern themselves. But there is an even greater affront than forcing taxpayers to fund bad art; it is to force them to fund art that mocks their most deeply held beliefs. Thomas Jefferson said that, "To compel a man to furnish contributions of money for the propagation of opinions which he disbelieves and abhors is sinful and tyrannical."[13]

Yet the NEA routinely funds artists whose main claim to fame is to mock religion, particularly Christianity. This makes sense for the modernist: If all ideas are relative, why should religion get any special protection, even if the Constitution says it should? As NEA Chairman Alexander told an interviewer, "It's hard to say at this point if there is *any* grant I might reject."[14] Alexander's relativistic outlook hardly seems in keeping with the NEA's mission as stated in its charter: to improve access to the arts for all Americans, to be a force for excellence, and the preservation of American heritage and cultural diversity.

By routinely denying traditional artists access to peer panel membership or grants, the NEA has affirmed the narrow concerns of a secular, modernist, often nihilistic elite. The NEA hides behind a facade of relativism but works actively to attack religion. Artworks that contain religious content are rejected for sponsorship unless they disparage religion in some way. A work affirming Christianity's foundational role in our culture is dismissed as an establishment of religion. A case in point is the NEA's turndown of sculptor Frederick Hart's project to draw designs for the facade of the National

Cathedral. Hart, who sculpted the soldiers statue at the Vietnam Veterans Memorial in Washington, D.C., was told to take a hike. "An NEA bureaucrat told me that they didn't do religious things. Separation of church and state and all that," Hart recalled.[15] He went on anyway to design and oversee the scepters, which now grace the cathedral. A stunning work of representative art, the "Creation" bas-reliefs show the universe emerging out of darkness and humanity emerging out of a muddy, swirling mass. Hart also sculpted statues of Adam, the apostle Paul, and Jesus. The total effect is an exhilarating celebration of God's love for humanity.

On the other hand, artists who specialize in mocking religion seem to have no trouble walking off with NEA grants, as do art institutions that show their works.

In June 1993, the Whitney Museum of American Art in New York, which received two hundred thousand dollars in NEA money during 1992–1993, staged "Abject Art: Repulsion and Desire in American Art." The exhibit's journal explains the focus: "Although 'abject art' is a play on 'object art,' the term does not connote an art movement so much as it describes a body of work which incorporates or suggests abject materials such as dirt, hair, excrement, dead animals, menstrual blood, and rotting food in order to confront taboo issues of gender and sexuality . . . Employing methodologies adapted from feminism, queer theory, post-structuralism, Marxism, and psychoanalysis, our goal is to talk dirty in the institution [of art] and degrade its atmosphere of purity and prudery by foregrounding issues of sexuality in the art exhibited."[16]

Included in the Whitney show were Joel-Peter Witkin's "Maquette for Crucifix," a naked Jesus Christ surrounded by sadomasochistic, obscene imagery and many grotesque corpses and body parts. Suzie Silver contributed a film entitled *A Spy*, in which Jesus is depicted as a naked woman with her breasts exposed. It was reminiscent of the Easter event in 1984 at the Episcopal cathedral of St. John the Divine in Manhattan, when a statue of "Christa" was unveiled to give the world an image of Jesus Christ as a buxom, bare-breasted goddess.

The Whitney exhibit also included the famous Andres Serrano work "Piss Christ," a photo of a crucifix in a beaker of the artist's own urine, and a film by porn star Annie Sprinkle titled, "The Sluts and Goddesses Video Workshop, or How to be a Sex Goddess in 101 Easy Steps."

During the summer of 1993, the Christian Action Network staged an exhibit on Capitol Hill that contained some of the photos from the Whitney exhibit. It caused a sensation, as several Congressmen and their staffs found themselves gazing at photos of corpses in sexual situations, a severed head kissing itself, and a man being lifted by his testicles, which were tied to a weight held over this head. Created by Joel-Peter Witkin, who had received four previous fellowship grants from the NEA, the "artworks" were cited by NEA reformers in a failed effort to defund the agency.

Other anti-Christian artists funded by NEA include the late David Wojnarowicz, who took photos of men engaged in homosexual acts. An essay in one of his exhibits described New York's Cardinal John O'Connor as "a fat cannibal from that house of walking swastikas up on Fifth avenue," and "a creep in black skirts."[17]

In 1990, the NEA gave twenty thousand dollars to an arts festival in Lewiston, New York, that planned to hold a "Bible Burn" put on by Survival Research Lab (SRL). The group said it would "create large sexually explicit props covered with a generous layer of requisitioned Bibles. After employing these props in a wide variety of unholy rituals, SRL machines will burn them to ashes."[18] A public protest caused cancellation of the exhibit, triggering a lawsuit by SRL against the event's sponsors.[19]

In 1987, NEA and the New York State Council on the Arts gave grants to the Franklin Furnace Theatre to help fund performances by Cheri Gaulke. In *Virgin* and other shows, Gaulke used her naked body to "explore female sexuality in relation to religion, myth, fashion, and eroticism in a partly Christian worship service, part pagan ritual."[20] The trend toward using Christian imagery in celebrations of Dionysian excess was mirrored in the popular culture in the work of the rock star Prince, who writhes in erotic dance while flashing around a Christian cross, and rock singer Madonna, who has a statue of a saint come to life to make love to her in a church setting in the video *Like a Prayer.* There is nothing new about this, of course. The unleashing of sexual excess in the name of religion dates back to Dionysos as well as to fertility rites in primitive cultures around the world. What is new is the mainstreaming of hedonistic sacrilege in America through popular art and government-funded NEA grants.

Appalled by NEA's excesses, Congress adopted language in 1989 instructing the NEA, in very detailed description, to refrain from funding works that most people would judge to be obscene, things such as child pornography, explicit sex, and overtly blasphemous works. To facilitate this, NEA Chairman John Frohnmayer instituted a policy requiring grant recipients to sign a pledge not to produce such works using the public dole. In no way did this usurp the artists' First Amendment rights, since none of them has a constitutional right to taxpayers' money. Of course, grant recipients, not used to any oversight, screamed like stuck pigs. How dare the lumpen proletariat taxpayers demand accountability? How dare the keepers of the public purse make any demands at all on the recipients of the largesse?

In 1989, Senator Jesse Helms (R-NC) suggested a standard that is constitutionally sound and would actually curb some of the worst of NEA's excesses. The Helms Amendment was taken from the Federal Communications Commission's definition of indecency which was declared constitutional by the Supreme Court in *FCC v. Pacifica* in 1978. The amendment bans federal funding for "patently offensive" depictions of sexual organs, sexual acts, and excrement. Together with the *Rust v. Sullivan* decision in which the Supreme

Court ruled that the government may establish standards on how federal funds are used, the Helms Amendment was a reasonable way to rein in NEA. But nothing appeared to have helped. The NEA continued to fund performance theaters in New York and California that specialize in explicit, offensive-by-design productions by radical activists, even after the November 1994 "GOP Revolution," when a conservative social agenda propelled the Republican Party into the majority in Congress. In 1995, Congress voted to give the NEA funding through 1997, after which the agency, which had had no authorizing legislation since 1990, was to expire.

In 1997, a battle royale raged between NEA defenders and the Congressmen who were trying to keep the deal by pulling the plug. Although the House Appropriations Committee voted to cut the NEA's budget to ten million dollars to pay for closing costs, few in Washington thought that it was time to play taps over the NEA's grave. They were right. The Senate, and then the full Congress, restored nearly one hundred million dollars in funding to save the NEA for another year.

The government funding issue will not go away, however. The Smithsonian museums have come under attack for posting politically correct "explanations" of time-tested exhibits. And as for censorship, that is an unending battle in an Age of Consent culture that has embraced relativism. The argument will always be heard: *Whose* standards will prevail?

Some of the late Robert Mapplethorpe's works easily qualify as being obscene under the Supreme Court's definitions. They are explicit, pornographic works that shock and scandalize all but the most jaded. Yet a jury in Cincinnati failed to convict on obscenity charges a museum director who displayed the Mapplethorpe works, including the famous photo of the artist naked with a bullwhip up his posterior. Jurors polled after the trial overwhelmingly said they personally felt the works were obscene, but that "art experts" who testified at the trial said it was really art, so who were they to question?

People have become so unsure of their own moral acumen that they trust the opinion of an "expert" over the evidence seen by their own eyes. A relativistic moral climate has created a citizenry that is terrified to be seen as out of step with the modern age.

Drawn by the enormous amount of publicity generated by the exhibit, thousands of people lined up at the museum to see the show. This was less a testament to Mapplethorpe than a tribute to the Yankee character, which might be summarized by the statement, "What? Somebody is telling me I can't see something? I don't care what it is, I am going!" This type of reaction poses a dilemma for those genuinely hurt and offended by public presentations of objectionable works. If they protest, they draw attention to the project. If they meekly pass up the opportunity to protest, they tacitly condone it. Setting the limits on expression is an extremely difficult business, and it is a debate that will never be resolved. Since the government wields enormous force (actually, it has a monopoly on force), it should be kept out of the art business.

As to access to art, whether it be mass media or single works, different standards should apply. The airwaves and the Internet can be accessed by anybody. An adult book store can bar anyone under the age of consent. Reasonable distinctions can be made. But communities should have the right to protect their moral climates. Private actions such as boycotts or picketing or sheer consumer rejection are useful, but local ordinances have a role, too. Not every community has to be like every other community. If one community wants to permit massage parlors to exist between residential homes, people who disapprove of this should have the option to move to one that does not allow it. Otherwise, if anything goes, the pornographer gets to set the standards for the entire community. In the name of individual rights, one individual could trump the rights of many other individuals. Civil rights are almost always a question of one right over another. Rarely are they starkly wrong versus right, but the triumph of one person's rights over that of another. There is one area that should be beyond debate, and that is the protection of children from exploitation. Child pornography or exposure of children to pornography should not be tolerated in any form. Children are vulnerable, cannot give meaningful consent, and may be scarred for life by an early sexual experience. Even hard-core libertarians usually agree at least on this point, if only on the technical grounds that granting children unwarranted competency would hurt the concept of contracts, which are the soul of private property.

Finally, the "censorship" debate can take on political dimensions far beyond the intrinsic worth of a particular piece of art.

In 1993, an exhibition called "Degenerate Art" was held in Los Angeles and then in Washington, D.C., and Chicago. Consisting entirely of works banned by the Nazis, the exhibit seemed timed to help critics make the connection between Adolf Hitler and current critics of the national Endowment for the Arts. The idea is that anyone who criticizes federal arts subsidies is similar to Adolf Hitler, who banned innovative art and established an official style consisting of socialist realism. Anything Hitler disliked must be great art. And Hitler hated modern art. This is the flip side of "guilt by association." We might call it "merit by disassociation."

In 1937, Hitler ordered that modern art be confiscated from museums all over Germany. Eventually, sixteen thousand artworks were rounded up, with 650 being exhibited in "*Entartete Kunst,*" or "Degenerate Art." The traveling show drew more than three million viewers around Germany. Journalist William Shirer recalls trying to get into a showing that had a line reaching out into the street. Embarrassed because the exhibit was outdrawing the "official" show of Nazi-approved works at the House of German Art, the propaganda minister, Paul Joseph Goebbels, ordered it closed.[21]

With a 175,000-dollar grant from the National Endowment for the Arts and another 350,000 dollars from the National Endowment for the Humanities, plus some German money, the

American exhibitors managed to retrieve 175 of the banned works for "Degenerate Art: The Fate of the Avant-Garde in Nazi Germany," which first ran at the Los Angeles County Museum of Art.[22] Amid the lesser-known works were some genuine historically significant paintings, such as Marc Chagall's *Purim*, Max Beckmann's *Descent from the Cross*, George Grosz's *Metropolis*, and some works by Bauhaus alumni Paul Klee and Wassily Kandinsky.

The idea of government rounding up art simply because it does not like it (apart from truly obscene art) is sobering and scary. In that regard, the exhibitors did everyone a favor by reminding us of the dangers of unbridled state power. In assessing the exhibit, however, the critics generally missed two striking aspects: the socialist realism that Hitler championed is nearly identical to the art that Stalin imposed on the Soviet Union during the same period, illustrating that the socialist totalitarianism in communism and national socialism spring from the same root. The second point is that most of the art that Hitler banned was not so much sensationally offensive but was merely bad art, poorly executed, and ugly. As the art world, like the rest of German society in the 1920s, slid into decadence, it was no wonder that Hitler could clamp down on the "degenerates" without fear of offending the German people. Excess led to an excess of reactionary order.

Before Hitler's crackdown, Germany was the center of Europe's most decadent art, film, and theater. The Weimar Republic had the least restrictive censorship laws on the continent. As historian Paul Johnson notes (and as the 1972 movie *Cabaret* so evocatively showed), "Stage and nightclub shows in Berlin were the least inhibited of any major capital. Plays, novels, and even paintings touched on such themes as homosexuality, sadomasochism, transvestism, and incest . . . In the *Weltbuhne*, the smartest and most telling of the new journals, sexual freedom and pacifism were exalted, the army, the state, the university, the Church and, above all, the comfortable, industrious middle classes, were savaged and ridiculed."[23]

One reason Hitler was able to turn so much wrath on Germany's hapless Jewish minority is because they became identified with so much that was wrong with German culture. Jews happened to own the most influential art galleries and "were dominant in light entertainment and still more in theatre criticism . . . In every department of the arts, be it architecture, sculpture, painting, or music, where change had been most sudden and repugnant to conservative tastes, Jews had been active in the transformation, though rarely in control," writes Paul Johnson in *Modern Times*.[24]

Hitler's mass appeal was his plan to restore greatness of all kinds to Germany in the aftermath of the humiliation of World War 1 and the Versailles treaty. And he needed a scapegoat class as a steppingstone to his agenda. Whereas Christianity sees Satan as the author of evil, Johnson notes, "modern secular faiths needed human devils, and whole categories of them. The enemy, to be plausible, had to be an entire class or race."[25]

Hitler was a dictator (and a painter himself) with questionable taste in art, but the flip side of his arts crackdown was a false respect for "degenerate" art in the West—again, the "merit by disassociation" syndrome. Because Hitler had banned it, the left-wing arts establishment automatically embraced it. In many ways, we are still stuck with it.

The same thing occurred in architecture, when the Bauhaus, Germany's school of modernist architecture, was shut down by the Nazis. Fleeing to America, the communist-oriented architects quickly became the darlings of the critics, creating a politically correct architecture. Out went classical design, and in came the relativistic modernism that turned buildings into boxes.

13

Boxing Up the Art of Architecture

> *Every new $900,000 summer house in the north woods of Michigan or on the shore of Long Island has so many pipe railings, ramps, hob-tread metal spiral stairways, sheets of industrial plate glass, banks of tungsten-halogen lamps, and white cylindrical shapes, it looks like an insecticide refinery. I once saw the owners of such a place driven to the edge of sensory deprivation by the whiteness & lightness & leanness & and bareness & spareness of it all. They became desperate for an antidote, such as coziness and color.*
>
> Tom Wolfe

IN 1919, architect Walter Gropius opened the Bauhaus School in Weimar, the capital of post World War I Germany. As Tom Wolfe notes, "It was more than a school; it was a commune, a spiritual movement, a radical approach to art in all its forms, a philosophical center comparable to the Gardens of Epicurus."[1]

The seminal idea of the International School as championed by Bauhaus architects in the first decades of the twentieth century was the socialist doctrine of smashing all traditions and leveling all social distinctions. The movement's founding manifesto, penned by Gropius for the Workers Council for Art, proclaimed: "Together let us desire, conceive, and create the new structure of the future, which will embrace architecture and sculpture and painting in one unity which will one day rise toward heaven from the hands of a million workers like the crystal symbol of a new faith."[2]

Bauhaus architects tried out their ideas on massive housing projects commissioned by the German government in the wake of World War 1. Subsequent buildings were deliberately made to resemble "German worker housing," to destroy the distinctions between the rich and poor and to incorporate a spirit of modernism derived from replication of technology into design. Gropius and the other modernists believed that each architectural movement needed to be rooted in the ethos of the culture in which it takes root. In the early twentieth century, the industrial revolution was giving way to the technological revolution. Thus, buildings should reflect technology: streamlined, geometric shapes, colorlessness, and metallic, glass, cement, and plastic surfaces. Many Bauhaus designs were starkly geometric, utilizing white, black, tan, and gray.

The driving philosophy behind Bauhaus was "functionalism," which is the belief that if things are designed specifically to meet a purpose, then beauty will emerge as a result. Or maybe not. It doesn't really matter, since function is supreme. But there is a more fundamental reason that function was emphasized over form; comparatively beautiful forms created distinctions between the social classes. The rich could afford better-looking buildings than the poor. Hence the Internationalists dictated that all buildings had to have a uniform look of utility. Out went archways, curves, cornices, gables, peaked roofs, decorative art, and other classical forms that make buildings interesting. In came glass and steel boxes with flat roofs and no distinguishing characteristics other than a decided coldness and functional appearance.

Like other socialists, Gropius wanted to create something entirely new—New Art for the New Man. That meant consciously rejecting what had come before. This hostility to tradition was, in Gropius's words, "starting from zero." And it was inspired by an announced solidarity with the oppressed masses whom the socialists would deliver from the capitalists. A group of left-wing German artists called the Novembergruppe put out this manifesto in 1919: "Painters, Architects, Sculptors, you whom the bourgeoise pays with high rewards for your work—out of vanity, snobbery, and boredom—Hear! To this money there clings the sweat and blood and nervous energy of thousands of poor hounded beings—Hear! It is an unclean profit . . . [W]e must be true socialists—we must kindle the highest socialist virtue: the brotherhood of man."[3]

Eventually driven out of Weimar, Gropius designed a permanent home for the Bauhaus in Dessau—Germany's most avant-garde city. Built in 1923, the series of interconnecting boxes became the prototype for countless nondescript buildings to follow. In 1932, the Bauhaus was moved to Berlin, where it finally was shut down by the Nazis in 1934. Gropius fled first to London and then took a chair at Harvard. Modernist architect Ludwig Mies van der Rohe, who had been appointed director of the Bauhaus in 1930, kept it afloat for a few years by fending off attacks from the communists and Nazis, both of whom accused him of toadying to the other. Mies himself was nearly apolitical, with his modernist vision serving as his religion. "I don't care whether the man who mixes cement is a Nazi or a communist," Mies said often. "I'm just interested in whether or not he makes good cement."[4]

Humiliated by Hitler's constant rejection of his work and having closed the Bauhaus in 1933, Mies left Germany in 1937 and accepted a new post as head of the Armour Institute architectural school in Chicago in 1938. From this perch, like Gropius at Harvard, he influenced two generations of architects in the modernist style. It was in the United States that modernism seemed to take shape, timelessly, out of sheer intellectual force. Historian Elaine Hochman comments: "Mies freely admitted his indebtedness to nineteenth century German neoclassicism, a style that also influenced Albert Speer and Hitler, the latter implacably opposed to modernism. Transposed to foreign shores, where this stern, indigenous tradition did not exist, the notion of modernism became severed from its cultural, philosophical, and stylistic roots, and its most notable émigré proponents, such as Mies and Gropius, anxious to minimize their Germanic roots, came to assert the style's independence from tradition and context."[5]

Like many modernists, Mies worshipped art above all. He married a socialite, Ada Bruhn, in 1913 and had three daughters, but he abandoned them all within five years. In 1948, two of his daughters managed to obtain visas so they could visit him in Chicago. When they showed up, the staff was stunned; Mies had never mentioned that he had a family.[6]

During its short but influential reign, the Bauhaus attracted the cream of modernist Europe, with artists such as Paul Klee giving lectures while architects like Mies designed glass and steel boxes that came to dominate modern architecture. Meanwhile, in France, Edouard Jeanneret of Switzerland, who affected the pseudonym Le Corbusier, formulated his ultramodern "Citrohan" model for houses, which he called "machines for living." In 1927, Gropius, Mies, Le Corbusier, and other avant-garde architects came together in Stuttgart, Germany, to put together an exhibition of "worker housing." The result became the dominant force of architecture for the next several decades.

Worker housing was intentionally spare to simulate the conditions that workers faced at factories. It was the perfect "cage" in which to place the human subjects, who, ratlike, became the fodder for socialist experiments in reordering society. As Tom Wolfe explains, the units had "flat roofs, with no cornices, sheer walls, with no window architraves or raised lintels, no capitals or pediments, no colors, just the compound shades, white, beige, gray, and black.

The interiors had no crowns or coronets, either. They had pure white rooms, stripped, purged, liberated, freed of all casings, cornices, covings, crown moldings (to say the least!), pilasters, and even the ogee edges on tabletops and the beading on drawers. They had open floor plans, ending the old individualistic, bourgeoise obsession with privacy."[7] Out, too, were wallpaper, drapes, and warm, wooden features. The floors were cold linoleum in blacks and grays. Furniture consisted of International style tubular steel and straight, figure-resistant structures that no one could sit in for long without discomfort.

The workers themselves complained bitterly of the inhumane boxes, but that was only because, in the words of Le Corbusier, they were not yet "reeducated," or in the words of Gropius, the workers were "intellectually undeveloped." No matter. The worker-loving socialist architects would help free the people from exploitation, including their own tendencies to cling to older, more comfortable modes of living. Part of the problem with the new housing was that it was constructed rapidly and was often very shoddy. In the eyes of many Germans, modernism became associated with the cheap and shabby.

Meanwhile, in America, Frank Lloyd Wright (1869-1959) had been building form-oriented houses for three decades. Wright differed from the Bauhaus modernists in that he sought to emphasize the interiors, making them pleasing to his clients. Pioneering his concept of "organic architecture," Wright's houses were designed with the idea that the form would grow out of people's needs and the character of the surrounding countryside. Wright-designed dwellings were built to take advantage of the natural environment, whether it was hills or near water. This was in contrast to the Bauhaus set, who built not to complement nature but triumph over it. Wherever they sprang up, stark Bauhaus buildings stuck out like a sore thumb—precisely the intended effect. Since man was the measure of all things, why should man subordinate his will to the natural world made by a creator God, who existed only in the imaginations of the unenlightened anyway? The relativistic subjectivism that is at the heart of all man-centered philosophies begins by doing away with God, then inventing one. In architecture, Gropius served that function, as hordes of young designers bent their will to his.

Ironically, while Bauhaus collectivists were churning out designs to minimize tradition, an ideological opponent, the Russian émigré writer Ayn Rand, was writing a towering work of fiction that challenged socialism head-on: *The Fountainhead.* Published in 1943, *The Fountainhead* is the story of architect Howard Roark, who devotes himself solely to his own vision, undaunted by the collectivist politics around him. In Russia, Rand had seen totalitarianism close up, and she bitterly opposed any claim by anyone else to a person's work or imagination. As the New Deal took shape and America was transformed into a social welfare state, Rand provided a powerful counterpoint of individualism among intellectuals. The problem was that her vanity—the original sin—knew no bounds. She embraced the Bauhaus's modernist philosophy, railing against architecture that retained classical elements, and criticized the idea of an architect submitting his craft to the whims of a patron. The true artist, she said, is the one who creates solely for himself, independent of the expectations of others. This mirrored the attitude of Mies, who contended that clients should be treated as "children."

Rand's Objectivist philosophy was a relativistic theory of the sacred Self, combined with a virulent dislike of religion. Employing the latest Freudian nomenclature, she promoted the romantic notion of the lone visionary. Speaking through Roark, she declares: "The first right on earth is the right of the ego. Man's first duty is to himself. His moral law is never to place his prime goal within the persons of others . . . The savage's whole existence is public, ruled by the laws of his tribe. Civilization is the process of setting man free from man."[8]

After getting expelled from a design institute, Roark explains to the dean why he could never include elements from any other work in his: "The Parthenon did not serve the same purpose as its wooden ancestor. An airline terminal does not serve the same purpose as the Parthenon. Every form has its own meaning. Every man creates his meaning and form and goal. Why is it so important, what others have done?"[9]

When the dean tells Roark that successful architects take the wishes of their clients into account, Roark finds this contemptible: "Well, I could say that I must aspire to build for my client the most comfortable, the most logical, the most beautiful house that can be built. I could say that I must try to sell him the best I have and also teach him to know the best. I could say it, but I won't. Because I don't intend to build in order to serve or help anyone. I don't intend to build in order to have clients. I intend to have clients in order to build."[10]

In an introduction to a new issue of her book twenty-five years after its first publication, Rand quotes Nietzsche, rejecting his "psychological determinism" but accepting his emotional end-goal as an individual's quest for "an inner state of exalted self-esteem . . . I would identify the sense of life dramatized in *The Fountainhead* as *man-worship*."[11] In her contempt for Judaism and Christianity and her embrace of an atheistic, man-centered religion of her own making, Rand had much in common with the socialists with whom she did intellectual battle. The relativistic (and therefore constantly changing) modern notion of man as the sole maker of his own fate was preached every day in the Bauhaus, whose communist leanings finally drew the attention of the National Socialists. Though they sprang from the same socialist roots, the Nazis and communists were blood enemies. The Nazis embraced nationalism and an occultic rebirth of Germany's pagan past, while the communists sought an international revolution based on Marx's "scientific socialism." Both saw the State as the unchallenged authority, rejecting the American notion of limited government.

In America, Gropius helped spread socialistic philosophy through his leadership of the school of architecture at Harvard; Lazlo Moholy-Nagy (1895-1946), his Hungarian colleague, founded the New Bauhaus, which became the Chicago Institute of Design; Joseph Albers, a German artist, opened a rural version of the Bauhaus at Black Mountain College in North Carolina; at Chicago's Armour Institute, Mies designed the entire campus of the Illinois Institute of Technology. In the rush to embrace the immigrants, Frank Lloyd Wright was unceremoniously cast aside, becoming a sort of architect emeritus even though he had many productive years ahead of him.

Another influential American designer, Buckminster Fuller also had less than warm relations with the expatriate modernists. Few of them adopted his geodesic dome (which, like the flat roofs, tended to leak) in any of their designs, and they were not sure what to make of this man who dabbled in an array of interrelated disciplines. As Wolfe remarks, "It was hard to tell whether he was an architect, an engineer, a guru, or simply that species of nut known all around the world: *the inventor*."[12]

Under the influence of the Bauhaus socialists, the American Left conjured a romantic vision of Nazism as consummate evil, with communism, or something close, as the benign alternative. The "German invasion" of left-leaning partisans helped instill the false ideological dichotomy of Nazism at one end of an ideological scale, with communism at the other. But the true scale has anarchy (total lawlessness) at one end, with totalitarianism at the other. Both Nazism and communism would be at the far left end, with American-style limited government somewhere near the right side of the middle.

Bauhausers helped confuse further an already credulous American academia, but their greatest impact was on the nation's skylines. Under their tutelage, city after city, beginning with New York and Chicago, swept aside older buildings to make room for the glass boxes. Where ornately decorated brick and bronze facades once marked the downtowns, built by thousands of skilled artisans, a new cityscape arose, made of giant rectangular high-rises of concrete, steel, and glass. The spirit of classless, German-worker housing had triumphed, pushing aside hundreds of years of organic city growth. The process was accelerated by "urban renewal," in which entire neighborhoods were bulldozed to make way for public housing projects so ugly that their passing was not exactly mourned when the residents destroyed them. As for the high-rent downtowns, the haunts of the elites became desolate landscapes peppered with Bauhaus-cold office buildings. The irony is that some of the new buildings, which were supposed to be severely functional, did not even live up to that. Flat roofs leak, and yet the Internationalists insisted on the inclusion of flat roofs regardless of climate. As any homeowner in a northern climate can tell you, flat roofs make no sense with a couple of feet of snow on them. At Harkness Commons, which Walter Gropius designed for Harvard University, stalactites formed on the concrete overhangs shortly after construction.

Everywhere, in the most incongruous environments, the Bauhaus diaspora penetrated with shocking effect. In Paris, towers of glass and steel arose as "edge cities," clashing with the older, elegant Parisian cityscape. The French, mindful of their heritage, at least managed to put some distance between the modern boxes and the Louvre, the old Opera House, and the rest of the ancient city. When the Eiffel Tower was erected for the Paris exposition of 1889, it changed the skyline of Paris forever. Even though most Frenchmen have come to accept it, they have not been noticeably keen on having any more oversized monoliths looming over their City of Lights.

Bauhaus made its impact precisely where the buildings were most glaringly out of place. In fact, the more incompatible the locale, the better. Wellesley College in Wellesley, Massachusetts, boasts one of the prettiest campuses in the United States. Built on rolling hills, the ivy-covered brick halls seem like an idyllic archetype for what most people think of as a college campus. But an observer could be left speechless when, rounding a small hill, he spies a monstrosity of concrete and glass with outside stairways and industrial railings smack in the middle of this bucolic setting. The spectacularly ugly Bauhaus-inspired science building accomplishes all that a shock artist could hope for. It looks so out of place that it must be acknowledged, much as a child's tantrum is unavoidably obvious during a classical concert. Perhaps the overseers of Wellesley were persuaded that they needed to be among the vanguard of progressive architecture to show that they were in the vanguard of progressive thought in general. As a fountainhead of radical feminism and lesbian politics in the 1990s, Wellesley is not likely to soon lose its progressive reputation.

At Yale University, Bauhaus adherent Louis Kahn was tapped in 1953 to design an addition to the elegant, Italian Romanesque art gallery, originally built in 1928 by Yale architect Egerton Swartout. Kahn's addition shocked the Yale community, even though it was already accustomed to the Bauhaus invasion. Tacked onto the side of the older building was a flat box with tiny beige bricks and four narrow bands of concrete at ten-foot intervals. "In the gallery's main public space the ceiling was made of gray concrete tetrahedra, fully exposed. This gave the interior the look of an underground parking garage."[13]

Although most average Americans looked aghast on such "innovation," they were not personally subjected to the worst of the Bauhaus influence. They did wind up working in offices in the giant glass boxes and sent their children to school in long, flat industrial-looking factories. But middle-class dwellings, at least, retained many classical features that worked aesthetically as well as functionally, such as peaked roofs. It was the very rich and the very poor who took the brunt of the Bauhaus invasion, the rich by choice and the poor by default.

In 1951, Mies completed the Farnsworth House in Illinois, a square, white structure of plate glass and steel. *Architectural Forum* hailed it as "a concentration of pure beauty, a distillation of pure spirit."[14] The only problem was that the house had no working windows, making it unlivable. The home's disenchanted owner sued Mies.

As with art, architectural patrons could buy demonstrations of their progressive views, but on a much larger scale. An eyesore painting could be viewed by only a few people in a home or gallery, but an entire building foisted this modern conceit on all who passed by. That takes a lot of money, of course, and so the Bauhaus looked to America's monied class to project their vision. They found willing clients in people like the Rockefellers and the Goodyears, who helped commission the boxlike Museum of Modern Art in New York, which opened in 1929. Soon, boxes began sprouting in other places around town. In 1958, the Seagram Building, a thirty-eight-story box of glass and steel designed by Mies van der Rohe took the International School to new heights on Park Avenue. His assistant on the project was American architect Philip Johnson, who designed countless Bauhaus-style buildings for several decades before breaking with the box-format in his famous drawings of the proposed AT&T building in the late 1970s. Built in the early 1980s, the AT&T building has a gothic arch and columns at the bottom and, most un-Bauhaus of all, a Chippendale nook at the very top. Given that Bauhaus requires strict adherence to spare, functional forms, the eye-catching nook was a major rebuke and a throwback to the age of conspicuous decoration. The Johnson apostasy triggered more American innovations.

Even before Johnson made his break, a handful of Americans designed buildings that restored imagination and beauty to the urban landscape. In the mid-1960s, a Philadelphia architect, Robert Venturi, wrote essays and books that called for, essentially, the overthrow of modernist asceticism. *Complexity and Contradiction in Architecture* (1966) opened the floodgates for criticism of the International style and freed architects to, once again, borrow freely from the past and to incorporate different styles in single projects.[15]

"Architects can no longer afford to be intimidated by the puritanically moral language of orthodox Modern architecture,"[16] Venturi proclaimed. He praised the much-despised "Main Street" concept of buildings that appealed to ordinary people and began designing buildings that included "ironic references," such as the giant gold-colored television antenna he set atop The Guild House, an apartment complex built in Philadelphia in 1963. By making sure that everyone knew he was only joking, Venturi managed to stay within the modernist vein while systematically undermining it.

In 1964, the Huntington Hartford Gallery of Modern Art, designed by former Bauhaus adherent Edward Durrell Stone, was built in New York. An elegant, angular structure with deliberately ornamental elements, the building annoyed the establishment critics. As Tom Wolfe relates, Stone was so savaged that he took to defending his building by saying things such as "Every taxi driver in New York will tell you it's his favorite building!" He might as well have said that the drivers also appreciated Norman Rockwell, for all the good it did him in critical circles.

Another breach in the Bauhaus line was the TWA terminal at New York's Idlewild Airport (now Kennedy International). Built in 1956, the design by Eero Saarinen incorporates the usual elements of glass, steel, and concrete, but its elegant roof line suggests the form of an eagle. Airport visitors found themselves saying, "Hey! Here is something new and modern that I actually like!" It must have annoyed the Bauhaus disciples every time they flew in or out of the airport. Or when they flew to the nation's capital. Saarinen, who drafted the plan for St. Louis's Gateway Arch, also designed the Dulles Airport terminal, which has a long, sweeping wing as its ceiling, supported by pagoda-like columns. Decades later, it is still one of the most striking buildings in America. A major expansion in the late 1990s incorporated and expanded Saarinen's design.

In the 1980s and 1990s, American architects outside academia began to break out of the International School in droves and to include neoclassical elements in "post-modern" buildings. Out went the boxes and in came triangles, arches, domes, trompe l'oeil ("fool the eye" illusions), and other forms that make architecture interesting. Architects like Johnson began combining the best of the modern (clarity of line and simplicity) with classical forms to create a neoclassical school.

Aesthetics returned with a fury, as shopping centers abandoned the strip look and began to take on the appearance of small villages or villas, complete with nooks and crannies and decorative art, some of it even representational. Horton Plaza in San Diego, taking advantage of a perfect climate, conveys an indoor-outdoor ambiance with overhangs, cornices, circular stairways, arches, turrets, pastel colors, and flags. Built in the early 1980s, the multistory shopping center's sheer size is minimized by the feeling of being in the winding streets of a Mediterranean village. Elsewhere in San Diego, as in Hartford, Connecticut, playful architecture abounds, with huge slanted roofs, graduated sidings and giant geometric shapes. One hundred miles north of San Diego in Costa Mesa, the Orange County Performing Arts Center (1988) rises out of a former lima bean field, stealing the show from surrounding glass boxes with its giant classical arch.

Not all communities have been as fortunate. Many contain nondescript high-rises and concrete canyons that are anything but inviting. In Rosslyn, Virginia, directly across the Potomac River from Washington, D.C., a series of boxy Bauhaus high-rises is relieved only by the USA Today building, a giant, blue-glass high-rise curved like the bow of a ship. With auto-clogged streets and few shops, Rosslyn's downtown is accessible mainly by skywalks between buildings. The steel-glass-concrete coldness is inescapable. Office dwellers can escape over the river to historic Georgetown, which maintains much of its pre-modern charm. Even recently erected buildings in Georgetown reflect a conscious effort to keep things in a historical perspective. Unlike Rosslyn, Georgetown's office complexes blend in with an older architecture that invites strolling and window shopping. From a distance, Rosslyn has a striking, typically urban skyline that is almost identical to those of countless mid-sized cities. The idea seems to be that because it is so close to Washington, it doesn't need to be pretty. You can always look over the river at the monuments. But at certain times, such as sunset, Rosslyn *is* pretty to look at, with its glass boxes sending shimmering reflections of gold and red into the Potomac. The lamplit Francis Scott Key Bridge, loaded with Virginia-bound commuters and their red taillights, leads the viewer's gaze up into an Oz-like skyline. Like many urban monstrosities, Rosslyn's glass and concrete canyons are better appreciated from a distance.

In Cleveland, which has suffered from an undeserved moniker as "the mistake on the lake," the Rock 'n' roll Hall of Fame, designed by Bauhaus believer I. M. Pei, opened in 1995. In addition to trying to attract tourists, perhaps Cleveland's city fathers have an alternative motive for hosting the rockers. In the future, the "mistake on the lake" could refer specifically to the Rock 'n' roll Hall of Fame instead of the entire city. The whole thing may be a clever way to shift the ignominy, like a sacrifice to the ancient gods of taste.

The ninety-two million dollar metal and glass pyramid faces the shore of Lake Erie, yet provides no views of either the lake or the skyline of downtown Cleveland. Instead, the focus is on a nondescript street and a railroad track. Inside, the museum glorifies rock 'n' roll as if the nation were done a cultural favor by rock's emergence as the dominant beat in every aspect of our lives. It is played in supermarkets, elevators, dentists' offices, and it provides the musical backdrop for television and movies. The rock 'n' roll generation has imposed its impoverished music on an entire nation, all the while complaining that it doesn't get enough respect.

Critic E. Michael Jones attended the opening of the museum and found it to be "a sort of quasi-Egyptian monument to dead drug addicts." He notes that the ultra-slick Bauhaus-style of the building is at first glance incongruent with the ragged vulgarities of rock 'n' roll. But he decided that it is appropriate after all because "Pei's architecture gave expression to the real message of modernity, which was, 'We have technology; we don't need restraint'... Modernity always felt it could unleash primeval forces of this sort and then control them with technology."[17] The nation's addiction to drugs of all kinds is one manifestation of this quick-fix tendency. Government-sponsored needle and condom distribution is another.

Iconoclasts are after much more than altering their worlds of art, architecture, science, literature, politics, or economics; they are or have been working to overthrow morality itself to usher in an Age of Consent that is indifferent to sex outside marriage and, more generally, indifferent to whether men will be cads. In a world of anonymous high-rise boxes and abstract art, morality-free literature, and widespread pornography, it is easier for men to hide their wicked ways. Since art reflects life, it is appropriate that a "Culture of Death" that is comfortable with abortion and increasingly fascinated by euthanasia is saddled with lifeless buildings and lifeless art. Has anyone noticed how much those Bauhaus high-rises resemble tombstones?

14

Music: Roll Over, Apollo

*About the only thing to do on the Rock of Gibraltar was to
go up to where the famous monkeys were and watch them
at play. So that's what we decided to do. And when the
monkeys came and clustered around us, Brian decided to
play them his music. He turned on the tape recorder and
after a few bars the monkeys, with a collective shriek, ran
pell-mell away, tearing off into the distance. Brian took it
as a terrible rejection. He screamed at the monkeys, trying
to get them to come back, and then when they wouldn't, he
began to revile them in terrible language . . . A kind of
madness, shouting, "The monkeys don't like my music!"*[1]

Marianne Faithfull, recalling the late
Rolling Stones guitarist Brian Jones

THE 1984 MOVIE *Footloose* has a very catchy soundtrack and
a typical Hollywood "youth" theme; the kids are not
understood by their bewildered parents, but the elders
eventually see the light courtesy of their progressive offspring.

What sets *Footloose* apart from other films of this genre is the backhanded respect that it shows religion; even the new kid in town, played by Kevin Bacon, who becomes a sort of clean-cut town rebel, attends church with his mom. And there is a key scene in which the central adult figure, the pastor of the town church, played by John Lithgow, is listening to Bach while writing a sermon. His daughter (Lori Singer) has been campaigning to end the town's ban on dancing, a stricture initiated and sustained by her father's tyrannical influence.

Dad thinks, with plenty of justification, that rock 'n' roll is the devil's music. But he had gone overboard by forbidding dancing via the town council. As it turns out, he went off the deep end because of a terrible tragedy for which he feels responsible. He gets over this by the end of the film, after the rebel quotes a bunch of Bible verses about dancing that the pastor's daughter finds for him. (Who says the devil can't quote Scripture?)

Anyway, the daughter comes in and asks Dad why he doesn't find his own classical music sinful, and he replies that it uplifts the soul because it is harmonious and brilliantly structured. This music appeals to the spirit, he says, unlike other varieties, which bruise the soul by miring it in animalistic urges. This is basically what Allan Bloom said in his famous passages on the dangers of rock 'n' roll in *Closing of the American Mind:*

> But rock music has one appeal only, a barbaric appeal, to sexual desire—not love, not *eros*, but sexual desire undeveloped and untutored. It acknowledges the first emanations of children's emerging sensuality and addresses them seriously, eliciting them and legitimating them, not as little sprouts that must be carefully tended in order to grow into gorgeous flowers, but as the real thing. Rock gives children, on a silver platter, with all the public authority of the entertainment industry, everything their parents always used to tell them they had to wait for until they grew up and would understand later.[2]

While rock has perfected the art of inciting the young and irritating their elders, it is also the continuation of a family quarrel begun among the Greeks more than two thousand years ago.

When the Greeks believed in multiple gods, each god had its own cult. Apollo, the god of the intellect and the higher spirit, was worshipped with the *kithara*, or lyre, which is much like a harp. Dionysos, on the other hand, represented the wild, sensual, emotional side of the human psyche. Dionysian cults conjured up fertility rites, orgies, and possibly human sacrifices to the tune of the *aulos*, a shepherd's pipe. The pipe played two basic tones—a bass tone and a higher, shriller sound. As related by one music historian, legend holds that "Apollo protected his style of music, and made King Midas grow asses's ears for daring to prefer the sound of a shepherd's pipe to that of the lyre."[3] Although the Greeks eventually came to use both instruments in their festivals, the conflict is with us still. According to critic Martha Bayles, the tension between the Apollonian preference for reason over the sensual and emotional Dionysian style epitomizes the struggle of Western civilization to "sustain the priority of reason over will and passion."[4]

In Bayles's view, the problem was resolved in the American art form of jazz, in which the sensual and intellectual are woven into uniquely satisfying moods. Bayles likes jazz a lot and thinks modernism ought to have delineations; some of modernism is destructive, some constructive. What is wrong with most modern music, she says, is that it no longer satisfies the soul.

To begin to understand why, let's go back to Greece, where formal Western music began with the theories of Pythagoras (ca. 582–500 B.C.), who discovered the mathematical principles of the musical scale. Having studied for twenty-two years in Egypt, where the city of Thebes had boasted of the Royal Academy of Music for over a thousand years, Pythagoras probably borrowed Egyptian concepts to construct his musical theory.[5]

To the Greeks, music was an expression of the ideal. Plato (ca.

427–347 B.C.) saw the teaching of music as an important part of educating the young, noting that, "rhythm and harmony find their way into the inward places of the soul, on which they mightily fasten, imparting grace, and making the soul of him who is rightly educated graceful."[6]

Throughout the centuries, music reflected the highest aspirations of people as well as the rhythms of everyday life. Whether it was formal orchestral works sponsored by kings or folk songs that arose out of peasant culture, music had to be musical, that is, pleasing to the ear. It also tended to have religious themes. In the sixteenth century, notable secular composers accounted for about 47 percent of the total number of composers, 54 percent in the seventeenth, and 56 percent by the eighteenth. As for secular music itself, it rose from 58 percent of the total to 95 percent in the nineteenth century.[7] But it was not until the late nineteenth century and for much of the twentieth century that composers began to dispense with beauty and meaning. As with the visual arts, music was commandeered by a critical elite that captured the discipline and interpreted it. One might even say it was a calculated offensive to make music offensive.

In the mid-nineteenth century, Europe was a hothouse for socialist doctrines, which began to find expression in music. Composer Richard Wagner, who later became the musical voice of National Socialism (Nazism), shocked the music world in the late 1850s with his opera *Tristan und Isolde*, in which traditional harmonies were shattered by primitive, sexually suggestive musical bursts. Wagner saw Christianity as a negative force holding back humanity from rising to its potentially godlike powers, which were rooted in a mythical, magical past. He saw art as the means by which the human spirit could free itself from the Christian world view of sensual restraint. "True art is revolutionary, because its very existence is opposed to the ruling spirit of the community," Wagner wrote in 1849.[8]

In 1861, Friedrich Nietzsche, who posthumously became the philosopher-king of Hitler's Third Reich, listened to a piano score of *Tristan* and was captivated. He heard the beat of a revolution that would smash the moral order in order to pave the way for the Superman who would be uninhibited by the old strictures. Although he was later to rescind his Wagnerian devotion, Nietzsche had found the cultural tool to unlock the sensual excess that he craved. Here is his own description of his reaction to *Tristan*: "The world is a poorer place for those who have never been sick enough to appreciate this 'lust of hell.' It is permissible, in fact, it is practically obligatory to come up with some sort of mystical formula. I suspect that I knew better than anyone the monstrosities of which Wagner is capable, the filthy worlds of alien delight, which no one but he had the wings to reach, and since I'm strong enough to turn even the most dangerous and questionable aspects to my advantage, I name Wagner as the greatest benefactor of my life."[9]

Nietzsche's arrogance is palpable, as he proclaims himself godlike, able to use good or evil to his advantage. The only distinction is whether something helps him achieve personal power.

Writer Thomas Mann cites Nietzsche's statement as support for his own contention that "Wagner's *Tristan* is a thoroughly obscene work."[10] As for Nietzsche, who eventually went insane and died from syphilis, with which he deliberately infected himself in a bordello, his arrogant vision of man harnessing all powers and ascending to "superman" status pervaded the Nazi movement. Springing from pagan roots, Nazism was at bottom an attempt to overthrow the Christian order of Europe, with the ultimate intent of eliminating the despised religion's foundation—the Jews and their scriptures. Nietzsche was thrilled by Wagner's musical passion, seeing it as an antidote for what he considered the impossible, man-made requirements of Christianity and, indeed, of Western Civilization. The Christian view of man existing under an objective reality (that is, God's design) to which man could only par-

tially see, was an extension of the Platonic ideal. Plato postulated
an ideal realm in which perfect forms of all types existed. Man
could detect the form, including the moral form, but only as much
as his sensual and intellectual limitations allowed him. Proclaiming boldly that "God is dead," Nietzsche set out to smash all limits
on the human will. Nietzsche scoffed at Christianity as "Platonism
'for the people'" in an 1886 book aptly titled *Beyond Good and Evil*.[11]
Throughout his life and works, Nietzsche discussed the power of
music, particularly that of Richard Wagner. Describing his reaction upon hearing Wagner's overture to the opera *Die Meistersinger*,
Nietzsche finds it disturbing and exciting: "Now it seems archaic,
now strange, acid, and too young, it is as arbitrary as it is pomp-
ous-traditional, it is not infrequently puckish, still more often rough
and uncouth—it has fire and spirit and at the same time the loose
yellow skin of fruits which ripen too late."[12]

In short, it fulfilled Nietzsche's anarchic yearnings, as exemplified
by this passage: "I could imagine a music whose rarest magic would
consist in this, that it no longer knew of anything of good and evil,
except that perhaps some sailor's homesickness, some golden shadow
and delicate weakness would now and then flit across it; an art that
would see fleeing towards it from a great distance the colors of a
declining, now almost incomprehensible *moral* world, and would
be hospitable and deep enough to receive such late fugitives."[13]

In disparaging the idea of an objective reality, Nietzsche
expounded a relativistic view of the universe, with each man deriving
his own morality from his own tapping of creative power. Judaism
and Christianity had interfered with that process by inserting a
very specific and demanding God between humans and their
potential. By mixing politics with the sensual power of the revolt
against order, Nietzsche and Wagner unleashed an unholy force
that would sweep Europe both culturally and politically.

"It was Nietzsche's evil genius to see that no social revolution
can proceed in the presence of a stable sexual morality," writes social

critic E. Michael Jones. "Wagner wanted social revolution because he wanted sexual liberation; Nietzsche wanted sexual liberation because he wanted social revolution. Wagner's sin was primarily sensual, Nietzsche's intellectual."[14]

In Adolf Hitler, both temptations took root to create an emotion so intense that it swept an entire world into war. Hitler himself explained that he drew his inspiration from the Wagnerian operas that he heard yearly, beginning as a boy of sixteen: "When I listen to Wagner, I feel as though I am hearing the rhythms of an earlier world. It is my guess that one day science will find, in the wavelengths set in motion by the *Rhinegold*, secret connections with the order of the world . . ."[15]

While Hitler saw in Wagner's operas an occultic vision of a shining new world without the corruptions of Judaism or Christianity, others saw a musical iconoclast whose passion broke barriers. Liszt, Berlioz, Schumann, and Mendelssohn became the heart of a romantic movement in which emotion played a larger role in composition. Inviting the listener to be swept away with feeling, the romantics paved the way for more sensual styles down the road. Bach's power lies in its majestic formulations that achieve sublimity, while Liszt or Wagner put the listener on an emotional roller coaster. But some composers found romanticism still too constricting.

Arnold Schoenberg was one of them. In his native Vienna, Schoenberg heard Wagner's siren song of sensual excess at the turn of the century and carried it a step further. Thematically and musically, he shattered the final bonds of tradition. While Wagner's adulterous protagonists in *Tristan* are eventually destroyed, Schoenberg's expositions of sexual license have benign consequences. Eschewing his Jewish heritage, Schoenberg began reading poetry that espoused free love and socialism. In his first major work, *Verklarte Nacht* (Night Illuminated from Within), Schoenberg casts adultery in a romantic light, with a husband easily forgiving his wayward wife. Taking Wagner's concept of *verklart* (transfigured or illuminated from within) from Act Two of *Tristan*, he captures the excitement of forbidden love while mitigating the consequences. As E. Michael Jones puts it, "The sexual revolution is on, but everything's going to be okay."[16]

But it was not okay for Schoenberg himself, whose wife committed adultery, with her lover committing suicide. After his marriage fell apart, Schoenberg abandoned formal structure, creating works that increasingly were based on atonality. From 1924 on, with the help of his pupil Anton Webern, he composed and popularized the "twelve-tone technique," in which musical tones are given equal prominence, as are pitches. This resulted in the evolution of atonality, in which musical tunes are eliminated altogether.

The late John Oesterle, who taught philosophy at Notre Dame, described the practical effects of the twelve-tone technique: "In the 12-tone progression (which has an artistic, limited use), they adopted the completely arbitrary and inartistic principle that no tone of the series could be used until all the other tones had been employed. As a consequence, themes and progressions sounded just as well played backwards as forewards, and were written accordingly, which is the logical conclusion of attempted atonalism in music."[17]

Atonal "music" is difficult to play since the human ear delights in the movement of pitches to create contrasts and melodies. Schoenberg and his followers went far beyond Wagner's moments of musical anarchy and "freed" music from all traditional constraints. What resulted is the antithesis of music, and it cultivated a whole school of critics who were employed to explain why atonal "music" was worth listening to even though most people found it boring and annoying. The German government poured funds into the effort to promote the technique, demonstrating that the Germans were as "progressive" as anyone else. Innovative composers such as American Aaron Copland and Russian Igor Stravinsky tried the twelve-tone system, minimizing distinctions and winding up "sounding like everyone else who composed in that mode . . . Twelve-tone technique was the great musical internationalizer, democratizer, and homogenizer," Jones writes. As the trend away from the traditional took hold, it became a runaway train, ending in absurdity.

American minimalist composer John Cage, who found more acceptance in Europe than he did in America, tried one bizarre stunt after another, breaking all musical rules. As *Los Angeles Times* music critic Mark Swed wrote, Cage in the early 1950s "began to seriously embrace chance and chaos, to advocate the inclusion of all sounds and silences as useful for music, and to employ the I Ching as a device for removing his own ego and tastes from his composition."[18]

In 1954, Cage reached his ultimate existentialist destination when he staged his piano work *4'33"*; it was four minutes and thirty-three seconds of the soloist contemplating the piano—without playing at all.[19] Although the work received mixed reviews at the time, with some critics actually dismissing it as silly, the minimalist spirit is alive and well in Germany, where intellectual pretensions seem to no know bounds. At Frankfurt Fest in 1992, no less than twenty-five concerts of Cage's music were held. When *4'33"* was played, the audience sat raptly, "in its own worshipful, utter silence—not a cough, not a shuffle, not an audible breath."[20]

In *Concert for Piano and Orchestra* (1958), Cage "gave a far greater degree of challenge to the players and challenged them not to be silly. Here a violinist snaps rubber bands; a wind player squawks on his mouthpiece; a saxophonist sets loose some windup ducks that circle the conductor, who acts as a human clock."[21] Of course. Who could find that silly? Well, for starters, a New York audience, which nearly rioted when the piece premiered nearly four decades ago. But in 1992, *Concert for Piano and Orchestra* received a full ten-minute ovation from a grateful German festival audience.

Rocking Around the Clock

As "classical" music suffered decay, popular music became all-encompassing, the heartbeat of a fast-paced culture. Moving from folk melodies to fusions of classical, folk, and even black gospel, musicians produced middle-brow styles such as swing and Dixieland jazz. In 1949, *Billboard* magazine abandoned the "hillbilly" chart heading and made it "country and western," prompted by the success of Texas swing band leader Bob Wills and singing cowboy Gene Autry.[22]

American popular music adopted and shed styles the way a fussy customer sheds shoes. During the 1920s, it was the Jazz Age. Duke Ellington, Bessie Smith, and Louis Armstrong took the peculiarly American music form around the world. Popular tunes were smithed in Tin Pan Alley for Broadway shows, which eventually found their way into motion pictures. Dance crazes such as the Charleston and the Jitterbug swept the college campuses, aided by the new medium of radio. Swing, boogie-woogie, hillbilly, and western swing carved out their niches, and the Big Bands continued in popularity until the late 1940s, frontlined by singers such as Nat King Cole, Frank Sinatra, Tony Martin, and Teresa Brewer. In the 1950s, 1960s, and even into the 1990s, Sinatra, Tony Bennett, and Johnny Mathis carried on the crooner tradition in the face of a music development that changed American culture profoundly. Jazz trumpeter Miles Davis pioneered a new style of jazz called "cool jazz" after World War II. Propelled by the invention of the long-playing (LP) vinyl record, the recorded music industry grew exponentially, spelling the end for ballrooms as the center of popular music, as music historian Edith Borroff relates:[23] "The days of the touring bands were over, and musical reputations were subsequently made or broken with records. The disc jockeys, with their power to feature or ignore new releases, had become the kingpins of the record industry . . . They were responsible in part for such phenomenal hits as Irving Berlin's 'White Christmas'; over 40 million records and 5 million copies of sheet music of this song were sold by 1962, probably the greatest sale in the history of the music industry."[24]

At the same time, some "white" music stations began playing rhythm and blues, which evolved into "soul" music. Then a few white singers began to pick up the infectious beat and make it their own. In 1956, Bill Haley and the Comets recorded "Rock Around the Clock." That is when rock began to really sell records and when Dionysos began to win the tempo battle, hands down. Elvis Presley took rock into a wilder realm with "Hound Dog," "Jailhouse Rock," and many other songs that have since become standards. Rockers Jerry Lee Lewis, Bo Diddley, and Little Richard added fuel to the fire. *The Rolling Stone History of Rock & Roll* described Diddley's first recording, "I'm a Man," as being "loaded with sexual braggadocio and seething with menace."[25]

Rock 'n' roll began as a combination of Afro-American folk music (rhythm and blues) and white country folk music—hillbilly ballads. Elements of jazz, such as horns, abounded, at least early on. Unlike the earlier forms, the spirit of rock was always about rebellion. At first, it was a high-spirited form that celebrated life and youth. The anthems of Ricky Nelson, the Everly Brothers, and the early Beatles are mostly about love and love lost. During the 1960s, the Beach Boys, along with Jan and Dean, invented a genre of bouncy surf rock that extols the California youth culture. Their sunny lyrics and upbeat stage shows wouldn't have fooled Allan Bloom however, who insisted that the rock beat is always a musical metaphor for sexual intercourse. Numerous rock stars agree.

Debbie Harry of the eighties group Blondie puts it this way: "I've always thought the main ingredients in rock are sex, really good stage shows, and really sassy music. Sex and sass. I just dance around and shake. Rock 'n' roll is all sex. One hundred percent."[26]

Mick Jagger of the Rolling Stones: "I often want to smash the microphone up because I don't feel the same person on-stage as I am normally. I entice the audience . . . [W]hat I'm doing is a sexual thing. I dance, and all dance is a replacement for sex."[27]

Black music, which white disc jockeys called "race" music in the 1940s, turned the gospel sound into the blues, and rhythm and blues. Artists such as Mahalia Jackson and Aretha Franklin made the crossover into R&B seem almost effortless. Certainly the energy level was the same if the message wasn't. Gospel's power comes from its cathartic ability to take the performer and audience into the heart of Dionysian emotion only to emerge from it, harnessing it for a higher purpose. As Bayles explains, "In gospel, suffering is the path to God, and God will respond to the most agonized cry by turning it into the most jubilant shout. So there's no reason to hold back. Needless to say, the resulting taste for extremes takes on a very different cast when transferred to the realm of sexual pain and pleasure."[28] The switch was exemplified in Marvin Gaye's album, *Let's Get It On*, in whose liner notes Gay proclaimed, "I can't see what's wrong with sex between two consenting anybodies. I think we make far too much of it." Voodoo influenced the music of Screamin' Jay Hawkins, Muddy Waters, Bo Diddley, and later, Jimi Hendrix, who openly sang that he was a "Voodoo Child" in a song by that name.

In terms of impact on the emerging music, the hard-driving Little Richard took it to orgiastic heights in his private life as well as on stage. Fashioning his high-top hair after a homosexual musician named Esquerita who had had sex with him and then taught him to play piano, Little Richard became the inspiration for a whole generation of pop musicians. Combining a driving rock beat and screaming vocals, Little Richard set the standard for rock flamboyance. Among the stars who have cited his work are Elvis Presley, Sam Cook, Otis Redding, John Lennon, Elton John, Janis Joplin, David Bowie, Paul Simon, Marty Balin of Jefferson Airplane, Jon Lord of Deep Purple, and Smokey Robinson, who proclaimed

"Little Richard is the beginning of rock & roll."[29] In fact, it would be hard to find a major rock star who has not at some time cited Little Richard as a major influence. Mick Jagger said it for many when he proclaimed, "Little Richard is the originator and my idol."[30]

The wild antics that Little Richard threw himself into on stage were nothing compared with the orgies he threw backstage or at his hotel rooms. And as pop musicians mimicked his performance style, they also began mimicking his total abandonment of sexual mores—even "clean" bands like the Beatles, who took ample advantage of lovestruck fans before these hapless girls were known as "groupies."

The secularization of black music was also shaped largely by the development of the blues, which Mahalia Jackson said were "songs of despair," as opposed to gospel songs, which are "songs of hope."[31] Blues historian Paul Oliver writes that, "The blues is primarily the song of those who turned their backs on religion."[32] As such, the blues were the perfect vehicle for the emerging white bands from Great Britain and America who wanted to demonstrate their liberation from a Christian-based culture. John Mayall and the Bluesbreakers did their best to sound like American bluesmen and sold a lot of records in the process. Groups like Led Zeppelin appropriated not only the basic blues structure but also some of the seedier lyrics of the more earthy bluesmen. Many of the English blues songs are centered around sexual passion.

If rock is mainly about shedding sexual constraints, it is also about shedding moral constraints of any kind, leaving the listener in a relativistic universe with a morality of his own making. Parental authority was rock's first target, followed by a succession of complaints about "society" in general. From youthful exuberance in the 1950s, albeit an upbeat innocence only in comparison with what was to come, "mainstream" rock gradually began to cease criticizing the culture from within to become a force against civilization itself. Instead of arguing in the parlor, it began throwing rocks at the house from the street.

A major innovation occurred in 1981 when Music Television (MTV) was launched. Originally a twenty-four-hour cable television channel that played music videos, MTV became an all-purpose, electronic youth central, with news programs, situation comedies, game shows, and animated features such as the futuristic "Aeon Flux" and the cynical "Beavis and Butthead." The advent of MTV meant that youth rebellion had its own visual/audio outlet instead of depending on handouts from the established media the way the Beatles had to do on "The Ed Sullivan Show" in 1964 to promote their first big American hit, "I Want to Hold Your Hand."

In the late 1980s, shocked by the proliferation of obscene and violence-strewn lyrics on many rock and rap albums, the Parents Music Resource Center won agreements from the recording industry to put parental warning labels on albums. Even this modest concession to a shell-shocked culture was too much for libertines, who denounced the move as "censorship."

When culture critics William Bennett and Delores Tucker prevailed upon Time-Warner executives to sever ties in 1996 with Interscope Records, a maker of some of the most nihilistic, pornographic albums, they were met with the argument that their own parents were once shocked by Elvis, so they should relax. But while Elvis hinted at seduction, he also sang straight love songs and even made gospel and Christmas albums. The current crop of shock rockers hints at rape, but also sings straight songs—about female genital mutilation and sodomy.

In the scheme of things, rock's transformation occurred almost overnight. It was only a few years between Elvis Presley's gentle protest song "In the Ghetto" to the Rolling Stone's "Street Fighting Man" and "Sympathy for the Devil."

Meanwhile, another American musical force was rising fast, partly as a reaction to the excesses of rock 'n' roll. Country music had been popular in the South and West since the 1940s, but it broke into the "mainstream" culture after Bob Dylan did his crossover

Nashville Skyline album in 1969 and novelist Kurt Vonnegut and other celebrities admitted a taste for country music. Manhattan sprouted country music bars, followed by Texas-style chili parlors. Even George Bush, while running for president in 1992, allowed as to how he and his wife Barbara enjoyed country music—and ate pork rinds. It was one thing for the Georgian Jimmy Carter to appear on stage with pony-tailed Willie Nelson; it was another for the hyper-establishment Bushes to own up to a taste for country twang. The music that was despised as the province of the unsophisticated was suddenly in, and the market expanded wildly. In the 1990s, country performers such as Garth Brooks and Dolly Parton achieved star power equal to that of anyone in the television, rock, or film genres. In 1991, for example, Brooks's "Ropin' the Wind" was the top album, with about seven million units sold.

Apart from its catchy tunes and pun-laden lyrics, country music's broader appeal was its reiteration of the themes of family, religion, patriotism, and hard work. Folks who formerly thought of country as hillbilly music found themselves saying, "That stuff speaks to me; it's what my life is all about." While rock 'n' roll careened into nihilism, bloodlust, and sexual explicitness, country borrowed the rock beat and set its homey lyrics to it, spinning tales of real people and real-life situations. Unfortunately, many country bands borrowed liberally from their rock 'n' roll counterparts when creating television videos. Although far more wholesome generally than the fare on MTV or VHS, some of the videos on country music channels feature frenetic pacing and overtly sexual themes. Some of the country bands perform warmed-over, countrified rock tunes, indicating that part of the country music movement is merely rock 'n' roll wearing a cowboy hat and ten years behind the times.

As for rock, its rebellion runs far deeper than the desire to be different. Modernist conceits such as self-absorption as the key to enlightenment or unlimited sexual intrigue are merely the tools by which young minds are seduced away from religion, parents, and individual responsibility. Sex is the prime magnet, but many stars of rock were and are serving another god, to whom sex was just the best possible lure—the occult.

On album cover after album cover of best-selling records of the sixties through the nineties, occultic symbols abound. References to the occult are sprinkled through interviews with stars such as the late Jim Morrison, the self-proclaimed "lizard king" of The Doors. While on stage, Morrison often fell into a shamanic trance, summoning up powers from below. Doors keyboardist Ray Manzarek recalls that he was in awe of Morrison's other-worldly qualities:

> When the Siberian shaman gets ready to go into his trance all the villagers get together and shake rattles and blow whistles and play whatever instruments they have to send him off. There is a constant pounding, pounding, pounding. And these sessions last for hours. It was the same way with the Doors when we played in a concert. The sets didn't last that long, but I think our drug experiences let us get into it that much quicker. We knew the symptoms of the State, so that we could try to approximate it. It was like Jim was an electric shaman and we were the electric shaman's band pounding away behind him. Sometimes he wouldn't feel like getting into the state, but the band would keep pounding and pounding, and little by little it would take him over. God, I could send an electric shock through him with the organ. John could do it with his drumbeats. You could see every once in a while —twitch—I could hit a chord and make him twitch . . . And the audience felt it, too.[33]

Heavy metal groups such as Motley Crue and Black Sabbath openly displayed their loyalty to Satan, as did the Knights in Satan's Service (KISS), which became a mainstream attraction for teenyboppers. Ozzy Osbourne, whose song "Suicide Solution" was cited as the final straw that led at least one young listener to kill himself, wrote often of satanic themes, even penning a tribute to the British Satanist Aleister Crowley entitled *Mr. Crowley*.

Around 1970, Led Zeppelin guitarist Jimmy Page began to shift his focus from songs about sex to songs about the occult after meeting with Church of Satan founding-member Kenneth Anger, a disciple of Aleister Crowley. Album covers, beginning with Led Zeppelin III, began to carry Crowley's motto, "Do What Thou Wilt." By the fourth album, the band began identifying openly with Satanic imagery, including a hexagram on the cover that emanates light, an occultic symbol for Satan. The hit song of the album, which has since become a classic of the seventies, "Stairway to Heaven," is a pleasant ballad musically, but it is also a paean to Crowley's secret society of Satanists.

The lyrics were by Robert Plant, who said that as he wrote the song, his pen was moving across the paper almost by itself, as if automatically. In the occult world, "automatic writing," refers to the possession of the writer by a demonic spirit who uses the writer to "channel" the message. It's the principle behind the innocent-seeming Ouija board, another occultic device that has been mainstreamed as a harmless diversion. According to rock historian Mark Spaulding, the line, "There's a feeling I get when I look to the West and my spirit is crying for leaving," is a reference to an initiation rite included in Aleister Crowley's book *MAGICK: In Theory and Practice.* On page thirty-nine, there is this: "After further purification and consecration he [speaking of the initiate] is allowed for one moment to see the Lord of the West, and gains courage to persist." This is an allusion to an initiate being blindfolded, but permitted a moment to gaze at the West. Crowley later states of the initiate that, "In the West he gains energy."[34]

It was the Rolling Stones who first popularized not only references to Satan in rock, but the mixing of sex and violence. Jagger warned his listeners in the *Let It Bleed* album that rape was "just a kiss away" and that the Midnight Rambler wanted "to stick a knife right down your throat, baby, and it hurts." Those lyrics quickly became almost tame compared with the complete embrace of perverse sex and violence by Stones clones such as WASP, which began as the black magic band Sister. Here's a sample of WASP lyrics from their first album:

> I am a sinner, I kiss the breast
> I am a sadist that RIPS THE FLESH
> I take the women, curse those who enter
> I am a killer and tormentor

This is still kids' stuff when compared to lyrics from some rap and rock groups in the nineties, such as Getto Boys, 2 Live Crew, Nine-Inch Nails, and others. They freely sing of masturbation, suicide, rape, mutilation, murder, and dismemberment of women (before and after). In November 1997, MTV shattered another barrier by featuring full frontal nudity in the video "Smack the Bitch Up," in which strippers and other women are abused by an unknown assailant, who is revealed to be a woman.

Civil libertines say that such themes are not taken seriously by the youngsters who buy these albums and videos by the millions. All they listen to is the beat, they say. But for a generation brought up on Jungian suggestion and subconscious communication, who spy messages in everything from advertising to soap labels, it is amazing how easily they exempt rock from any mental or moral impact.

But it takes no more than common sense to understand that a constant diet of sleaze makes one more accepting of sleaze, either on one's own part or when it is embraced by others. This is what is known as becoming "jaded." Second, there are troubled people on the margin of sanity who are greatly affected by perverse entreaties from rock idols, and they are usually receiving these messages while in a drugged or drunken state.

Charles Manson, who was rejected in a tryout for the Monkees band and became a rock 'n' roll cult figure in his own California commune, led a group of young people into unspeakable carnage in the Sharon Tate murders in 1969. His hypnotic mixture of personal charisma and a rock-induced drug subculture allowed him to override any decency that was left in his followers. One week after the murders, five hundred thousand people gathered in a New York farm to form "Woodstock Nation."

A heady mix of rock music, politics, drugs, and sex, Woodstock was more than an extended concert. As noted by Rabbi Daniel Lapin of Toward Tradition, Woodstock was a giant "finger in the eye of God," a throwing off of the old moral system. As a cultural landmark, Woodstock was the high point of the New Age of moral relativism that engulfed America. To the mud-soaked, stoned partyers, it all seemed so innocent, so devoid of negative consequences, apart from an overdose here or there. But the Aquarians lost their innocence later that year when a Rolling Stones performance at the Altamont race track in California ended in an orgy of beatings and one killing by blood-crazed Hells Angels who had been hired as "security" for the concert.

The trouble had begun in the early evening, as the sun went down and the crowd had grown restless. As F. Michael Jones relates: "By the time Jefferson Airplane took the stage, a pattern had been established for the day. The band would bellow out some incitement to revolution, and then stand back in befuddlement as the crowd actually acted on what they were saying. Jefferson Airplane, a group that had always billed itself as front men for the encroaching anarchy and disorder, now seemed at a loss, if not genuinely terrified, as the understanding dawned on them that what they had been preaching in their songs was now happening before their very eyes."[35]

As the Airplane began singing a song about putting people "up against the wall," the Hell's Angels began beating a young black man with lead-filled pool cues. The crowd was both repelled and energized by the blood in the air, and it reached maximum pitch in the middle of the Stones' portion of the concert. Stones insider Tony Sanchez recalled that an unending supply of girls, many in trancelike states, took off their clothes and crawled toward the stage, "impelled as if by some supernatural force, to offer themselves as human sacrifices to these agents of Satan." The Hell's Angels beat the girls senseless, and Jagger began asking the crowd to "cool out now." Violence broke out as soon as the band began the song "Sympathy for the Devil" and continued until a young black man who was carrying a gun was beaten to death by the Hell's Angels. The Stones, who were too frightened to stop playing, finally finished their gig and took off in a helicopter as the beatings began anew, growing to a bloody crescendo. In a film clip of Jagger watching a tape of the carnage, his face is ashen and confused.

The moral restraints that his band had discarded had finally led to murder. As he turned to leave the room, Jagger wore an expression that seemed to indicate he knew that he had been used by something or somebody to bring it about. If God was dead and no longer in control of things, then somebody else was in charge, and it wasn't Jagger.

15

It's Not So Relative After All

Puritanism and paganism—the repression and the expression of the senses and desires—alternate in mutual reaction in history . . . Probably our excesses will bring another reaction; moral disorder may generate a religious revival; atheists may again (as in France after the debacle of 1870) send their children to Catholic schools to give them the discipline of religious belief. Hear the appeal of the agnostic Renan in 1866: "If Rationalism wishes to govern the world without regard to the religious needs of the soul, the experience of the French Revolution is there to teach us the consequences of such a blunder."[1]

Will and Ariel Durant

I N THE AGE OF CONSENT, personal preferences are regarded as supreme. But this extreme individualism is unsustainable because it destroys family, community, and national life—the soil in which freedom grows.

Like a man awaking from a hangover, America is beginning to right itself, painfully, gingerly taking steps back toward coherence.

Amidst the clutter of media-fed confusion, voices of sanity are being heard sounding timeless themes that transcend the fad deities of "sexual freedom," "multiculturalism," and "diversity."

Liberal commentators were bewildered by the Christian men's movement, Promise Keepers, whose historic "Stand in the Gap" rally on the Mall in Washington on October 4, 1997, was utterly devoid of self-serving political messages. On the lookout for hints of a Nuremberg-style Nazi gathering, some liberal observers admitted that the men who knelt on the Mall to confess their sin were not about to be herded into a fascistic plot to subjugate nonbelievers. When a million or more men pledge to be better husbands and fathers, the only losers are divorce lawyers, pornographers, and homosexual activists—the latter of whom attacked Promise Keepers with at least as much enthusiasm as the feminists. Strident commentary from the National Organization of Women's Patricia Ireland and the Fund for a Feminist Majority's Eleanor Smeal came across on national television as curiosities from a 1960s time warp. Even some liberal commentators shook their heads while the feminists embarrassed themselves with hysterical warnings and accusations.

Maybe it is because we are approaching the second millennium, or maybe it is because baby boomers are aging, or maybe it is because relativism has made such a mess of things, but something powerful is occurring. A major reassessment is underway that has the possibility of stemming the tide of decay and decadence that has swept America over the past few decades.

For starters, church attendance is up. What the mainstream Protestant denominations have lost in membership has been made up in the spectacular growth among evangelical churches. A new spirit also has reinvigorated many Catholic churches and synagogues as baby boomers return to the faiths of their childhood. There is a growing realization that secular government does not have all the answers; a growing distrust of mainstream media with a concurrent rise in alternative media, and a general feeling that things have gone too far in the wrong direction.

America may just be pulling back from the edge because the forces of relativism have given it a good look at what awaits in the abyss: children killing children because life is so cheap, and a popular culture that dwells on mindless rebellion, aberrant sexuality, suicide, and palpable hatred for all things bright and beautiful. Sometimes the best way to differentiate good from the bad is to stare directly into the face of evil. Relativism is increasingly being exposed as a malevolence that wears a mask of benign tolerance. People are getting tired of not only evil but all the excuses that are made on its behalf.

Feminist novelist Erica Jong, whose books such as *Fear of Flying* helped celebrate sex without commitment, has had something of an epiphany. Recently, Jong has acknowledged that the sexual revolution was a disaster for women, for men—for everyone.

Cultural signs abound that people are craving romance more than sex, commitment more than experimentation. In the mid-nineties, singer Tony Bennett made a huge comeback, not as a caricature of an earlier era or as an ironic, campy icon. To a new audience of twenty-somethings, Bennett is a genuinely moving singer whose ballads touch the heart and give the hope that romance is not dead after all. On the cable television network Nickelodeon, the "Nick at Nite" television programs from earlier eras, such as "I Love Lucy," "Mary Tyler Moore," and "Bob Newhart" are drawing millions of viewers who have tuned out of the constant sexual innuendo, violence, and foul language of current programs. To get to these "classic" programs, they have to endure the campy tone of Nick's promos, which are the progenies of the more cynical comics' mockery of middle-American life. But the viewers do have access to what Nick celebrates as "our television heritage." Other "clean," quality shows are thriving in syndication, such as "The Waltons," "Bonanza," "Family Matters," and "The Young Riders." A handful of wholesome network shows such as "Touched by an Angel" and "Home Improvement" are outright hits.

At the movies, the times seem to be changing, too. Whereas in 1993, the Best Picture category was littered with movies about dysfunction, culminating in the Best Picture Award for the cannibalism flick, *Silence of the Lambs*, the 1995 nominees were positively wholesome, dealing with heroism (*Apollo 13, Braveheart*) and human relationships (*Babe, Sense and Sensibility,* and *Il Postino*). Okay, Babe is a pig, but he personifies human qualities that audiences are hungering for: loyalty, bravery, perseverance, and trustworthiness, not to mention likeability.

In popular music, country has continued its climb toward domination of the charts, with Garth Brooks and other artists who sing clean (well, relatively clean) songs about life, love, family, and country. Christian rock has become a major business, grossing big money annually. Christian rockers Amy Grant and Michael W. Smith have had crossover hits in the mainstream pop market, while artists virtually unknown outside Christian circles—Steven Curtis Chapman, Kathy Troccoli, Wayne Watson, Cheryl Keagy, Carman, Twila Paris, the Newsboys, Audio Adrenaline, Jars of Clay, d.c. Talk, Point of Grace, and the Supertones—collectively have sold tens of millions of albums.

In the same way, Christian authors like James Dobson and Frank Peretti typically sell over a million copies to a market that is virtually ignored by the *New York Times Book Review*, whose bestsellers can reach the chart by moving as few as fifty thousand copies.

Two of the largest countercultural forces to hit America since the 1960s have picked up more speed in the mid-1990s. By publicizing the horrors of "partial-birth abortion," the pro-life movement has moved the moral high ground away from the relativistic totem of "choice," with a vast majority of Americans agreeing that abortion should be illegal in many circumstances.

The home-schooling movement and the Christian school

movement, the backbone of the next counterrevolution, continue to enroll more pupils. By 1998, an estimated 1.5 million children were being home-schooled, representing a powerful counterforce to the educational "blob" that has steered the public schools away from academic excellence and toward condoms, "gay pride," and self-esteem exercises.

The power of the home-schooling segment of the population became painfully evident to congressmen in the spring of 1995. Faced with an education bill that contained a provision that would have, in effect, ended home schooling by requiring state licensing for parent-teachers, the home-schoolers inundated Congress with more than a million phone calls, plus thousands of letters, telegrams, and personal visits. The phones were shut down for days. Awestruck by this show of force, Congress quickly deleted the offending provision. Aware that they had averted a crisis but not slain the growing federal education beast, home-schoolers began working with libertarians and other foes of big government to get rid of the federal education establishment entirely. Items on the education reform agenda are: easing the financial burden on parents who opt out of the public schools; defunding Goals 2000; and abolishing the federal Department of Education.

Americans have learned to talk back to their government and to the media and are relishing the freedom. Revolution—better yet: Restoration—is in the air, and it goes far beyond the political upheaval that began in 1980 with Ronald Reagan's election, was stalled under George Bush, and was reborn in November 1994 when voters ousted the Democrats from control of Congress. Although the Republican Party seems more often to be the political vehicle for this new, populist movement of traditional family values and revulsion against Big Government, the GOP is merely that—a vehicle. As numerous polls and Ross Perot's capture of 19 percent of the vote in 1992 showed, fed-up Americans could easily become disillusioned with a "go along to get along" Republican Party that refuses to provide effective opposition to the liberal, big-government agenda. Bill Clinton's easy reelection in the face of mounting scandal showed just how out of touch much of the GOP remains.

What makes the populist revolt so mystifying to the liberal media is its insistence on freedom from government as opposed to using government to benefit its members. For decades, liberals have assumed that the argument was over who gets to run things. They became accustomed to people who wanted to create more programs to please more constituencies. But now, the grass-roots activists are looking not for more government programs but to protect their families from further encroachment. And that holds for liberalization of the concept of "civil rights." Although the ever-expanding universe of newly coined "rights" groups may seem to their constituents to be an expansion of freedom, the average person is beginning to realize that the ultimate beneficiary is a larger, more powerful government, with activists in charge.

Because the emerging populist majority understands that relativism has led to license and hence excuses for more government power, there is growing support for a minimum of government effort to ensure a moral climate. Unlike liberals, who use government to meddle in virtually every aspect of people's lives, social conservatives want mainly to keep dirty old men from killing babies, preying on children, and turning the entire nation into an x-rated bookstore or movie house via the Internet and other media. Social conservatives want the government to stop subsidizing illegitimacy, divorce, and homosexuality, and to stop seizing so much family income that it forces millions of mothers into the workplace, hobbles family-owned businesses, or makes parents work longer hours to make ends meet. Most people don't want to be bribed by government to accept an inferior form of care for their children. They are not particularly enticed by the feminist vision of a world in which all mothers work and all children are raised in institutions in which they can learn the equality of relativism.

An entire movement of professional, well-educated women who

are opting to make their home and children their primary focus is emerging. Linda Burton, who edits a newsletter for full-time mothers (*Welcome Home*) and co-wrote the 1986 book, *What's a Smart Woman Like You Doing at Home?*, is working to change the cultural climate so that full-time mothers are not made to feel worthless. In addition to challenging the pop culture's emphasis on careerism, Burton says that government can help, not by creating child care programs, but by providing tax incentives for child-rearing, the establishment of Social Security benefits to homemakers, and "the right to put into an IRA the same amount allowed her working spouse . . . Economic and social incentives for mothers who want to be at home would at last present women with a fair balance of opportunity—the first genuine 'choice' they've had in a long time."[2]

Instead of trying to impose their values on everyone else, the new populists see themselves as defending their beliefs and traditions from constant assault. Any parent who has been shocked by sex-saturated school materials and raised objections has felt this oppression firsthand. All viewpoints are welcome, they are told, except their own. Increasingly, the "culture war" in America is not over who gets to "use" the government but whether parents can regain the freedom to dissent, to keep most of their earnings, to direct the upbringing of their children, and to walk down the street or turn on the television or radio without being assailed by foul language, horrific violence, pornography, and all the other blessings of relativism-spawned license.

While some of the revolt against liberalism (and at a more fundamental level, against relativism) is taking political form, the real battle is going on in individual souls. Unquenched by the numbing pursuit of material and physical comfort and nonstop amusement, the soul is crying out for real sustenance, the kind that only God can fill because he happened to make us that way.

Relativists are scornful of the biblical idea of a God who seeks fellowship with men. The concept seems to contain so many contradictions. For example, if God is all powerful, why does he need us to worship him? If his ego is so small (or so large), why is this really necessary? G. K. Chesterton offered one explanation, which is that God doesn't need to be worshipped; man needs to worship God. Otherwise, man will wind up worshipping himself and his ungodly lusts. Chesterton, who would marvel at the sheer number and audacity of the multiple gods of our age, put it famously when he said that absent a faith in God, men are not so apt to believe in nothing as to believe in *anything*. Abandoning God is a bit like abandoning real food for junk food. The junk serves as a filler that keeps one from eating nutritious foods that sustain. The wages of sin are death because sin interferes with the sustenance of life—a relationship with God.

Relativists think they are immune to the need for connecting with God, and they suppress their growing guilt by embracing a variety of causes in order to prove just how "good" they are. The new populism consists not of forcing relativists to be spoon-fed religion or conservative ideas, but of getting out from under the tyranny of the relativists' misguided efforts.

Far from posing a threat to freedom, the people who hold traditional beliefs are beginning the rebuilding of the American moral ethos. To accomplish this, they are seeking less government intervention, more individual responsibility, and a lid on new claims of "rights."

In general, they are seeking a world in which:

- Parents would not have to shield the eyes of their children as they walked through the neighborhood corner store. Vulgar magazines and videos would be back where they belong—in the cultural backwaters on the edge of town. Pornography has plagued society since time immemorial, but it had been kept under control through public expectations of what is appropriate. Although tough enforcement of obscenity laws would help curb some of the excesses, there is nothing like public scorn to put the porn back in the closet.

- Hollywood would be far more responsible in its output, and those who would violate basic standards of decency would find themselves ostracized and shamed. The boycott of the Walt Disney Company by the Southern Baptists and other Christian groups is the equivalent of Concord in the war to reform the entertainment industry.

- Radical cultural activists would lose their power quickly because the federal tap would be turned off. They would have to compete in the marketplace of ideas like everyone else, and their ideas have already been found wanting. Taxpayers would no longer have to pay the fees of radical lawyers bent on limiting parental rights in the name of "children's rights." School children would no longer face an onslaught of federally-funded condoms and sex education that denigrates marriage and family and steers children into sexual experimentation. Radical homosexual activists would have to raise their own funds in order to attack sexual morality. And they could not rely on the law to impose their agenda on others. Only the institutions deserving of support would get it. Money targeted for AIDS research would not be sidetracked into radical coffers but would be used for its original intent—treating victims of the disease and funding medical research.

- Government intrusion into the art world would end, triggering a new golden era of creativity, unbound by bureaucratic decree. Bad art would soon dry up because nobody would be forced to pay for it. Beauty, meaning, and artistic skill would return as essential elements of artistic acceptance. No more would taxpayers wince at their own money being spent to support attacks on their most deeply held beliefs.

- Public television would operate without government subsidy, and it would continue to thrive, better than before. The best of PBS would form the nucleus of a privatized public broadcasting system, such as "Sesame Street" and other favorites. Gone would be the hard-left programs that few watch and which only government funds. Likewise, National Public Radio would survive—and thrive—with foundation, corporate, and listener support.

- In the courts, criminals would be punished swiftly but fairly. The practice of interminable appeals would end, and the fact of actual behavior would replace psychological frame of mind as the focus in criminal trials. Sociologist Charles Murray has written that you can tell whether civilization is present by what kind of attitude people have when they see a criminal being hauled off by police. If they say, "He's going to get it," then there is law and order. If, however, they say "He'll get off," there is no respect for authority and there is no law and order. The end of judicial relativism would produce a climate in which criminals knew instinctively that the odds favored stiff punishment if they victimized fellow citizens. Claims to redefine the family or to sanctify the logically impossible concept of homosexual "marriage" would be laughed out of court. Adoption agencies would put the needs of children first, not the dictates of groups with radical social agendas.

- The courts would return, at every level, to the business of seeing that the Constitution and subsequent laws were faithfully observed. The Supreme Court would no longer render decisions based on gut feelings and sociological analysis but rather faithful adherence to the letter and the spirit of the Constitution. And the justices would have a lesser role, because revival of the Tenth Amendment would shrink the federal government considerably, with all undefined powers returning to the states and the people.

- Abortion would be relegated to its historically low status, which means it would be illegal. Hippocrates' oath would be restored in its original meaning at the nation's medical schools, where the credo "first, do no harm" would apply to all human life. Dr. Jack Kervorkian, the suicide-assistance specialist, and his ilk would be put out of business.

- Education would undergo a renaissance, with phonics, math drills, drawing lessons and other classical methods and topics returning to the classrooms. Children would actually learn math, science, history, geography, logic, drawing, and maybe even Latin and Greek. Out would go self-esteem counseling, workshops, anti-American social studies, and other distractions.

- Divorce laws would be tightened, and people would be rewarded culturally and monetarily for marrying and staying married. Welfare would be radically overhauled and largely taken over by churches and other private organizations. Single mothers would not be tempted by a government check to have more children out of wedlock or to ignore the need for a father in children's lives. More children would be born into two-parent families, and more would grow up with a father in the house. The crime rate would drop dramatically within a generation.

- The Defense Department would return to its primary mission, that of defending America, and would not be harnessed to do social bulldozing for homosexual and feminist activists.

• Because social reforms, public and private, would mean less need for an overweening government and consequently less taxation, families would have more money with which to plan their lives. With newfound financial freedom, families could make their own decisions about schooling, care of aging parents, and even where to live. They could spend their own, hard-earned money without strings attached.

In short, there would be a decidedly nonrelativistic culture with clear moral values, less government, more intact families, a healthier, child-friendly moral climate, an artistic renaissance, and a renewed commitment to ordered liberty, religious freedom, and individual responsibility. Radical pests could no longer count on mandatory taxation to fill their coffers, and they would leave the rest of us alone to live our lives and raise our children as we see fit. The relativistic doctrine of the late twentieth century would be deemed incomprehensible and even pathetic.

Everywhere, the Age of Consent is being ridiculed. People are becoming aware of how much of their culture has been commandeered by a virulently relativistic force that fronts for secularism. They are reasserting their freedom to disagree. In Alabama, Judge Roy Moore defied another judge's order in 1997 to take down his plaque of the Ten Commandments that Moore had made himself and hung on the wall of his courtroom for several years. Reciting prodigious amounts of scripture, constitutional language, and the writings of America's founders, Moore made his liberal attackers seem petty and mean. Following Judge Moore's example, thousands of Alabama students and faculty defied another liberal judge's order to cease all mention of religion in the public schools. When the liberal judge authorized the appointment of monitors to ensure compliance, they were quickly ridiculed as the "prayer police."

In Washington, thousands of teenagers gathered in the spring of 1995 to pledge that "true love waits." They planted pledge cards on the mall representing more than two hundred thousand other teens who had vowed to remain sexually pure until marriage.

Promise Keepers, a movement designed to call men back to their primary duties as men of faith, as husbands and fathers, is exerting a powerful pull, with sold-out stadium rallies all across the nation. Their massive rally on the Mall in Washington was the largest religious gathering in American history, signaling a higher stage in the resistance to the Age of Consent.

The National Day of Prayer also has gained momentum. First held in 1775 when the First Continental Congress issued a proclamation, the custom was revived in 1863 by Abraham Lincoln and was made official in 1952 by a Joint Resolution of Congress signed by President Truman. In 1988, Congress amended the resolution to designate that the event be held annually on the first Thursday of May. Since then, the National Day of Prayer has grown, with public Bible readings, national media campaigns, prayer circles, and public pronouncements. It has ensured that millions of Americans, for at least one day a year, are praying in unison for the restoration of the United States as a nation under God. The event takes inspiration from II Chronicles 14, in which God offers this promise: "If my people, which are called by my name, shall humble themselves, and pray, and seek my face, and turn from their wicked ways; then I will hear from Heaven, and will forgive their sin, and will heal their land."

A new alliance of people of faith is taking shape, as Catholics and Protestants put aside their doctrinal differences to concentrate on defeating the forces of relativism that are choking off religious and family freedom. Christians and observant Jews are forming alliances, such as Toward Tradition, which seeks the reestablishment of biblical values in public life and a common culture that allows faith-minded people the freedom to worship without government interference.

The revolt of the populace through the medium of talk radio is the major communications story of the 1990s. Although the Internet is poised to revolutionize public discourse, it is talk radio that has broken the monopoly of the liberal news and entertainment media. And the liberal establishment knows only too well how they have been circumvented. In hysterical tones, a *Time* magazine cover story attacked Rush Limbaugh and the whole genre, even suggesting that Congress was receiving too much input from the people back home. The television networks' grip on America has been broken by cable television and new technologies such as the VCR, satellite transmissions, computer hook-ups, and, again, the talk radio phenomenon.

Much of the value of the new media is in reinforcing what people already know to be true. Many people had rejected relativism but had felt isolated and helpless as the media giants relentlessly pushed their toxic brew of cynicism and sensationalism. Rush Limbaugh gave them a common focus and an outlet for their frustration with political correctness of all kinds. As multimedia specialist Robert Chitester told an April 1995 conference at the Hoover Institution, the hugely successful PBS series "Free to Choose," based on economist Milton Friedman's bestseller, "helped people understand what they already believed . . . [I]t confirmed and clarified the ideas they already had."[3] Chitester, who created the series, warned that broadcasting is a medium so superficial that it is dangerous to assume that the truth will win out just by saying it once. "If you can change people's minds in an hour using television, the next day someone else is going to change their mind back the other direction. You must hook them to go beyond television."[4]

Amidst what, at first, seems like a mindless media cacophony, clear strains of sanity are being heard. There is plenty of chaff along with the grain, but more people are learning to listen for the music instead of the noise, the eternal melody instead of the din.

Paradoxically, with the explosion in information, it is becoming clearer that life is not as complicated as it has been made out to be. The relativistic sirens who, for a time, wooed us away from the truth, have been unmasked, and their song seems foolish. Although the truth is so powerful that it does not need the same amount of repetition required by a lie, the challenge in the next millennium will be to redress the cultural imbalance so that evil will not drown out the good. This may not be such a tall order. The truth has its own sweet sound, and the rest is just noise. The Age of Consent may just have set the stage for an Age of Faith.

Notes

Foreword

1   W.P. and F.J.T. Garrison, *William Lloyd Garrison* [1885-1888], vol. 1, p. 268.

2   Marilyn Ferguson, *The Aquarian Conspiracy: Personal and Social Transformation in the 1980s* (Los Angeles: J. P. Tarcher, distributed by St. Martin's Press, New York, 1980), p. 29.

3   Such as English professor Eugene Narrett, whose teaching position was eliminated at Framingham State University in 1997 after he clashed with university authorities over his politically incorrect articles dealing with feminism and homosexuality.

1 The Way We Were

1   Richard Severo, "Red Skelton, Knockabout Comic and Clown Prince of the Airwaves, Is Dead at 84," *The New York Times*, 18 September 1997, p.D-20.

2   Ibid.

2 Relativism: The Siren Song of Decadence

1   Allan Bloom, *The Closing of the American Mind* (New York: Simon and Schuster, 1987), p. 25.

2 Stewart Emory, *Actualizations: You Don't Have to Rehearse To Be Yourself; Transform Your Relationships!* (Dolphin Books, Doubleday, 1978), pp. 112, 113.

3 Ibid, p. 101.

3 Materialism: The Religion that Fails

1 Aleksandr Solzhenitsyn, "A World Split Apart," *Solzhenitsyn at Harvard,* ed. Ronald Berman (Washington: Ethics and Public Policy Center, 1980), p. 17.

2 Checko Sonny, "Magazine Publisher Gives Farm a Laugh," *The Stanford Daily,* 2 November 1989, p. 1.

3 Ps. 26:22, New International Version. (The Authorized [King James] Version reads: "The words of a talebearer are as wounds, and they go down into the innermost parts of the belly.")

4 Jeffrey Satinover, *Feathers of the Skylark* (Westport, Connecticut: Hamewith Books, 1996), p. 14.

5 Nena O'Neill and George O'Neill, *Open Marriage,* (New York: M. Evans and Company), 1984, p. 25.

6 David Popenoe, "A World Without Fathers," *Wilson Quarterly,* Spring 1996, p. 20.

7 In 1997, the Rockford Institute compiled summaries of research from hundreds of studies indicating remarkable consistency in difficulties encountered by children reared in situations other than the father-mother household. The Institute concludes that there is no body of credible research that shows children doing as well in situations other than the "traditional family," notwithstanding the best intentions and loving efforts of single parents. The intention is not to disparage single parents, many of whom do a superb job of parenting, but to acknowledge that fatherless or motherless children have a documentable disadvantage in life regardless of any other factor, including socioeconomic status.

8 Patrick F. Fagan, "The Real Root Causes of Violent Crimes: The Breakdown of Marriage, Family and Community," Cultural Studies Project, The Heritage Foundation, Washington, D.C., No. 1026, 17 March 1995, p.36.

4 The Sexual Revolution: Relativizing Eros

1   Pitirim Sorokin, *The American Sex Revolution* (Boston: Porter Sargent, 1956), p. 19.

2   Ibid, pp. 16, 17.

3   Ibid, pp. 3, 4.

4   Peter Kostenbaum, *Existential Sexuality: Choosing to Love,* eds. Charles Hampden-Turner and Rollo May (Englewood Cliffs, New Jersey: Prentice-Hall, 1974), p.17.

5   Elizabeth Mehren, "What We Really Think About Adultery," *Los Angeles Times,* 2 June 1991, p. E-1.

6   Ibid.

7   Jeffrey Zaslow, "Different is OK," *USA Weekend,* 16–18 February 1996, p. 18.

8   Ibid.

9   C. S. Lewis, *The Abolition of Man* (New York: MacMillan, 1955), p.90.

10   Margaret Sanger, *Pivot of Civilization* (New York: Brentano's, 1922), p. 253, quoted in Charles A. Donovan and Robert Marshall, *Blessed Are the Barren: The Social Policy of Planned Parenthood* (San Francisco: Ignatius Press, 1991), p. 59.

11   David Kennedy, *Birth Control in America: The Career of Margaret Sanger* (New Haven: Yale University Press, 1970), p. 99, and Madeline Gray, *Margaret Sanger: A Biography of the Champion of Birth Control* (New York: Marek, 1979), p. 192, both cited in Donovan and Marshall, *Blessed Are the Barren,* p. 7.

12   Mildred Dodge, quoted in Gray, *Margaret Sanger,* p. 59.

13   Margaret Sanger, *The Woman Rebel and the Rise of the Birth Control Movement in the United States* (Stony Brook, New York: State University of New York at Stonybrook, 1976), vol. 1, no. 2, p. 10; vol 1., no. 3, p. 20; vol. 1, no. 5, p. 33, as quoted in Donovan and Marshall, *Blessed Are the Barren,* p. 7.

14   Ibid, p. 7.

15   Ibid, p. 9.

16   Letter from Margaret Sanger to Dr. Clarence J. Gamble, 10 December 1939, quoted in Donovan and Marshall, *Blessed Are the Barren,* p. 18.

17 Jean-Michael Angebert, *The Occult and the Third Reich* (New York: MacMillan, 1974), p. 121.

18 William L. Shirer, *The Rise and Fall of the Third Reich* (New York: Simon and Schuster, 1960), p. 241.

19 quoted in Donovan and Marshall, *Blessed Are the Barren,* p. 25.

20 "Really, Dr. Kinsey?", *The Lancet,* vol. 337, no. 8740, 2 March 1991, p. 547.

21 Judith A. Reisman, Ph.D., Edward W. Eichel, with J. Gordon Muir, M.D., and John H. Court, Ph.D., *Kinsey, Sex and Fraud: The Indoctrination of a People* (Lafayette, Louisiana: Huntington House, 1990).

22 Alfred C. Kinsey, Wardell B. Pomeroy, and Clyde E. Martin, *Sexual Behavior in the Human Male* (Philadelphia and London: W. B. Saunders, 1948), pp. 668, 669.

23 James H. Jones, *Alfred C. Kinsey: A Public/Private Life* (New York: W. W. Norton, 1997).

24 Ibid, p. 512.

25 Ibid, pp. 620, 621.

26 Judith A. Reisman, *Soft Porn Plays Hardball* (Lafayette, Louisiana: Huntington House, 1991), pp. 36, 37.

27 Thomas Landess, "The Evelyn Hooker Study and the Normalization of Homosexuality," *Insight,* Family Research Council, May 1995, p. 4.

28 Ibid, p. 1

29 Ronald Bayer, *Homosexuality and American Psychiatry: The Politics of Diagnosis* (New York: Basic Books, 1981), quoted in Charles Socarides, *A Freedom Too Far* (Phoenix: Adam Margrave Books, 1995), pp. 165, 166.

30 Peter LaBarbera, "Major Media Underwrite, Recruit at Gay Journalists Convention," Lambda Report on Homosexuality, January 1995, p. 1.

31 Socarides, *A Freedom Too Far,* p. 183.

5 *Television's Relativistic World*

1 S. Robert Lichter, Linda S. Lichter, Stanley Rothman, *Watching America: What Television Tells Us About Our Lives* (Prentice Hall Press, 1991), p. 277, and quoted in Michael Medved, *Hollywood vs. America: Popular Culture and the War on Traditional Values* (New York: HarperCollins Publishers/ Zondervan, 1992), p. 109.

2   J. Fred MacDonald, *One Nation Under Television: The Rise and Decline of Network TV* (New York: Pantheon Books, 1990), p. 31.

3   Herbert S. Laufman, "Television's Impact," *Radio & Television News,* July 1949, p. 127, quoted in MacDonald, *One Nation Under Television,* p. 44.

4   Variety, 16 July 1952, p. 37, cited in MacDonald, *One Nation Under Television,* p. 54.

5   Cited in *One Nation Under Television,* p. 100.

6   Ibid, p. 101.

7   Ibid.

8   Ibid, p. 100.

9   "Is Television an Asset or a Liability to Education?", America's Town Meeting of the Air, 13 February 1951, cited in MacDonald, *One Nation Under Television,* p. 53.

10   Carol Traynor Williams, "The Television Family: The Genre Beneath the Genres," *The Popular Culture Reader, Third Edition* (Bowling Green, Ohio: Bowling Green University Press, 1983), p. 317.

11   MacDonald *One National Under Television,* p. 105.

12   Ibid p. 109.

13   Ibid, p. 77.

14   Ibid, p. 69.

15   "The Team Behind Archie Bunker & Co.," *Time,* 25 September 1972, quoted in Kathryn C. Montgomery, *Target: Prime Time: Advocacy Groups and the Struggle Over Entertainment Television* (New York: Oxford University Press, 1989), p. 29.

16   Ibid, p. 30.

17   Ibid.

18   Ibid.

19   Ibid.

20   Ibid, pp. 30–31.

21   Ibid, p. 31.

22   Terry Pristin, "The Filmmakers vs. the Crusaders," *Los Angeles Times, Calendar,* p.7 at 31.

23   Montgomery, *Target: Prime Time,* p. 79.

24   Steve Weinstein, "Back in the Closet," *Calendar, Los Angeles Times,* 7 April 1991, p. 5.

25   Ibid, p. 7.

26   David Ehrenstein, "More Than Friends," *Los Angeles* magazine, May 1996, p. 62.

27   Ibid, p. 63.

28   Ibid, p. 64.

29   Ibid, p. 66.

30   Ibid, p. 170.

31   Linda S. Lichter, S. Robert Lichter, and Stanley Rothman, "Hollywood and America: The Odd Couple," *Public Opinion,* December/January 1983, p. 58, quoted in Medved, *Hollywood vs. America,* p. 294.

32   Ibid.

33   Ibid, p. 295.

34   Lee Margulies, "Gary David Goldberg and the Great American Family Tour," *Television and Families,* Spring 1988, pp. 32–33.

35   Diane Haithman, "Geraldo Turns Up His Nose at Sensationalism," *Los Angeles Times,* 18 January 1990, p. F-1 at F-12.

6   *Television Sex and Violence: The Jading Game*

1   Medved, *Hollywood vs. America,* p. 184.

2   Ted Turner's testimony, Hearings before the Subcommittee on Telecommunications, Consumer Protection, and Finance, 21 October 1981, Social/Behavioral Effects of Violence on Television (Washington, D.C., U.S. Government Printing Office, 1982), p. 5, quoted in Macdonald, *One Nation Under Television,* p. 213.

3   Ibid.

4   Montgomery, *Target: Prime Time,* p. 104.

5   Ibid.

6   Elizabeth Jensen and Ellen Graham, "Stamping Out TV Violence: A Losing Fight," *The Wall Street Journal,* 26 October 1993, p. B-1 at B-8.

7   "Violence in Prime Time Television 1992–1993," Center for Media and Public Affairs, Washington, D.C., February 1994.

8   Press conference at the National Press Club, Washington, D.C., in April 1997 in which Valenti introduced the age-based ratings.

9   "1993—The Year in Review," Media Monitor, Center for Media and Public Affairs, Washington, D.C., January/February 1994, p. 1.

10 Cited in Don Oldenburg, "Primal Screen, Kids: TV Violence & Real-Life Behavior," *The Washington Post,* 7 April 1992, p. E-5.

11 Quoted by Sen. Paul Simon during Television/Film Meeting on Violence in Los Angeles, 2 August 1993.

12 Testimony of Brian L. Wilcox before the U.S. Senate Subcommittee on the Constitution, Committee on the Judiciary, 21 May 1993.

13 Neil Lewis, "Court Strikes Down FCC restriction on Adult TV," *The New York Times,* in *Seattle Post–Intelligencer,* 24 November 1993, p. A-3.

14 Testimony of William H. Dietz, American Academy of Pediatrics, before the Subcommittee on the Constitution, U.S. Senate Committee of the Judiciary, 8 June 1993.

15 "Standards for the Depiction of Violence in Television Programs," ABC, CBS, and ABC joint issuance, December 1992.

16 Kevin Merida, "Pop Culture Takes the Rap as Congress Battles Violence," *The Washington Post,* 10 May 1994, p. A-1.

17 Donna Gable, "Cable is recruiting monitor in war on TV violence," *USA Today,* 7 March 1994, p. 3-D.

18 Telephone interview with Robert Knight on 20 May 1994. Ms. Bressan's full title is Vice President and Assistant to the President of the CBS Broadcast Group and head of Program Practices.

19 "Station Managers: Television is too violent," *Electronic Media,* 2 August 1993, p.1.

20 Telephone interview with Robert Knight on 20 May 1994. Ms. Hikawa's full title is Vice President, Broadcast Standards, Capital Cities/ABC, Inc.

21 "A Message from Sen. Paul Simon (D-Ill.), Chief Sponsor, Television Violence Act," Violence on Television: A Symposium sponsored by the editors of TV Guide, 2 June 1992, p. 15

22 Robert H. Knight, "Cultural Pollution: The Pernicious Effects of TV Sex and Violence," *Family Policy*, Family Research Council, Washington, D.C., 1995, pp. 1–8.

23 Quoted in Oldenburg "Primal Screen, Kids," p. E-5.

24 Cooper, CRS Report, p. 13, regarding George Gerbner, "Gratuitous Violence and Exploitative Sex: What Are the Lessons?" Prepared for the Study Committee of the Communications Commission of the National Council

of Churches hearings in New York, 21 September 1984, Annenberg School of Communications, University of Pennsylvania, Philadelphia, p. 2.

25 U.S. Department of Health, Education, and Welfare, The Surgeon General's Scientific Advisory Committee on Television and Social Behavior, "Television and Growing Up: The Impact of Televised Violence," Report to the Surgeon General, United States Public Health Service, Washington, D.C., 1972, p. 18, cited in Edith Fairman Cooper, "Media Entertainment Sex and Violence: Impact on Society, Especially Children," CRS Report for Congress, Congressional Research Service, 2 December 1986, p. 8.

26 L. A. Joy, M. M. Kimball, M. L. Zabreck, "Television and Children's Aggressive Behavior," in T. M. Williams, eds., *The Impact of Television: A Natural Experiment in Three Communities* (Orlando, Florida: Academic Press), 1956, cited in Brandon S. Centerwall, "Television and Violence: The Scale of the Problem and Where to Go From Here," *Journal of the American Medical Association,* vol. 267, no. 2., 10 June 1992, pp. 3,059–3,063 at 3,060.

27 David Pearl, Lorraine Bouthile, and Joyce Lazar, eds., "Television and Behavior: Ten Years of Scientific Progress and Implications for the Eighties," v. 2, *Technical Reviews,* U.S. Department of Health and Human Services, National Institute of Mental Health, Public Health Service, Alcohol, Drug Abuse, and Mental Health Administration, Rockville, Maryland, 1982, p. 155, cited in Cooper, *CRS Report,* p. 11.

28 G. Comstock and H. Paik, "The effects of television violence on aggressive behavior: a meta-analysis," preliminary report to the National Research Council for the Panel on the Understanding and Control of Violent Behavior, Syracuse, New York, S.I. Newhouse School of Public Communications, Syracuse University, 1990, cited in testimony of Brian L. Wilcox on behalf of the American Psychological Association before the U.S. Senate Subcommittee on the Constitution, Committee of the Judiciary, 21 May 1993.

29 Ibid.

30 Remarks made at The Industry-Wide Leadership Conference on Violence in Television Programming, 2 August 1993, Beverly Hills, California, in *National Council for Families & Television Report,* p. 12.

31 CQ Researcher, "TV Violence."

32 George Vradenburg III, Executive Vice President, Fox, Inc., testimony before the U.S. Senate Subcommittee on the Constitution, Committee of the Judiciary, 21 May 1993.

33 Telephone interview with Robert Knight on 24 May 1994.

34 CQ Researcher, "TV Violence," p. 170.

35 Vradenburg, loc. cit.

36 Neil Malamuth and Edward Donnerstein, *Pornography and Sexual Aggression,* (New York, Academic Press, 1984), quoted in Victor B. Cline, "Pornography's Effects on Adults & Children," monograph, (New York: Media and Morality, 1993), p. 7.

37 Edward Donnerstein, "What the Experts Say," a forum at the Industrywide Leadership Conference on Violence in Television Programming, 2 August 1993, Beverly Hills, California, in *National Council for Families & Television Report,* p. 9.

38 Cline, "Pornography's Effects," p. 7.

39 Reisman, *Soft Porn Plays Hardball.*

40 Lewis, "Court Strikes Down FCC Restriction on Adult TV."

41 Ben Stein, *The View from Sunset Boulevard: America as Brought to You by the People Who Make Television* (New York: Anchor Press/Doubleday, 1980), pp. 10–11.

42 Ibid, p. 84.

43 The Bible, Authorized (King James) Version (London: Oxford University Press, first published in 1611), p. 1145.

44 Stein, *The View From Sunset Boulevard,* pp. 120–21.

45 "The View from Hollywood and Stein," *Television & Families,* Spring 1987, p. 7.

46 Medved, *Hollywood vs. America,* p. 242.

7 *Television Families: Relativizing the Relatives*

1   Gary L. Bauer, "That's Entertainment," in Dr. James Dobson and Gary L. Bauer, *Children at Risk: The Battle for the Hearts and Minds of Our Kids* (Dallas: Word Publishing, 1990, updated in 1995), p. 208.

2   Bradley S. Greenberg, et al, "Black Family Interactions on Television," in *Life on Television: Content Analyses of U.S. TV Drama* (Norwood, New Jersey: Ablex Publishing Corporation, 1980), p. 183.

3   Stein, *The View from Sunset Boulevard,* p. 91.

4   Ibid, p. 6.

5   Williams, "The Television Family," p. 317.

6   Ella Taylor, quoted in *Television & Families,* Fall 1987, pp. 50–51.

7   Ibid, p. 53.

8   Ibid, p. 54.

9   Lee Margulies, *Television & Families,* Winter 1988.

10 Greenberg, op. cit., p. 181. Emphasis added.

11 MacDonald, *One Nation Under Television,* p. 249.

12 Bill Cosby on "Larry King Live," CNN, ca. 1990.

13 MacDonald, *One Nation Under Television,* p. 250.

14 Dan Olmstead and Gigi Anders, "Turned Off: TV Survey: Sex & Vulgarity," *USA Weekend,* 2–4 June 1995, p. 4.

15 Ibid.

16 Ibid, p. 5.

17 Tim Funk, "Networks Abandon Kids Hour," *Modesto Bee,* 15 September 1995.

18 Joyce Sunila, "Art Imitates Family Life: For These Couples, a Show That's True to Life," *Television & Families,* Spring 1988, p. 40.

19 "A Vanishing Haven: The Decline of the Family Hour," A Special Report of *TV Etc.,* Media Research Center, vol. 7, no. 12, December 1995.

8   *Whose Beliefs? Television vs. God*

1   Don Feder, *A Jewish Conservative Looks at Pagan America* (Lafayette, Louisiana: Huntington House Publishers, 193), p. 149.

2   Mark Lasswell and Ed Weiner, "Getting Religion," *TV Guide,* 29 March–4 April 1997, p. 31.

3   Peter D. Hart Research Associates of Washington, D.C., poll of 804 adults conducted February 21 and 22, 1997, and published in *TV Guide,* op. cit.

4   George Sim Johnston, "Break Glass in Case of Emergency," in *Beyond the Boom: New Voices on American Life, Culture & Politics,* ed. Terry Teachout (New York: Poseidon Press, 1990), p. 58.

5   Jack Miles, "Prime-Time's Search for God," *TV Guide,* p. 27.

6   Jay Bobbin, "Richard Chamberlain returns in 'Thorn Birds' sequel," *The Washington Times,* 11–17 February 1996, p. T-1.

7   "Religion on Television News: Still Scarce," a MediaWatch analysis reported in *TV Etc.,* Media Research Center, April 1995, p. 6.

8   Thomas Skill (University of Dayton), John Lyons (Northwestern University), and David Larson (Duke University), "television Censors Religion as a Normal Part of Life," a study commissioned by the American Family Association and released in January 1992.

9   Thomas Johnson, "How Prime Time Boxes in Religion," a summary of the study "Faith in a Box," *TV-Etc.*, Media Research Center, vol. 6, no. 4, April 1994, pp. 1–2.

10   Ibid, p. 2.

11   Feder, *A Jewish Conservative*, p. 134.

12   Sandra Crawford, "Amazingly Void," *TV-Etc.*, May 1995, p. 7.

13   Ibid.

14   Lichter, "Hollywood and America," pp. 54–56.

15   Quoted in Medved, *Hollywood vs. America*, p. 71.

16   "Missing Mangers, *TV-Etc.*, Media Research Center, December 1995, p. 6.

17   "Getting Religion," *Beyond the Boom*, p. 30.

18   Quoted in Johnston, *Beyond the Boom*, p. 50.

19   Johnston, *Beyond the Boom*, p. 51.

9   Hollywood Films: The Real Plot

1   Bauer, "That's Entertainment," p. 208.

2   William Manchester, *The Last Lion: Winston Spencer Churchill, Visions of Glory 1874–1932* (Boston: Little, Brown, 1983), p. 826.

3   Medved, *Hollywood vs. America*, p. 291.

4   Ibid, p. 282.

5   Ted Baehr, *Hollywood's Reel of Fortune: A Winning Strategy to Redeem the Entertainment Industry* (Fort Lauderdale, Florida: Coral Ridge Ministries, no date), pp. 92–93.

6   MacDonald, *One Nation Under Television*, p. 284–285.

7   Ibid, p. 214.

8   William Goldman, *Adventures in the Screen Trade: A Personal View of Hollywood and Screenwriting* (New York: Warner Books, 1983), p. 39.

9   Bob Thomas, *King Cohn: The Life and Times of Harry Cohn* (New York: G.P. Putnam's Sons, 1967), p. 92.

10 Raymond Carney, *American Vision: The Films of Frank Capra* (Cambridge, England: Cambridge University Press, 1986), p. 6.

11 Frank Capra, *The Name Above the Title*, 1971, pp. 480–81, 486 Quoted in Medved, *Hollywood vs. America*, p. 279.

12 Leslie Halliwell, "The Decline and Fall of the Movie," an essay in *Halliwell's Film Guide* (New York: Charles Scribner's Sons, 1987), p. 1,177.

13 Halliwell, *Halliwell's Film Guide*, p. 689.

14 Ibid, p. 1,181.

15 Ibid, p. 1,182.

16 Medved, *Hollywood vs. America*, pp. 19–20.

17 Richard Grenier, *Capturing the Culture: Film, Art, and Politics* (Washington: Ethics and Public Policy Center, 1991), p. xxxvii.

18 Ibid, p. 360.

19 Baehr, *Hollywood's Reel of Fortune*, p. 59.

20 Ibid.

21 Ibid, pp. 59–60.

22 Grenier, in *Capturing the Culture*, pp. 135–149.

23 Ibid, p. 141.

24 Ibid, p. 145.

25 Medved, *Hollywood vs. America*, p. 72.

26 Ibid, p. 66.

27 David Welch, *The Third Reich: Politics and Propaganda* (New York: Rutledge, 1993), p. 77.

28 Ibid, pp. 77, 78.

29 William L. Shirer, *The Rise and Fall of the Third Reich: A History of Nazi Germany* (New York: Simon and Schuster, 1960), pp. 242–252.

10 Whatever Happened to Art?

1 Douglas Cooper, *The Cubist Epoch* (London: Phaidon Press, 1970), p. 31.

2 Edith Borroff, *Music in Europe and the United States: A History* (Englewood Cliffs, New Jersey: Prentice-Hall, 1971), p. 10.

3 Gen. 31:27, New International Version (Grand Rapids, Michigan: The Zondervan Corporation, 1984).

4   Borroff, p. 13.

5   William Fleming, *Art, Music and Ideas* (New York: Holt, Rinehart and Winston), p. 359.

6   Joseph Sobran, "Shakespeare and Fascism," *Sobran's*, January 1996, p. 5.

7   Ibid.

8   Carl A. Raschke, *Painted Black: From Drug Killings to Heavy Metal— The Alarming True Story of How Satanism Is Terrorizing Our Communities,* (San Francisco: Harper and Row, 1990), p. 94, as cited in E. Michael Jones, *Dionysos Rising: The Birth of Cultural Revolution Out of the Spirit of Music* (San Francisco: Ignatius Press, 1994), p. 165.

9   Jones, *Dionysos Rising,* p. 61.

10 Ibid, p. 139.

11 Ibid, p. 7.

12 Fleming, *Art, Music and Ideas,* p. 36.

13 Ibid, p. 360.

14 Ibid, p. 359. Emphasis added.

11 From the Sublime to the Incomprehensible

1   Tom Wolfe, *The Painted Word* (New York: Bantam Books, 1975), p. 36.

2   Frederick Turner, "On Religious Art," *American Arts Quarterly*, vol. XII, no. 3, Summer 1995, p. 22.

3   James H. Billington, *Fire in the Minds of Men: Origins of the Revolutionary Faith* (New York: Basic Books, 1980), p. 100.

4   Ibid, p. 176.

5   Francis Bacon, *Novum Organum*, Book I, Aphorisms 129, 88, 81, cited in James Burnham, *Suicide of the West: An Essay on the Meaning and Destiny of Liberalism* (New York: The John Day Company, 1964), p. 53.

6   Alexis de Tocqueville, *Democracy in America*, trans. Richard D. Heffner (New York: The New American Library, 1956), p. 172.

7   E. H. Gombrich, *The Story of Art* (London: Phaidon Press, 1967), p. 381.

8   Ibid, p. 385.

9   Ibid, p. 436.

10 Jones, *Degenerate Moderns,* p. 141.

11 Ibid, p. 150.

12 Ibid, p. 150.

13 Cooper, *The Cubist Epoch,* p. 28.

14 Gombrich, *The Story of Art,* p. 463.

15 William Rubin, Helene Seckel, Judith Cousins, *Les Damoiselles d'Avignon* (New York: Harry N. Abrams, 1994), p. 205.

16 Gombrich, *The Story of Art,* p. 463.

17 Wolfe, *The Painted Word,* p. 21.

18 Ibid, pp. 21–22.

19 Gaugh, *de Kooning* (New York: Abbeville Press, 1983), p. 116.

20 Ibid, p. 77.

21 Ibid, p. 77.

22 Wolfe, *The Painted Word,* p. 63.

23 Ibid, p. 51.

24 Ibid, p. 83.

12 The Perils of Government Sponsorship

1   Quoted in Laurence Jarvik, "Pull the Plug," *The National Endowments: A Critical Symposium,* eds. Laurence Jarvik, Herbert I. London, and James F. Cooper (Los Angeles: Second Thoughts Books, 1995), p. 104.

2   Quoted in Kim Masters, "Obscenity Pledge Ruling," *The Washington Post,* 10 January 1991, p. B-2.

3   Brochure for A New Deal for the Arts, an exhibition at the National Archives and Records Administration, Washington, D.C., 28 March 1997–11 January 1998.

4   Annual Report, 1989, National Endowment for the Arts, p. vi.

5   Mary Abbe, "Minneapolis Performance Raises Concerns About AIDS," Minneapolis–St. Paul Star–Tribune, in *The Washington Times,* 26 February 1994, p. A-3.

6   Jacqueline Trescott, "Art on the Cutting Edge: Bloody Performance Renews Funding Debate," *The Washington Post,* 3 March 1994, p. C-1.

7   Chris Bull, "See Jane Run the NEA," *The Advocate,* 22 February 1994, p. 35 at 38.

8   Elizabeth Kastor, "Funding Art That Offends," *The Washington Post,* 7 June 1989, p. C-1.

9   *Webster's Third New International Dictionary of the English Language Unabridged,* (Merriam Webster, 1967), p. 150.

10   Robert Mapplethorpe: The Perfect Moment, an exhibition by the Institute for Contemporary Art in Philadelphia that went on tour in 1988 with a $30,000 grant from the NEA.

11   Joe Brown, "Bared Soul: Tim Miller's Art Gets Under the Skin," *The Washington Post,* 1 April 1994, p. D-1, and Mark Sullivan, "A riotously funny Body," *The Washington Blade,* 1 April 1994, p. 61.

12   Joseph Epstein, during "Crisis in the Arts," a panel discussion taped at San Diego State and aired on PBS in early 1991.

13   Original draft, Virginia Statute of Religious Freedom.

14   Bull, "See Jane Run the NEA," p. 38.

15   Frederick Hart, interviewed by the author on 4 January 1991.

16   From exhibit flyer, with thanks to Christian Action Network.

17   Valerie Richardson, "Artists Deliberately Bite Hand That Feeds, *The Washington Times,* 15 February 1990, p. A-1.

18   "Arts Group Planned to Burn Bibles to Ashes," *Religious Rights Watch,* September 1990, *The Washington Post,* 15 August 1990, p. C-1,

19   Judd Tully, "Rejected Artists File Suit," *The Washington Post,* 9 September 1990.

20   "This Week's News From Inside Washington," *Human Events,* 17 February 1990, pp. 3, 4.

21   Shirer, *The Rise and Fall of the Third Reich,* p. 244.

22   Suzanne Muchnic, Hitler's Sordid Little Art Show," *Los Angeles Times, Calendar,* 10 February 1991, p. 9.

23   Paul Johnson, *Modern Times: The World from the Twenties to the Eighties* (New York: Harper & Row, 1983), p. 114.

24   Ibid, pp. 115–116.

25   Ibid, p. 117.

13   Boxing Up the Art of Architecture

1   Tom Wolfe, *From Bauhaus to Our House* (New York: Farrar Straus Giroux, 1981), p. 10.

2   Elaine S. Hochman, *Architects of Fortune: Mies van der Rohe and the Third Reich* (New York: Fromm International, 1990), p. 49.

3   Wolfe, *From Bauhaus*, pp. 14–15.

4   Hochman, *Architects of Fortune*, p. 124.

5   Ibid, p. 318.

6   Ibid, p. 307.

7   Ibid, pp. 31–32.

8   Ayn Rand, *The Fountainhead* (New York: MacMillan, 1943, reprinted in 1968), pp. 714–715.

9   Ibid, p. 12.

10 Ibid, p. 14.

11 Ibid, p. xi.

12 Wolfe, *From Bauhaus*, p. 57. Italics in original.

13 Ibid, pp. 63–64.

14 Jonathan Hale, *The Old Way of Seeing* (Boston: Houghton Mifflin, 1994), p. 130.

15 Ibid, p. 136.

16 Ibid, p. 137.

17 E. Michael Jones, "Fear and Loathing at the Rock and Roll Hall of Fame," *Culture Wars,* November 1995, pp. 22, 27.

14   Music: Roll Over, Apollo

1   A. E. Hotchner, *Blown Away: The Rolling Stones and the Death of the Sixties* (New York: Simon and Schuster, 1990), p. 273.

2   Bloom, *The Closing of the American Mind*, p. 73.

3   Martha Bayles, *Hole in Our Soul: The Loss of Beauty and Meaning in American Popular Music* (New York: The Free Press, 1994), p. 58.

4   Ibid.

5   Borroff, *Music in Europe and the United States*, p. 7.

6   Fleming, *Art, Music, and Ideas*, p. 35.

7   Sorokin, *The American Sex Revolution*, pp. 29, 30.

8   Jones, *Dionysos Rising*, p. 24.

9   Ibid, p. 54.

10 Ibid, p. 55.

11 Friedrich Nietzsche, *Beyond Good and Evil*, trans. R. J. Hollingdale (London: Penguin Books, 1973), p. 14.

12 Ibid, Section 240, p. 151.

13 Ibid, Section 255, p. 168.

14 Jones, *Dionysos Rising*, p. 102.

15 Angebert, *The Occult and the Third Reich*, p. 153.

16 Jones, *Dionysos Rising*, p. 107.

17 John A. Oesterle, "Music, Order and the Soul," *The Thomist*, vol. xiv, no. 3 (July 1951), pp. 323–334, reprinted in *Culture Wars*, November 1995, p. 35.

18 Mark Swed, "Wall-to-Wall Cage," *Los Angeles Times, Calendar*, 20 September 1992, p. 50.

19 Borroff, *Music in Europe and the United States*, p. 628.

20 Swed, "Wall-to-Wall Cage," p. 50.

21 Ibid, p. 51.

22 Bayles, *Hole in Our Soul*, p. 109.

23 Borroff, *Music in Europe and the United States*, p. 674.

24 Ibid.

25 Mark Spaulding, *The Heartbeat of the Dragon* (Sterling Heights, Michigan: Light Warrior Press, 1992), p. 42.

26 Ibid, p. 14.

27 Ibid.

28 Bayles, *Hole in Our Soul*, p. 272.

29 Spaulding, *The Heartbeat of the Dragon*, p. 28.

30 Ibid, pp. 119, 120.

31 Bayles, *Hole in Our Soul*, p. 189.

32 Ibid, p. 189.

33 Jerry Hopkins and Danny Sugerman, *No One Gets Out Alive* (New York: Warner Books, 1980), pp. 158–160.

34 Spaulding, *The Heartbeat of the Dragon*, p. 93.

35 Jones, *Dionysus Rising*, p. 178–179.

15 It's Not So Relative After All

1 Will and Ariel Durant, *The Lessons of History*, (New York: Simon and Schuster, 1968), p. 50.

2   Linda Burton, Janet Dittmer, and Cheri Loveless, *What's a Smart Woman Like You Doing at Home?* (Washington, D.C.: Acropolis Books, 1986), pp. 176–177.

3   Robert Chitester, "The Limits of Advocacy," a summary of his remarks at the Agents of Change conference at the Hoover Institution, sponsored by the Hoover Institution and the Pacific Research Institute, 20–22 April 1995.

4   Ibid.

Index

This book was designed and set into type
by Mitchell S. Muncy,
with cover art by Stephen J. Ott,
and printed and bound
by Quebecor Printing Book Press,
Brattleboro, Vermont.

❦

The text face is Adobe Caslon,
designed by Carol Twombly,
based on faces cut by William Caslon, London, in the 1730s,
and issued in digital form by Adobe Systems,
Mountain View, California, in 1989.

❦

The paper is acid-free and is of archival quality.

8